THE
HISTORY OF
SERBIA

ADVISORY BOARD

THE
HISTORY OF
SERBIA

John K. Cox

The Greenwood Histories of the Modern Nations
Frank W. Thackeray and John E. Findling, Series Editors

Greenwood Press
Westport, Connecticut • London

Library of Congress Cataloging-in-Publication Data

Cox, John K., 1964–
    The history of Serbia / John K. Cox.
        p.   cm.—(The Greenwood histories of the modern nations, ISSN 1096–2905)
    Includes bibliographical references and index.
    ISBN 0–313–31290–7 (alk. paper)
    1. Serbia—History.   I. Title.   II. Series.
DR1965.C69   2002
949.71–dc21   2001040599

British Library Cataloguing in Publication Data is available.

Copyright © 2002 by John K. Cox

Library of Congress Catalog Card Number: 2001040599
ISBN: 0–313–31290–7
ISSN: 1096–2905

First published in 2002

Greenwood Press, 88 Post Road West, Westport, CT 06881
An imprint of Greenwood Publishing Group, Inc.
www.greenwood.com

Printed in the United States of America

∞™

The paper used in this book complies with the
Permanent Paper Standard issued by the National
Information Standards Organization (Z39.48–1984).

10 9 8 7 6 5 4 3 2 1

Contents

Series Foreword

The Greenwood Histories of the Modern Nations series is intended to provide students and interested laypeople with up-to-date, concise, and analytical histories of many of the nations of the contemporary world. Not since the 1960s has there been a systematic attempt to publish a series of national histories, and as series editors, we believe that this series will prove to be a valuable contribution to our understanding of other countries in our increasingly interdependent world.

Over thirty years ago, at the end of the 1960s, the Cold War was an accepted reality of global politics, the process of decolonization was still in progress, the idea of a unified Europe with a single currency was unheard of, the United States was mired in a war in Vietnam, and the economic boom of Asia was still years in the future. Richard Nixon was president of the United States, Mao Tse-tung (not yet Mao Zedong) ruled China, Leonid Brezhnev guided the Soviet Union, and Harold Wilson was prime minister of the United Kingdom. Authoritarian dictators still ruled most of Latin America, the Middle East was reeling in the wake of the Six-Day War, and Shah Reza Pahlavi was at the height of his power in Iran. Clearly, the past thirty years have been witness to a great deal of historical change, and it is to this change that this series is primarily addressed.

With the help of a distinguished advisory board, we have selected nations whose political, economic, and social affairs mark them as among the most important in the waning years of the twentieth century, and for each nation we have found an author who is recognized as a specialist in the history of that nation. These authors have worked most cooperatively with us and with Greenwood Press to produce volumes that reflect current research on their nation and that are interesting and informative to their prospective readers.

The importance of a series such as this cannot be underestimated. As a superpower whose influence is felt all over the world, the United States can claim a "special" relationship with almost every other nation. Yet many Americans know very little about the histories of the nations with which the United States relates. How did they get to be the way they are? What kind of political systems have evolved there? What kind of influence do they have in their own region? What are the dominant political, religious, and cultural forces that move their leaders? These and many other questions are answered in the volumes of this series.

The authors who have contributed to this series have written comprehensive histories of their nations, dating back to prehistoric time in some cases. Each of them, however, has devoted a significant portion of the book to events of the past thirty years, because the modern era has contributed the most to contemporary issues that have an impact on U.S. policy. Authors have made an effort to be as up-to-date as possible so that readers can benefit from the most recent scholarship and a narrative that includes very recent events.

In addition to the historical narrative, each volume in this series contains an introductory overview of the country's geography, political institutions, economic structure, and cultural attributes. This is designed to give readers a picture of the nation as it exists in the contemporary world. Each volume also contains additional chapters that add interesting and useful detail to the historical narrative. One chapter is a thorough chronology of important historical events, making it easy for readers to follow the flow of a particular nation's history. Another chapter features biographical sketches of the nation's most important figures in order to humanize some of the individuals who have contributed to the historical development of their nation. Each volume also contains a comprehensive bibliography, so that those readers whose interest has been sparked may find out more about the nation and its history. Finally, there is a carefully prepared topic and person index.

Readers of these volumes will find them fascinating to read and useful in understanding the contemporary world and the nations that comprise it. As series editors, it is our hope that this series will contribute to a heightened sense of global understanding as we enter a new century.

Frank W. Thackeray and John E. Findling
Indiana University Southeast

Preface

This book is designed to help readers understand Balkan history. Interest in this subject has recently become much more widespread and emotionally charged, due to the outbreak of war in the former Yugoslavia in 1991. The author hopes that this work will promote a better understanding of the Serbian idea of nationhood, of the richness of Serbian culture, and of the ways Serbs have dealt with the many political, military, and socioeconomic challenges in their history. This book endeavors to remove the veil of stereotypes and myths obscuring the significant details and developmental processes in Serbian history and, to some extent, in the history of the neighboring peoples.

Many books treating the explosive twentieth-century relations between Serbs and their neighbors are characterized by readers as "pro-Serb" or "anti-Serb," or "pro-Croat," or "anti-Albanian," etc. But here every effort has been made to take a balanced approach to controversial issues, using the best sources available in a variety of languages. The author speaks or reads Serbian, Croatian, Slovene, German, Russian, and Hungarian and has lived and traveled fairly extensively in the South Slav lands and the surrounding region.

This book addresses the massive, negative weight of twentieth-century events on the relations of Serbs with their neighbors. Events from the

Balkan wars and World War II are the main source of the collective bad memories recently whipped up by demagogic leaders and conveniently but erroneously labeled "ancient ethnic hatreds." Granted, old rivalries, and in some cases very bitter ones, do plague Serbian history, as they do the history of all nations. And self-determination, that essentially liberal but seemingly unavoidable corollary to modern national belief, was bound to swell the seams of even Tito's federalist, socialist Yugoslavia. But history has been instrumentalized in frightening and illegitimate ways in the 1990s, as politicians carved up the dying country of Yugoslavia and tried to come to terms with the legacy of communism.

Among the many conventions for writing Balkan history is the distinction between the words Serb and Serbian, or Croat and Croatian. Serbian and Croatian often refer to members of those national groups living inside their own country, while Serb and Croat denote co-nationals living beyond the borders of their "motherland" or "fatherland." Examples of this would be the Serbs of Croatia as opposed to the Serbians of Belgrade, or the Croatians of Dalmatia as opposed to the Croats of Chicago. For ease of understanding, I have generally ignored this distinction, relying on the context to make clear the intended meaning. Most Serbian words have been spelled in the Latin variant of the Serbo-Croatian language and have not been anglicized, except for a few readily recognizable terms like the city Belgrade (instead of the Serbo-Croatian "Beograd").

In the interest of readability, certain kinds of shorthand sometimes appear in the text. For instance, "the West" refers generally to the countries of Western Europe, the United States, and Canada; "Bosnia" usually stands for Bosnia-Hercegovina; the Habsburg Empire or Austria-Hungary is sometimes rendered as "Austria" but never as just "Hungary"; and "Eastern Europe" refers to the countries of the former Soviet bloc plus Albania and Yugoslavia. Following the time-honored tradition of diplomatic history, sometimes the capital city of a country indicates the government or political leaders: for instance, when one refers to "Vienna," the Austrian (or Austro-Hungarian, or Habsburg) government is meant, except when the context is obviously a discussion of the city itself. "Bosnian" as an adjective or noun expressing nationality generally refers to the group early known as "Bosnian Muslim" and today sometimes called "Bosniak." It is indeed important to remember that Bosnian was a regional designation for centuries and not a national or even religious one, but sadly, that symbiosis among the several ethnic groups living there is probably gone forever. Likewise, the term "Kosovars" is not generally used in this book to mean any and all residents of that important, multiethnic region; here, it stands for the Albanians who live in Kosovo (or Kosova in Albanian).

Serbian is usually, but not always, written in the Cyrillic alphabet. When it is written in the Latin alphabet, it contains certain letters that English does not have. These are used in this text and are indicated by the presence of a diacritical mark called a haček (ˇ) above them. The letters "č" and "ć" are prounced like the "ch" in church; "š" is like the "sh" in shirt; and "ž" is like the "š" in measure. Other letters are pronounced differently in Serbian than in English: "j" is like the English "y" and "c" is like "ts."

Many people helped make this book happen. Some were my teachers. Others assisted me in locating hard-to-find materials. Many provided patient answers to many electronic questions. All gave me guidance and inspiration. My special thanks and huge indebtedness for advice and resources go out to Bogdan and Svetlana Rakić, Murlin Croucher, Jeffrey Pennington, and Aleksandar Štulhofer; for the superb maps I am much obliged to Christopher Ferro. I also thank Božidar and Anka Blatnik, Henry R. Cooper, Jr., Ben Eklof, the late John Grice, Charles and the late Barbara Jelavich, Omer Karabegović, Kemal Kurspahić, Joseph Laker, Paul Lensink, Stan Markotich, Nick Miller, Bill Schmickle, Gregory Schroeder, Predrag Stokić, and Kim Vivian for tips and training in this field. These people bear no responsibility for errors in fact or interpretation in this book.

I would like to acknowledge, with gratitude, the able and friendly support of the staff of the Bishop Hodges Library at Wheeling Jesuit University, especially Eileen Carpino and Barbara Julian. Funding that aided greatly in the completion of this project was generously provided by the West Virginia Humanities Council and by the Research and Grants Committee of Wheeling Jesuit University.

This book is dedicated to Katy, for her good, tough questions.

Timeline of Historical Events

A.D. 500s–700s	Arrival of Slavic tribes in the Balkans
c. 1000	Growth of Serbian principalities of Raška, Zeta, and Hum
1169–1196	Reign of Stevan Nemanja
1219	Rise of Serbian Orthodox Church under Archbishop Sava
1276–1314	Reign of Jelena Anžujska and her son
1355	Death of Tsar Dušan, medieval Serbia's greatest ruler
1371	Battle of the Marica River resulting in the first major defeat of Serbs by Turks; Turkish rule begins spreading over Serbia and lasts into the 1800s
1389	Battle against the Turks at *Kosovo Polje* (Field of Kosovo)
1395	Death of real-life Kraljević Marko
1444–1459	Disastrous "Varna Crusade" and the fall of Smederevo seal the fate of the medieval Serbian kingdom. Serbian Church placed under Greek control
1557–1766	Renewed autonomy of Serbian Church, thanks to the patronage of Ottoman Grand Vizier Sokolović, who was a native of Bosnia

1804	Outbreak of Serbian rebellion against corrupt Ottoman military officers
1813	Karađorđje and other leaders flee to Austria
1814	Vuk Karadžić publishes his first volume of Serbian folk poems and a grammar of the Serbian language
1826–1830	Treaties and decrees making Serbia into an autonomous tributary state of the Ottoman Empire
1832	The Turkish sultan declares the Serbian Orthodox Church independent again
1844	Serbian Interior Minister Ilija Garašanin drafts the *Načertanije*, or plan for Serbia's territorial expansion into the lands of Tsar Dušan's medieval empire
1847	Petar Petrović Njegoš publishes *The Mountain Wreath*
1860s	Growth of parliamentary government and nationalism in Serbia
1878	Serbia declared completely independent by the Treaty of Berlin; small territorial gains as a result of wars against the Ottomans
1882	Prince Milan Obrenović upgrades Serbia to a kingdom
1887	Radical Party under Nikola Pašić comes to power
1903	Brutal assassinations of King Aleksandar Obrenović, his wife Draga Mašin, and others in palace in Belgrade
1903–1921	Reign of the popular and effective nationalist king, Petar Karađorđević
1912–1913	The First and Second Balkan Wars; severe brutality against civilians on all sides; Serbia wins massive territory in Kosovo and Macedonia; Montenegro expands greatly; the Ottoman Empire is almost completely expelled from Europe
1914	The assassination of the Austrian Archduke and his wife in Sarajevo by a Serbian nationalist. Outbreak of World War I; surprising Serbian defeats of Habsburg forces
1915	Serbs defeated by Austrian, German, and Bulgarian troops; perilous retreat of Serbian forces to the Adriatic Sea
1916	135,000 Serbian soldiers evacuated from northern Albania to the island of Corfu; eventually transferred to Thessaloniki, where they join the Allied armies fighting northward
1918	End of World War I; proclamation of the Kingdom of Serbs, Croats, and Slovenes, later known as Yugoslavia

1921	First Yugoslav constitution, highly centralized, put into effect; non-Serb population groups feel assimilation pressure
1928	Three Croatian politicians fatally shot in Parliament by a Montenegrin
1929	King Aleksandar declares a royal dictatorship
1934	King Aleksandar assassinated in Marseilles by Croatian and Macedonian fascists (the Ustaše and Internal Macedonian Revolutionary Organization)
1939	Yugoslav government grants Croatia considerable autonomy in an agreement called the *Sporazum*
1941–1945	Yugoslavia invaded by Germany, Italy, Hungary, and Bulgaria; various resistance groups fight on after official collapse; bitter rivalry emerges in Serbian-populated areas between Tito's Partisans and Mihailović's Chetniks; massive atrocities committed by Croatian Ustaše who now have a puppet state including all of Croatia and Bosnia; Partisans emerge as most potent fighting force, and Tito establishes one-party rule after war; federal system created to ensure equality of six chief national groups
1948	Tito-Stalin rupture spurs Yugoslavia to develop its own "national road to socialism"; also called the "third path" or "Yugoslavia's way"
1950s	Beginnings of workers' self-management and the nonaligned movement; Tito's Communist Party renames itself the League of Communists of Yugoslavia and seeks to guide society rather than dictate to it
1966	Aleksandar Ranković fired from his security and party posts
1967–1971	"Croatian Spring," or rise of nationalism in Croatia
1968	Student riots in Belgrade and other cities; nationalist riots in Kosovo; Soviet invasion of Czechoslovakia prompts creation of "territorial defense forces," or national guardlike militias, in each of the Yugoslav republics
1972	Tito purges Serbian and other liberals and nationalists
1974	Yugoslavia's fourth and final constitution is promulgated with no political pluralism is allowed, though economic and political power are further decentralized; Tito begins to rely more on the military to hold the country together

1980   Death of Tito; national mourning

1981   Riots in Kosovo

1986   Controversial Memorandum of the Serbian Academy of Science and the Arts, expressing an increasingly radical national critique of the Yugoslav system; Milošević becomes head of Serbian branch of the League of Communists

1987   Milošević becomes president of the Serbian republic within Yugoslavia

1988   Milošević declares martial law in Kosovo

1990   Multiparty elections begin in various republics; nationalist parties triumph

1991   Slovenia and Croatia declare themselves sovereign and secede from Yugoslavia; bloodshed begins

1992   Bosnia and Macedonia declare themselves independent; siege of Sarajevo and "ethnic cleansing" begin in Bosnia

1994   North Atlantic Treaty Organization carries out the first military action in its history, against Bosnian Serb forces near Goražde in April

1995   Decisive U.S. military and diplomatic intervention yields the Dayton Accords, which stop the war in Bosnia

1998   Slobodan Milošević begins a large campaign of "ethnic cleansing" against Albanians in Kosovo, who have recently formed a guerrilla force to fight for independence

1999   NATO conducts seventy-eight days of airstrikes against Serbia and Montenegro, the last two Yugoslav republics; Kosovo occupied by 50,000 troops from NATO and other countries

2000   Milošević loses a federal presidential election to an opposition coalition called DOS, tries to rig or annul the results, but steps down following massive demonstrations of 500,000 people in Belgrade; remains in the country and threatens a comeback but republican elections in December further erode his power base

2001   New, reform-minded Serbian and Yugoslav leaders try to regain confidence of world community and are readmitted to many international organizations; sanctions lifted; aid deliveries begin; war crimes issues remain unresolved; a new Albanian uprising in southern Serbia (but not in Kosovo) presents crisis for NATO and Serbian government; Montenegro threatens secession; Milošević arrested and flown to the Hague to face charges of genocide

1

Serbia Today

Serbian history has not followed a pattern that is familiar to most students of American or West European history. This does not mean that it is unintelligible or unworthy of study. Indeed, as the political crisis of the 1990s in the Balkans extends into the new millennium, it is more important than ever to try to understand both the issues that are important to Serbs today and the various ways in which Serbs have interacted with their neighbors throughout history.

One of the basic facts of Serbian history is that for many centuries Serbs were not the masters in their own house; in a sense, Serbia has been playing "catch-up" in the world of European nation-states since the mid-1800s. Their attempts to regain their political independence and annex neighboring regions where their fellow Serbs also lived have underlain all of the political experiences of modern Serbs, whether they are with monarchical or socialist forms of government.

It is also important to remember that Serbia, like much of the rest of Eastern Europe, entered the industrial age later than the countries of Western Europe or North America. This means that Serbia's society has, at least until recently, changed fairly slowly. Although it has always been an integral part of European civilization in its attitudes and institutions, only in the decades since World War II has Serbia moved rapidly toward turning into an urban, secular, and industrialized society similar to Great Britain, Canada, and the United States.

GOVERNMENT

Only two republics—Serbia and Montenegro—remain in the country that is still known as Yugoslavia. The official name of this country is the Federal Republic of Yugoslavia. This "third" or "rump" Yugoslavia, as it is also sometimes called, came into existence in 1992, after the secession of Slovenia, Croatia, Bosnia-Hercegovina, and Macedonia from the country that was officially called the Socialist Federal Republic of Yugoslavia. Serbia is by far the dominant partner in this third Yugoslavia. Its leaders of the last fifteen years have cemented their grasp on power by resuming the hundred-year-old struggle to unite all current and previous Serbian territories into one country. Serbia's confrontational policies with its Balkan and European neighbors are causing some Montenegrins to reconsider their alliance with the Serbs and it remains to be seen whether or not Montenegro will follow the secessionist path taken by the Croats, Slovenes, Bosnians, and Macedonians. Parliamentary elections in April 2001 gave a narrow edge to the coalition of President Milo Djukanović, who promised to hold a referendum soon on independence. These events are but a reminder that Serbian history is hard to study in isolation; the political, economic, and cultural life of Serbia has been intimately connected with that of its neighbors, both friends and foes, in ways that are characteristic of many other societies in Eastern Europe.

The political scene in Serbia today was until recently dominated by two parties—Slobodan Milošević's nationalistic Socialist Party of Serbia (SPS) and the Yugoslav United Left (YUL). Milošević was president of Serbia from 1989 to 1997; from 1997 to 2000 he was president of Yugoslavia.

In the 1990s there were numerous other parties, many of them small. These parties rose in prominence due to their resistance to Milošević's rule after NATO attacked Serbia for its abuse of human rights in Kosovo (1999). They were joined in public opposition by the mayors of important Serbian cities such as Velimir Ilić of a Čačak and Zoran Živković of Niš. The opposition has joined together in four large, diverse coalitions in the 1990s (the Democratic Movement of Serbia, "Together," the Alliance for Change, and currently the Democratic Opposition of Serbia, known as DOS). It took these parties a long time, however, to mobilize enough of Serbia's population to win at the ballot box. In late 2000 Vojislav Koštunica became the new president of Yugoslavia, and in early 2001 Zoran

Djindjić became the new prime minister of Serbia. Both men are now trying to rid the government of corruption and protect the civil rights of all of Serbia's citizens.

The federal government consists of fourteen major ministries (what in the United States would be called "departments") concerned with aspects of administration such as foreign affairs, defense, internal affairs, telecommunications, and foreign trade. Local government in Serbia takes place in subunits known as districts, of which there are thirty. These districts are basically equivalent to North American counties. Smaller administrative units, called *opštine*, are like municipalities or townships.

The current Serbian constitution was adopted in 1990. It guarantees for all of its citizens—of all ethnic and religious backgrounds—the basic civil rights familiar to citizens of all democratic countries. Many of these rights were not honored in the 1990s. Serbia did not have a typically autocratic government, because opposition parties did exist, and to a small degree opposition newspapers and television and radio stations were allowed to broadcast. But minority groups under Milošević faced severe discrimination; the government maintained a tight control on the economy, rewarding its supporters and engaging in great corruption; and opposition groups, academics, and journalists were regularly harassed, jailed, beaten, and sometimes murdered.

Serbia has a proud tradition of semidemocratic rule, with a strong traditional role for the Parliament, which dates back to the mid-nineteenth century. But Serbs have also been burdened with bad government for much of their history. During the Ottoman times, (c. 1370–1800s), most Serbs—to the extent that they were politically aware at all beyond the scope of local interests—learned simply to live with a government that they viewed as alien and to some degree predatory. Independent Serbia had its share of irresponsible monarchs in the nineteenth century. Under the socialist government of Tito (1953–1980), many Serbs felt equally shut out of politics. Serbia's current political and economic situation is very complex, and the democratic opposition is still in its infancy. Furthermore, the breakup of Yugoslavia and the transformation of many of the country's leaders from stalwart communists to hard-core nationalists has left Serbian society in confusion. For a fuller discussion of recent political issues see Chapter 10.

GEOGRAPHY AND ECONOMY

Serbia today comprises 34,116 square miles. This is about 35 percent of the total territory of the former Yugoslavia, as it existed from 1918 to

1991. Of this total, 21,609 square miles form what was called "narrow Serbia" in the former Yugoslavia, with the former autonomous republics of Kosovo and the Vojvodina accounting for 4,203 and 8,304 square miles, respectively. To put Serbia's size into perspective, think of the American states of South Carolina or Indiana. The European countries of Portugal and Austria are also roughly the same size as Serbia.

The Republic of Serbia has four main regions that are geographically distinct as well as historically important: the capital area around Belgrade, the plains of the north, the heavily forested region of the center, and the region of Kosovo (also called Southern or Old Serbia, which also use to include Macedonia) in the south. Serbia has a continental climate, which means it has both hot summers and cold winters, and most of its regions get forty inches of rain per year or less.

Belgrade has been an important administrative center for centuries. It sits at the confluence of the Danube and the Sava Rivers. Its northern location between the plains and the forest belt of Serbia has meant that, throughout history, the city was a constant bone of contention between the Ottoman and Habsburg (Austrian) empires. Belgrade has thus seen a lot of fighting and one of its chief landmarks is the former Ottoman fortress known as the Kalemegdan, which towers over the old town.

Today Belgrade is a large European city with a varied and sophisticated population, a large industrial base, the stately architecture of a national and republican capital, and large suburbs, especially to the north, where the land is flat. In its suburbs and nearby industrial cities such as Smederevo, factories produce steel, machine tools, electrical components, and tractors. In the nineteenth century the city was thought of as quaint and exotic by visitors from Western Europe. This was because the city was once home to many Turkish administrators and garrison soldiers and, later, because the Serbian population had adopted many Turkish habits in clothing, cuisine, and even vocabulary. From the late 1800s through the time of the second Yugoslavia, however, Belgrade had very much the opposite reputation. It was, for the Balkans at any rate, a cultivated and cosmopolitan urban area that was something of a magnet for artists and bohemians.

The flat, northern expanses of Serbia consist mostly of the region known as the Vojvodina. This area is the southern tip of the Pannonian plain, which covers much of Hungary and large parts of Slovakia and Romania. The Danube—one of Europe's biggest rivers, linking Germany and Austria with the Balkans and the Black Sea—flows through this area; its tributaries include two other large rivers, the Tisza and the Sava. The Vojvodina's rich, black soils produce important crops of wheat and sugar

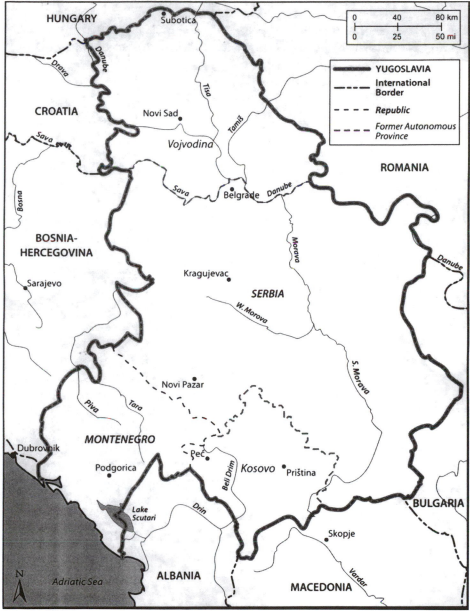

Christopher Ferro

beets. Natural gas and oil are also pumped here. This area includes parts of the historical regions of the Banat, Srem, and Bačka. The Vojvodina was part of the Habsburg Empire during much of the time that the rest of Serbia was under Turkish rule, and the area eventually became the new center of gravity for the Serbian culture. Today Serbs constitute a majority in the region, with Hungarians the biggest of the many minorities.

The central region of Serbia, known as the Šumadija, is heavily forested, hence the derivation of its name from the Serbian word *šuma*, or forest. Today this region is a patchwork of agricultural and mining areas and medium-sized industrial cities, the most important of which is Kragujevac, where automobiles and military products are manufactured. The several branches of the Morava River are the main waterways of the Šumadija. Historically this area was famous as the locale of the outbreak of the Serbian wars of independence in the early 1800s. These hilly forests had traditionally been the refuge of Serbian rebels and highwaymen known as *hajduks*. The grazing of sheep, cattle, and pigs has long been important here; hay, corn, barley, oats, and potatoes are also grown on a moderate scale. Plums (often used to make Serbian brandy, known as *šljivovica*) and other fruits are commonly grown here in orchards.

The southernmost region of Serbia generally goes by the name Kosovo today. It consists of high plains and mountains with significant mineral wealth and good, but overworked, soil. Over the centuries this area, which was the heart of the medieval Serbian monarchy, has come into ever more dispute between Serbs and Albanians. It contains many important churches, monasteries, palaces, and battlefields that attest to the grandeur of medieval Serbia, but the area was probably never purely Serbian in terms of the ethnic makeup of its people. Furthermore, its population profile has undergone steady change since at least the 1600s, and Serbs—even before the NATO bombing campaign of 1999—are now a small minority in this important region. The majority Albanians, who call the area Kosova, have resisted Serbian administration of the region in various ways since the Turks were driven out by the Serbs in 1913. Well over one third of all Albanians in the world live in Kosovo; the neighboring country of Albania has over 3 million people, but Kosovo itself contains over 1.5 million Albanians. Kosovo was the poorest part of the former Yugoslavia, despite substantial government investment in its industry; it had the lowest per capita income and highest literacy of any republic or province. Kosovo is even poorer today, because of the political repression and violence of the past thirteen years. Before the

1990s, many Albanians wanted autonomy (local self-rule) within Serbia; today most desire Kosovo to be independent. Serbs, for their part, generally resent any thought of giving up control over Kosovo. This is the case not just because of the region's cultural value, but also because it is rich in minerals and because its chains of hills form a logical and easily defended border for southern Serbia.

The highest mountain in Serbia is the peak Djeravica (2,656 meters, or 8,713 feet). This peak and many other high mountains of comparable height are found in the Prokletije and Šar Mountains of the south. Within central and northern Serbia, the Kopaonik Massif has the highest elevations and is famous for its ski slopes. The highest part of the Kopaonik is known as Pančić Peak (2017 meters), after Serbia's most famous nineteenth-century botanist and naturalist.

Serbia has 3,619 kilometers of railroad. It has 24,860 kilometers of paved and an additional 17,832 kilometers of unpaved roads. The country's main and biggest highway today runs southeast to northwest. Traversing the valleys of the Morava and Danube Rivers, it connects the major cities of Niš, Belgrade, and Novi Sad. A major east-west route, formerly known as the Highway of Brotherhood and Unity, parallels the Sava River and links Belgrade to Zagreb and points west. Important rail lines connect Belgrade to the neighboring capital cities of Budapest, Zagreb, Sofia, Podgorica (Montenegro), and Skopje (Macedonia).

The recent wars and blockades have seriously lowered the standard of living in the country, however. Unemployment fluctuates with the political situation but in the late 1990s was running somewhere around 25 percent. The biggest employment sector in the economy is mining and industry, with over 26 percent of the labor force. The government and military employ about 21 percent; 14 percent are involved in trade and just over 3 percent in agriculture.

POPULATION

With 10 million inhabitants, Serbia is comparable in size to Greece, Portugal, or the American state of Ohio. The capital, Belgrade, has more than 1.5 million persons; its population grew considerably in the 1990s due to an influx of Serbian refugees from other parts of the former Yugoslavia. Novi Sad is the second largest city, with 266,000 inhabitants. In the early 1990s, the Serbs of Serbia shared their country with over 1.5 million Albanians and nearly 350,000 Hungarians. There were smaller minorities of Slavic Muslims in the Sandžak region, Gypsies (Roma), Croats, Turks, and others. It should be remembered at this point that many members of the Serbian national or ethnic group live outside of Serbia. Although recent wars and waves of emigration, sometimes forced, are still changing the ethnic landscape of the former Yugoslavia, it is possible to state with certainty that in the early 1990s, more than one million Serbs lived in Bosnia and more than 500,000 lived in Croatia. Serbia's immediate neighbors on the territory of the former Yugoslavia, such as Croatia, Macedonia, and Bosnia-Hercegovina, are somewhat smaller in both size and population.

Nowadays, statistics just for Serbia are hard to find. This is because Serbia, along with the smaller republic of Montenegro, is technically still part of a country called Yugoslavia. Yugoslavia has a population that is not much larger than Serbia's. It has just over 10.5 million people, about two thirds of whom are Serbs. Montenegro has 520,000 people. It has considerable minorities too. In Yugoslavia as a whole, 52 percent of the population lives in urban areas.

THE MONTENEGRINS

The Montenegrins are a Balkan people usually considered to be a branch of the Serbian family, in terms of both ethnicity and culture. Sometimes they are called "first cousins" to the Serbs, but most people describe their relationship as even closer than that, arguing that they are the Serbs' "brothers and sisters" who have simply lived physically separated from the main branch of the nation since the fourteenth century. As the politician and novelist Milovan Djilas wrote, all Montenegrins are Serbs but not all Serbs are Montenegrins. Despite occasional political conflicts since World War I, most Montenegrins and Serbs feel extremely closely related.

The two groups share a common history up through the period of Tsar Dušan's empire. Another strong bond between Serbs and Montenegrins is their common religion of Orthodoxy. Traditionally the Montenegrin church is considered a branch of the Serbian church. Both peoples also speak Serbian and use the Cyrillic alphabet, even though Montenegrins have distinct pronunciation and spelling patterns. The language used today in Montenegro differs noticeably from that in Belgrade, but linguistic variety is a hallmark of modern Serbian, as it is of other European languages such as Italian and German. Finally, it should be noted that in Serbian history, it is more often than not the case that the Serbian nation spills over international borders. In fact, Serbs have only lived all together in a common state in the fourteenth and in the twentieth centuries; they are used to having their "brothers and sisters"—or, in more scholarly terms, their "co-nationals"—living in other countries. The borders of the cultural and ethnic collectivity called "Serbdom" have almost always been considerably bigger than the political boundaries of "Serbia," whether it was a medieval statelet, a Turkish province, or the dominant element in one of the three Yugoslavias.

There are also some important differences between Serbs and Montenegrins, however. Most of Montenegro was never effectively conquered by the Turks, who saw no reason to go all-out to pacify the backward region. As a result, a fierce spirit of independence but also a certain isolation characterize Montenegro's history. Even into the twentieth century, Montenegro's political scene was dominated by strong clans, which have sometimes been called "tribes." From the early 1500s until the 1850s, the country was basically ruled as a theocracy, with the chief Orthodox bishop also ruling as prince; this position was called the *vladika*, and its longevity meant that Montenegrins had far less experience with parliamentary government than the Serbs. (As in nineteenth-century Serbia, though, the central government was never extremely strong, because of the attitudes and habits of local leaders.) Finally, one of the salient features of traditional Montenegrin culture is the practice or institution of *krvna osveta*, or blood-feud. This was a Balkan form of the vendetta,[1] which was also common in Albania and Hercegovina and has long fascinated foreign travelers and scholars. In general, traditional Montenegrin culture was more patriarchal and less polished than the rest of Serbian culture; the differences between the rough-and-ready highlanders (sometimes compared to the Scots) and the educated, urban Serbian settlements of southern Hungary were especially great.

Montenegro gets its name from the Italian version of the Serbian term *Crna Gora*, meaning "Black Mountain." The name derives from the forbidding, rocky landscape of much of the country. Traditionally, most people in this poor and sparsely settled area have lived from animal herding or farming in a few river valleys. Many of the towns along the coast have traditional names, reflecting the great historical influence of such nearby powers as Venice. Kotor, for instance, was earlier known as Cattaro; Ulcinj was Dulcigno; and Bar was Antivari.

SOCIETY

By the late 1900s, Serbian society was one that would, for the most part, be thoroughly recognizable to someone from North America or Western Europe. Once famous for its colorful costumes, customs, and folklore, Serbia became increasingly modern after World War II. In global terms, Serbia has well-developed systems of education, transportation, and medical care. The country's birth rates, life expectancy, and major causes of death follow patterns similar to those of other East European countries.

Serbs speak Serbian, which until recently was considered by most people to be a variant of the Serbo-Croatian (or Croato-Serbian) language. Today it is the norm to speak of Serbian, Croatian, and Bosnian as three separate languages, even though they are mutually intelligible. This separation was caused in the 1990s primarily by political concerns, since Bosnia-Hercegovina, Croatia, and Serbia were at war. While it is true that the languages have some different vocabulary, pronunciation, and literary history, the biggest single difference is that most (but not all) Serbs have traditionally used a form of the Cyrillic alphabet and Croats and Bosnians have used a modified Latin alphabet. Serbian also uses more words of Turkish origin than does Croatian, and there are some small differences in grammar. Most scholars maintain that Serbian, Croatian, and Bosnian are about as different from each other as British and American English. These differences will doubtless grow over time, especially since the respective governments are promoting the differentiation through new school curricula and publishing standards. All three of these languages belong to the South Slavic branch of the Slavic language family, which makes them relatives of Russian, Polish, and Czech. Other South Slavic languages include Slovene, Macedonian, and Bulgarian.

Serbia had the beginnings of a public education system from the early 1800s on; the University of Belgrade was officially created only in 1905, although it already existed in all but name. Its core had existed as a lycée (classical high school) for nearly a hundred years. In the nineteenth century, many Serbs had to go abroad, especially to Paris or Vienna, for higher education, but in the twentieth century, the University of Belgrade developed a strong reputation. There are also newer major universities in Niš and in the capitals of the two former autonomous provinces, Novi Sad and Priština. All told, Serbia today has about 4,000 elementary schools and over eighty institutions of higher learning. There are more than 100 museums, including the National Museum (Serbian and international paintings and sculpture), specialized historical and military museums (including archaeological sites such as Lepenski Vir and many memorials to the late Yugoslav President Josip Broz Tito), and smaller commemorative museums honoring famous Serbs such as the inventor Nikola Tesla and the writers Dositej Obradović, Ivo Andrić, and Jovan

Sterija Popović. Many of the medieval churches and monasteries, with their priceless frescoes and paintings, are also open to the public.

Many journalists and authors of travel guides to the Balkans take it upon themselves to comment on a small set of attitudes that they consider to be "typical Serbian." Sometimes there is only a fine line between perceptive generalizations and demeaning stereotypes. This material is presented here only because students will certainly encounter it elsewhere, and one should realize that these are informal impressions rather than scholarly conclusions.

One common phrase in Serbian is *polako, polako*, meaning literally "slowly, slowly." This expression points to a relaxed pace and a tendency to live for the moment. Another term of which students should be aware is *inat*. This word usually connotes spite or stubborn—even irrational—defiance. Serbian politicians are said to display *inat* when they defy the world community on human rights issues, even in the face of overwhelming condemnation or military odds. It sometimes describes praiseworthy tenacity or devotion to principle.

One should also note that Serbs are famous for their warm hospitality to visitors and a generally Mediterranean lifestyle—more familiar to North Americans through contact with the Spanish and Italian cultures—that includes an emphasis on extended family gatherings, late dining, and a balance between work time and personal time that strikes many visitors from North America and northern Europe as refreshing.

Serbia has traditionally belonged to the realm of Eastern Orthodox Christianity. Its self-governing church, called the Serbian Orthodox Church, is headed by a patriarch, whose seat is in Belgrade. This church is related historically and theologically to the other Orthodox churches, such as those in Greece and Russia. Many of Serbia's minority groups are not Orthodox Christians. The Hungarians and Croats of the north are mostly Roman Catholic Christians, and in the south there are large Muslim communities among the Albanians, with smaller ones consisting of Turks and some Serbs.

CULTURE

High Culture

Literature, icon painting, and architecture are the artistic forms for which Serbia is best known. Of these branches of high culture, literature is probably the first among equals in quality and fame. Since many nations in the Balkans are defined by their languages, it is no wonder that literature—which is also easier to create and distribute than paintings, sculpture, or classical music—is the most developed aspect of modern Serbian high culture. Any cultural study of the Serbian experience would need to include, as a bare minimum, the following: the traditions of religious painting found especially in Kosovo, the Vojvodina, and parts of Bosnia; the Byzantine-style architecture of monasteries and churches; nineteenth- and twentieth-century realist paintings on historical themes; the moving epic poetry of the medieval "Battle of Kosovo" cycle; the violent, Romantic epic poem *The Mountain Wreath* of Petar Petrović Njegoš; surrealist and modernist poetry from the twentieth century; the psychologically complex and carefully crafted prose works of Ivo Andrić; and the historically tinged experimental prose of Danilo Kiš.

Serbian art and architecture, much of both reflective of the Byzantine traditions, are also justifiably famous. Between the early thirteenth and the early fifteenth centuries, many great works of art (icons, wall paintings, and manuscript miniatures) came into existence. Beautiful, beautiful architecture was created in monasteries and churches such as those at Studenica, Sopoćani, Gračanica, and Dečani. Serbian art in neighboring countries such as Bosnia-Hercegovina is also famous. Since the mid-1800s, Serbia has produced fine painters who are representative of general European artistic trends. The country has also attracted attention for its new but noteworthy traditions in classical music and philosophy.

Popular Culture

In the realm of popular culture, Serbs are definitely sports standouts. The Belgrade soccer teams Red Star (*Crvena Zvezda*) and Partizan are famous across Europe. The two teams are contentious rivals within Serbia, but they have produced international stars such as Dejan Savičević and have helped the former Yugoslav teams win medals in the Olympics.

Another team sport for which Serbia is famous is basketball. Teams representing the former Yugoslavia (which, as in the case of soccer, had many Serbian players) have won many Olympic medals—for men and women—in basketball. Many Serbian basketball stars, such as the current NBA standout Vlade Divac, are also famous around the world. Other outstanding basketball players of recent decades include Radivoje Korać and Dražen Dalipagić.

Serbia has had a wealth of talented filmmakers, many of whom have films that are available with English subtitles. The most famous Serbian film director is Dušan Makavejev, who has made many films in Yugo-slavia and elsewhere including *Man Is Not a Bird*. A powerful movie about the recent wars, directed by Srdjan Dragojević, is *Pretty Village, Pretty Flame* (1996). Serbia has also had, since the 1960s, a lively scene for rock and roll, punk, and alternative bands. *Riblja Ćorba* ("Fish Stew") was probably the most famous of these bands, along with the ballad singer Djordje Balašević. The breakup of Yugoslavia has changed the musical scene radically inside Serbia. Rock and punk are out; popular today are modes of music known as "neo-folk" (folk tunes and instru-ments with lyrics on modern themes) and "turbo-folk" (basically mass-produced dance music with patriotic themes). A Belgrade singer named Rambo Amadeus was the innovator of "turbo-folk," which originally seemed ironic or sarcastic, but has become commercialized.

The most important periodicals in Serbia in the last few decades have been the weekly newsmagazine *NIN* and the newspapers *Borba, Politika, Večernje Novosti, Politika Ekspres, Blic, Glas Javnosti,* and *Dnevni Telegraf*. An independent news weekly called *Vreme* became an important source of alternative news during the wars and censorship of the 1990s. There are many local newspapers and scholarly journals. In addition, small alternative radio (B-92) and television stations (Studio B) that operate in Belgrade supported the democratic opposition and antiwar movements, to the degree that the Milošević regime allowed them to function.

A NOTE ON SERBIAN NATIONALISM

Nationalism began as a European phenomenon in the eighteenth cen-tury and since then has spread throughout the world. It has mostly re-placed earlier ways of organizing countries, for instance, in the form of royal families known as dynasties or on the basis of religion. In its var-ious forms, nationalism is linked to the process of political and economic modernization in most countries. Today the world diplomatic scene has increasingly come to be dominated by nation-states, or countries built around one particular national or ethnic group. Nationalism is often praised for creating countries in which people rule themselves. Sadly, nationalism can also be a very destructive force when it leads to mili-tarism, aggression, and xenophobia (the fear of foreigners).

Nationalism is more than just patriotism, or love of one's country. It goes much deeper than simple affection for a region or wartime loyalty. Nationalism can be defined as a sense of group identity based on shared language, history, territory, sense of mission or destiny, and customs, and sometimes religion and race as well. People who share these characteristics are called a "nation." Sometimes, these basic factors of identity are also called "ethnicity." This sense of identity tends to become politicized, and in this way, nationalism becomes an ideology. The idea of people ruling themselves is part of the basic mindset of nationalism, and in this way, it is linked to democracy, which is another form of people ruling themselves. The technical name for the desire for self-rule in both nationalism and democracy is "popular sovereignty." In the modern era of European history, every "nation" has tended to try to become a separate and independent country, or "state." This process, which happens on other continents as well, is called the creation of "nation-states." It is one of the most basic political forces in the world today.

As the roster of the United Nations shows, there are over 180 countries or states in the world today. But there are many more peoples, or nations, than that. Not every national group has its own state. In Europe, until recently, there were several famous countries that consisted of many different national groups: Yugsoslavia, which had six "nations" within it, including Serbia; Czechoslovakia, which was home to both Czechs and Slovaks; and the Soviet Union, which consisted of Russia and fourteen other major national groups. Since 1990, all of these countries have broken up. In the Yugoslav case, this breakup and the ensuing formation of nation-states have been very violent.

Serbs have experienced two different forms of nationalism: civic and ethnic. The basic difference is that for civic (or political) nationalists, the "nation" is a political population—a group of people united by common political values, inspired by the same sense of mission, and linked by shared economic and political institutions. For ethnic nationalists, the "nation" is an ethnic or cultural population, consisting of people linked by real or imagined bloodline or genetic (or racial) similarity, or by customs, religion, and language. Both kinds of nationalism have political self-determination as their goal, but ethnic nationalism tends to be much more exclusive and politically intolerant.

Generally, ethnic nationalism has been more prevalent in Eastern Europe than civic nationalism. Scholars explain this by pointing out that nationalism began primarily as a response to social and economic change in Western Europe. It became a political phenomenon there and only later it made its way into Eastern Europe. Since the economic and political conditions in the two halves of Europe were very different, "imported" nationalism developed differently and had other effects in Eastern Europe than the "domestic" nationalism of Western Europe. In countries like France and England, nationalism was connected with the growth of political democracy in countries that had well-defined boundaries and stable, recognized cultures. The societies in these West European cultures were experiencing a great deal of economic growth in the 1700s and 1800s, and the populations there shared the same language and a lot of other common bonds.

In Eastern Europe, however, the situation was very different. The map there was not dominated by established territorial states like France and England, but rather by large multinational empires like those of the Ottoman Turks, the Habsburgs of Austria, and the Romanovs of Russia. The economies were developing a lot more slowly too, so there were fewer cities, fewer educated people, less social change than in the West. Nationalism was imported into countries like Serbia when intellectuals there saw that it had great potential for mobilizing people and for justifying new kinds of government that would include people other than the foreign kings and aristocrats who ruled over the local populations. Thus national feelings and political ideas involved a great deal of exclusivity, because people had to define themselves through their opposition to the existing order of things. In this way, too, we speak of nationalism as mostly a centrifugal and not a centripetal force in East European politics. It tended to break up the large, existing countries, which contained many national groups. The long-term goal of creating new countries was usually achieved too, but there was a great emphasis among ethnic nationalists on who was "with them" and who was "against them," usually defined in terms of ethnicity or language.

Today, many Serbs feel that their country should be bigger than it is. They believe they have a right to have all of Europe's Serbs living in one country. Since the Middle Ages, this has only happened in multinational countries such as the Ottoman Empire or Yugoslavia, where Serbs lived together with other national groups and where they did not have complete self-rule.

Furthermore, many Serbs claim that their fellow Serbs will be ill-treated in neighboring states. This political desire, to create a greater Serbia that includes all people who identify themselves as Serbian, might be logical in theory, and it certainly has a strong emotional appeal. But during the breakup of Yugoslavia it has created enormous problems with Serbia's neighbors. One can seldom draw clear dividing lines between ethnic territories in the Balkans, so it is very hard to redraw the map of Serbia fairly. The use of violence by the Serbian military and militias against civilian populations has also greatly complicated the resolution of other political issues. Furthermore, it is not morally justified to punish contemporary Muslim or Croatian populations for the anti-Serbian activities of their predecessors. Sometimes, too, Serbs claim territory where they used to be a significant or majority presence in terms of population but are now a minority. Claims to such territory are said to be based on "historic" rather than current "ethnic" rights. When a country claims territory using both sets of criteria, its neighbors rightfully perceive it as aggressive.

The final impact of forced and voluntary population movements resulting from the recent wars in Yugoslavia cannot yet be predicted. But it certainly has reduced Serbian populations in some areas. Areas that traditionally have had significant Serbian populations include Bosnia-Hercegovina, now an independent country, and three regions of another now-independent country, Croatia—Slavonia in the northeast, the Krajina region in the center, and parts of Dalmatia in the south. To many Serbs these areas are just as much "Serbia" as the land within the borders of the republic itself.

In Yugoslavia as it existed from 1945 to 1991, the Serbs were in many ways the dominant national group. But the federal structure of the socialist country kept Serbs politically separate, and President Tito's cultural policies did not allow much expression of nationalist sentiments or loyalties. Although other national groups in the second Yugoslavia, most notably the Croats, Albanians, and Slovenes, maintain to this day that the Serbs were unduly privileged in that country, most Serbs assert exactly the opposite: that their culture was singled out for persecution by the communist government. Two facts are undisputed, however: although Serbs were the biggest single population group in the second Yugoslavia, they comprised only 36 percent of the population. So, they were not a majority of the country and could not control it completely; yet neither their expectations nor those of their fellow Yugoslavs were met. More important, though, is the fact that about one in four Serbs (24 percent) did not live within the boundaries of the republic of Serbia. They lived for the most part, as we have already seen, in Croatia and Bosnia-Hercegovina. These figures underscore the potential for explosive conflict when the central government of Yugoslavia began falling apart and republics began to secede and form independent countries. Serbs would feel threatened, both in physical and political terms. Although Serbs would be unable to control the breakup entirely and although many individual Serbs would suffer enormously, their relatively dominant position in the country would give them as a group—or at least the increasingly autocratic claque of leaders acting supposedly on their behalf—a substantial amount of influence over the timing and destructiveness of events in the 1990s.

NOTE

1. See Christopher Boehm, *Blood Revenge: The Enactment and Management of Conflict in Montenegro and other Tribal Societies* (Philadelphia: University of Pennsylvania Press, 1987); for a fictional treatment, see the chilling novel *Broken April* (New York: New Amsterdam Books, 1990) by Albanian writer Ismail Kadare.

2

The Splendor of Medieval Serbia

PREHISTORY

The territory that is today known as Serbia was first densely settled by humans during the Neolithic period. On the Danube at Lepenski Vir and at Vinča near Belgrade, major excavations have revealed a great deal about the settled agriculture of the people of the time and their connections to Mediterranean cultures. During the Iron Age, the inhabitants were identifiable as Illyrians, Thracians, and Celts. In the middle of the first millennium B.C., Greeks settled in colonies along the Adriatic coast and moved into northern Macedonia as traders. By 10 A.D., the Romans had conquered all of today's Yugoslavia. Their long period of rule left mines, cities, and a good road network that was later to be used by incoming Slavic "barbarians" from the north.[1]

In the first millennium A.D., peoples called Slavs lived together in an undifferentiated group in northeastern Europe. In the sixth and seventh centuries, the ancestors of today's South Slavs arrived in the Balkans. They settled across the region, fought with the Byzantine Empire (the largely Greek successor state to the Eastern Roman Empire based in the great cosmopolitan city of Constantinople) and with Turkic peoples such as the Avars and Bulgars, and gradually coalesced into distinct tribes or principalities bearing mostly geographical names.

THE BEGINNINGS OF THE MEDIEVAL ERA

Across Eastern Europe, both the Roman Catholic Church and the Orthodox Church, based in Constantinople, were competing to convert the pagan Slavs. In the ninth century, the Glagolitic alphabet was created by two famous Byzantine missionaries, Cyril and Methodius. This alphabet was used mostly to the north and west of Serbia, but it was later replaced by another alphabet designed to fit Slavic sounds: the Cyrillic alphabet. Named in honor of the earlier missionary and based more closely on Greek characters, this alphabet provided the means for literacy and high culture to come to the Serbs.

Architecture, icons, and frescoes (of which those in the Sopoćani monastery near Novi Pazar are world famous) followed Byzantine Greek models. Most writing among the early Serbs, which of course followed their conversion to Christianity and their connection to the world of Byzantine culture, was on religious themes. Gospels, Psalters, apocryphal stories, menologies (religious calendars), hagiographies (lives of saints), and essays and sermons of the church fathers dominated. At the end of the twelfth century, two of the most important works of art were created, known as "Miroslav's Gospel" and "Vukan's Gospel." These priceless illuminated manuscripts combine handwritten biblical texts with painted initials and small pictures. There were also a few imported medical writings and some official documents. The language in which these things were written was actually not Serbian, but rather Old Church Slavonic (OCS), a kind of medieval international language in Eastern Europe that played the same kind of role Latin played in the West. The version of OCS used in Serbia did display certain specific local characteristics, but it would not be until the nineteenth century that modern Serbian was standardized and made official. By the high Middle Ages, the Serbian dialect, along with Eastern Orthodoxy, a sense of "spatial identity" (attachment to certain territories), and a set of social and political customs combined to create a sense of unity that distinguished Serbs from their neighbors. Such factors are more important, and demonstrable, than any sort of bloodline connections or supposed ethnic purity, although extended kinship ties doubtless formed the basis for political and social units.

Serbia came under Bulgarian and then Byzantine rule after 900. But Serbia's political history really begins with the reign of an independent prince named Stefan Nemanja, who ruled the territories of Raška and Zeta (modern-day southern Serbia and Montenegro) from 1169 to 1196. He was militarily strong and also built such famous monasteries as Studenica and, in his retirement, Hilandar at Mount Athos in Greece. He conquered neighboring Serbian territories in Kosovo, along the coast (Duklija), and in Hercegovina (Hum). He also gave his name to the dynasty that followed his reign, usually called the Nemanjić dynasty. His two sons cemented his legacy and made enormous contributions to Serbian history also. The older one, Stefan Prvovenčani ("the First-crowned") got international recognition to become Serbia's first king; his younger brother Sava became head of Serbia's self-governing Orthodox Christian church in 1219, when he became archbishop and founded a famous monastery in the town of Žiča. Today Sava, whose birth name was Rastko, is almost always called Saint Sava. One of his many achievements was the writing of the *Krmčija*, a code of church law based on a Byzantine model. Many Nemanjić rulers were quickly canonized, and church-state relations were very close.

Until the late fourteenth century, all the Serbian kings would be descendants of these men. Over the next 140 years, Serbia gradually expanded. Their cultural models remained Byzantine, but their political ambitions were also directed at Byzantium; they were staunchly Orthodox but also not averse to making tactical alliances with their Catholic neighbors to the north and west. Many of the most stunning Serbian artistic and architectural monuments originated at this time, such as the monasteries of Sopoćani (built by King Uroš) and Gračanica (built by King Milutin) and Dečani (built by Stefan Dečanski). German settlers, invited in by the kings, sparked a revival of mining. The use of money (instead of labor dues and barter) spread, and a great deal of trade was carried out with the independent city of Dubrovnik on the Adriatic.

THE GREAT TSAR DUŠAN

The medieval power and reputation of Serbia culminated in the reign of Dušan, who came to power in 1331 and took the title emperor in 1346. Until his death in 1355, he ruled an area extending from the Sava and Danube Rivers in the north to the Adriatic Sea in the West and the Aegean Sea in the south. He fought many wars and conquered many of Serbia's neighbors. His empire included Macedonia, northern Greece, Montenegro, almost all of Albania; the imperial title he took, reflecting both his aspirations to rival the Byzantine emperor and the ethnic makeup of his far-flung lands, was "Tsar of the Serbs and Bulgarians and Autocrat of the Greeks." Toward the end of his life he was in conflict with the Kingdom of Bosnia, with the more powerful Kingdom of Hungary to the north, and with the even more powerful Byzantine Empire

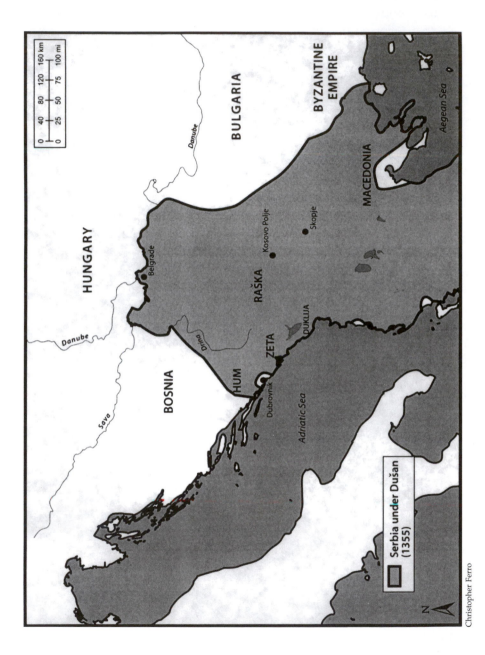

Christopher Ferro

to the south and east. Capturing the Byzantine capital city of Constantinople was his ultimate goal. He even considered an alliance with the Venetians and the Papacy, traditional foes of Orthodox countries like Serbia, to achieve this goal.

Dušan expanded on a key piece of St. Sava's legacy. On his own authority he upgraded the status of Serbia's Christian church, based in Peć, by making its leader a patriarch instead of an archbishop. This put the Serbian church on an equal footing with the older and more prestigious Greek-controlled church in Constantinople. Another of his signal achievements was his law code, issued between 1349 and 1354. Its provisions give us an invaluable glimpse into the nature of Serbian society at the time; the crimes it describes and harsh punishments it proscribes make fascinating reading. It also gives us a picture of Dušan as ruler trying hard to fight anarchy and corruption by keeping society stratified but also governing it efficiently and, by the standards of the day, justly.

DISINTEGRATION OF THE SERBIAN EMPIRE

When Emperor Dušan died, his son naturally took over the empire. But Serbia's expansion had been too rapid to build solid governmental foundations, and a variety of peoples, including Greeks, Bulgarians, Albanians, Vlachs, and Italo-Dalmatians, lived there together with Serbs. Stefan Uroš V (ruled 1355–1371), seems to have lacked his father's authority and reputation. Almost immediately several key Serbian lords (important landowners who were also usually key soldiers and administrators for the monarch) began to carve their own domains out of the recently united empire. Centralized authority and cooperation were rapidly eroding in the Serbian lands, and with it would go the country's ability to resist an important set of invaders just making their way to Europe: the Ottoman Turks.

The Turks are most famous today for their conquest of Byzantium in 1453—pulling off a victory that the Serbs only dreamed of—and for their two unsuccessful sieges of Vienna in 1529 and 1683. But they began conquering territory in the Balkans in the 1350s, and their armies had penetrated far enough inland to come into major conflict with Serbia. It is interesting to note that the Turks first appeared on European soil as allies of a Byzantine politician, John Cantacuzenus, who used them against three sets of his own political rivals. The Ottoman leader, Orkan, seized the Gallipoli area for himself in 1354, "[h]aving thus learned of the wealth and attractions of Europe, and also of its disunion and weakness."[2] In 1371 the first major battle between the Turks and Serbs took place. It is called the Battle of the Marica River (after the river in today's Bulgaria where it was fought) or the Battle of Chernomen (after a nearby town).

Two important Serbian leaders died in this battle, and the Ottomans began to rule many of the "front line" Serbian districts by indirect means: they forced local leaders into alliances or tributary status. The most famous of these dependent Serbian rulers, often called Turkish vassals, was a prince named Marko, who was later immortalized in folk songs and poetry for his many exploits. Ironically, Kraljević ("the Little King") Marko (died 1395) is often considered to be a prototypical Serbian freedom fighter, even though his legendary willfulness, cunning, rage, and fighting skills were often spent in plain mischief and in real life his service was often given to the Turks.

As circumstances would have it, the last emperor (Stefan Uroš), also died in 1371. A prince named Lazar was accepted as the titular Serbian leader because Milica, his wife, was a Nemanjić. He attempted to restore centralized rule from his fortress at Kruševac. He had considerable success making peace with Serbia's neighbors (except, of course, the Turks) and reviving Serbian culture. But he could not hold the fractious Serbian princes together. This disunity helped make the gradual Turkish conquest of Serbian lands possible. Lazar himself, after building a famous monastery at Ravanica, would die at the Battle of Kosovo in 1389.

SOCIAL STRUCTURE

The social structure in medieval Serbia was fairly straightforward. In terms of political and socioeconomic classes, there were four main groups. At the top of the pyramid was, of course, the king (and later emperor) and his family. Below them were the nobles; as was the case in other parts of Europe during the feudal era, the nobles held and used large amounts of the king's land in return for giving him military service. The majority of the population consisted of serfs, who had the right to use certain tracts of land but were also bound to that land and had to give their lords, the nobles, both taxes and labor dues. Below the serfs were the slaves. Slavery in medieval Serbia, as in the Ottoman and Roman Empires, was not based on race the way American slavery was. Often it was prisoners of war who became slaves; at any rate, Serbian slaves often functioned much like serfs.

The enormous stratum of society that provided the continuity in Serbian society from the fourteenth century all the way to World War II was the peasantry. Until the twentieth century it was organized on a type of extended family known as the *zadruga*. The head of a *zadruga* had powers that were far from absolute, and there were elements of shared power in the family. The *zadruga* included several generations, in-laws, and cousins, etc. In this way it was very different from the modern "nuclear" family, consisting simply of parents and one or two children, which is so common in industrialized countries.

The members of the *zadruga* farmed their lands, performed household labor, and made simple items for family use. The various families living near each other were grouped into villages, which also had a patriarchal head. This *knez* usually made decisions in consultation with a meeting or assembly known as a *zbor*. Some anthropologists and historians cite this as evidence of a fundamental pattern of democracy in Serbian culture. It was in this period that many Serbian religious traditions took root also. One of the most famous is the *slava*, an annual celebration of the name day of a family's patron saint.

One of the important legacies of this social structure is the anthropological concept (coined by the great Serbian geographer Jovan Cvijić) of "Dinaric" and "Zadruga" personalities. Balkan peoples who lived in rugged mountainous areas, such as the Montenegrins, Albanians, and some Serbs, Croats, and Greeks, did not live in *zadrugas*; as the theory goes, they developed a much different type of society and mind-set with implications for history into the twentieth century. The "Dinaric" personality type—named after the Dinaric Mountains where they lived—were, by virtue of their hardscrabble existence and isolation, fiercely individualistic and proud. They carried out "blood feuds," fought ferociously (and usually successfully) against invaders, and were not amenable to integration into modern society. These Dinaric characteristics, enshrined in literature and epic poetry, were once believed to have "programmed" Balkan peoples for violence. Modern scholars reject such deterministic notions, but the uses to which Dinaric "virtues" are put in the realms of politics and popular culture in the twentieth century do make important topics for study.

WOMEN IN MEDIEVAL SERBIA

The further back one takes an examination of any country's history, the fewer women appear in prominent roles in the historical narrative. History has traditionally been written by men, though it is created by all members of a society. Before the nineteenth century, most historians were mainly concerned with military and diplomatic affairs, in which women have traditionally played only marginal roles. A fuller appreciation of the role of women in a country's economic, social, and cultural life, not to mention their political ideas or influence, only began to attract serious scholarly and public attention in the twentieth century. Most accounts of Serbian history follow this general pattern.

Societies in medieval Europe were extremely patriarchal, but there was some cultural and political space in which women could operate. They usually wrote religious documents, ruled in the gaps between kings, and founded religious institutions. For the most part, however, women's lives were limited by custom and religious authority to the many kinds of work associated with daily family life; when they appear in traditional literature, it is almost always as the wives or mothers of warriors. Written documents about anyone's personal life in the Middle Ages are rare, especially for people who were not wealthy. A few such documents by women are discussed below; otherwise, historians rely on folklore, anthropology, the study of economics, and a few general documents about society such as Tsar Dušan's famous Law Code to figure out what life was like for most women.

In politics, only a few Serbian noblewomen have shown up on the historical radar. The British scholar Celia Hawkesworth has described the wives of Serbian rulers as functioning as "a kind of currency"[3] for making arrangements with foreign powers; this is indeed a striking image, because many of Serbia's early princesses and queens were of Greek, Hungarian, Bulgarian, or even French birth, and many of them were dropped or "sent away" by their husbands when the political winds changed. The most famous of these royal women was Queen Jelena, who was in all probability born Helene d'Anjou and was related to the kings of France and Naples. In Serbian she is often called "Jelena Anžujska." She was married to Uroš, the grandson of the founder of the Nemanjić dynasty. From her husband's abdication in 1276 until her own death in 1314, Jelena ruled part of the Serbian kingdom; her son Dragutin ruled the rest. She made her own policies regarding relations with Dubrovnik, and she supported both Orthodox and Roman Catholic religious institutions. She was born Catholic but became Orthodox; her policies may have been the result of her personal exposure to both religious traditions, or they may have been pragmatic in origin, since Serbia's population was far from homogeneous. A second interesting feature of Queen Jelena's reign was her interest in education. She amassed a large library and created a kind of vocational school for poor women. A beautiful religious lament about sin and salvation is also attributed to her.[4]

Two other important Serbian women of the time figure most prominently in cultural affairs. Their lives are both intertwined with that of

Prince Lazar. Kneginja (Princess) Milica was of Serbian noble descent and married Lazar in the 1350s; after his death, she ruled Serbia for four years. Her lament over her dead husband has been praised for its emotional power, and it puts the stamp of realistic human suffering and despair on the heroic sacrifices that abound in the history and legends of the time. The nun Jefimija is the other important cultural figure. She had been married to a Serbian leader who died at the Battle of the Maritsa River in 1371. She then took refuge at Lazar's court. In 1402 she embroidered a shroud for the tomb of Prince Lazar, already considered a martyr for the Serbian nation. The poem that she wrote and immortalized in sewn gold letters has been widely praised for its tone of intimacy and its scope of emotions.[5]

NOTES

1. Vladimir Dedijer et al., *History of Yugoslavia* (New York: McGraw-Hill, 1974), p. 10.

2. Leften S. Stavrianos, *The Balkans since 1453* (New York: Holt, Rinehart and Winston, 2000), p. 43.

3. Celia Hawkesworth, *Voices in the Shadows: Women and Verbal Art in Serbia and Bosnia* (New York: Central European University Press, 2000), p. 64.

4. Ibid., p. 70.

5. Ibid., pp. 84–85.

3

Living with the Turks: Ottoman Rule in the Balkans

THE BATTLE OF KOSOVO AND ITS LEGACY

The single most important date in Serbian history is June 28, 1389. That is when the Battle of Kosovo (or "Kosovo Polje," meaning Field of Blackbirds) took place in southern Serbia. There have been other important battles fought on the same "Field of Blackbirds," but the events of that June day more than six hundred years ago have come to define the Serbs' identity and mission as a people. The echoes of this one battle are still very much present in Serbian culture; the Battle of Kosovo and the myths surrounding it do not determine Serbian behavior today, but they can help explain it—especially when one examines how the battle has been represented and misrepresented by politicians and cultural figures.

There are no extant firsthand accounts of the battle, and there are many conflicting later reports about it. What is known is that a Christian army faced off against an invading Muslim army. The main Christian force was the Serbian contingent led by Prince Lazar Hrebeljanović—the most prominent leader on the territory of the fragmenting Serbian Empire. But there were also certainly Bosnians and Albanians, who were Christian at the time, among the Christian fighters. The Turkish force was led by the Ottoman Sultan himself, Murad I, and may have included

Greeks and Italians. The Ottoman army probably numbered between 30,000 and 40,000. They faced something like 15,000 to 25,000 Christian soldiers. Both leaders died in the fighting, and the Turks temporarily retreated after the battle. Travelers' and historians' accounts from the period after the battle depict the engagement at Kosovo as anything from a draw to a Christian victory.

The pope and other European leaders were alarmed at the Turkish incursions. Periodically, large international crusades set forth to try to drive the Ottomans off the continent. In 1364 and 1396 two such Crusades failed in and around Serbia. But the Serbs' fate was truly sealed by the vast and disastrous Varna Crusade of 1444. The Serb contingents were led—sometimes more into accommodation with the Turks than confrontation with them—by Đurađ Branković. Also involved were Hungarians under János Hunyadi, Romanians under Vlad Tepeş (also known as Dracul, the man who is the basis for the legend of Dracula), and Albanians led by Skanderbeg, their national hero. After the series of defeats in the Varna Crusade, Serbia collapsed. The Turks took their last fortress city, Smederevo on the Danube, in 1459.

The Battle of Kosovo was only one of many fought between the incoming Turks and the various, often multinational groupings of European feudal lords and their peasant soldiers. For Serbs the battle has come to signify the end of their medieval empire under Dušan. The year 1389 has also become synonymous with a loss of freedom and an enslavement at the hands of an ethnically and religiously alien people, the Turks; furthermore, the Battle of Kosovo reminds Serbs of the great sacrifice of their leader, Prince Lazar, who died there.

It is this last point that provided the seed from which an amazingly rich and prolific Kosovo legend has grown. In the Middle Ages, Prince Lazar's death came to be viewed in religious terms. He was said to have nobly offered himself as a sacrifice so that his people might one day recover their greatness. He had chosen the "heavenly kingdom"—rather than earthly compromise or retreat—in defending all of Christian Europe from the invading "infidels." Furthermore, the legend grew to include the Serbs' betrayal by one of their own commanders, an addition that helped soothe the bruised ego of a proud people and boosted the religious parallels of the legend as well. All of Serbian history after Dušan's reign could supposedly be explained by this cataclysmic defeat. There was also a religious parallel to the political decline. It contained the promise of resurrection or recovery. Kosovo became the light at the end of the tunnel, for someday Serbia would reclaim it and celebrate a return to freedom and greatness. Throughout the next centuries and all their changes, Kosovo continued to symbolize the importance of Serbia's sacrifices and its future mission. It is safe to say that the legend and memory of the battle, as reflected in culture and political discourse, is more important historically than the battle itself actually was.

Extensive studies of the growth of the Kosovo myth have been carried out by European and American scholars. Many versions of the legend exist. Most famous among them are the ones that developed as ballads or epic poems during the Middle Ages. Since the nineteenth century, the battle and its consequences have also been the subject of novels, plays, and poems of various types. The events connected with the battle are beautiful and moving. Much that is universal—especially about the themes of grief, loss, and duty—can be read with delight.[1]

Any complete understanding of the importance of the Kosovo story, however, must note the ways in which today's popular understanding of the battle differs from the historical realities of 1389. Most obviously, the Battle of Kosovo did not actually bring about the end of the medieval Serbian Empire; rather, the year 1389 is one milestone on the Serbian Empire's gradual downward slide. A significant degree of Serbian independence continued until the fall of the capital Smederevo in 1459. This was possible because the Turks usually favored indirect rule, even more so when they were hard pressed. Many Serb princes and princelings thus took oaths of loyalty to the Turks but found ways to preserve their own power. Prince Lazar's own son, as well as the famous Kraljević Marko, functioned as Turkish military commanders after 1389. As in Western Europe, they were tied to the Ottoman rulers through feudal ties known as "vassalage," which meant that they owed certain financial and military obligations to the Turks. But in many ways, the Serbian nobles continued to rule themselves for the seven decades it took the Ottomans to consolidate their hold.

It is also significant that in this battle the Albanians were on the same side as the Serbs. Albania had not yet been fully conquered by the Turks, and thus the Albanians had not yet converted to Islam in significant numbers. In the twentieth century, the polemics about reconquering and re-Serbianizing Kosovo have been aimed at Albanians, as if they were the ones who killed Prince Lazar in the first place. The issue, of course, is that most of the Albanians in Kosovo today are Muslim, and in the mindset of hardcore Serbian nationalists today, all Muslim populations in the Balkans share the "guilt" of the conquering Turks.

Over the centuries, the importance of Prince Lazar in the various poetic versions of the Kosovo story has grown. His widow, Milica, and son, Stefan, may have felt the need to secure their own political fortunes by playing up Lazar's death. The Serbian religious establishment quickly took up the cause of Lazar's heroism, and he was soon made a saint of the Orthodox Church. Later versions of the epic poems stressed the religious parallels and motivations in Lazar's life more and more. Material about the traitor in the Serbian ranks—pinpointed as Vuk Branković, though this is probably inaccurate—also appeared later. The story of how a Serb (later named as Miloš Obilić) managed to assassinate Sultan Murad on the day of the battle was also a later addition, underscoring the idea that victims can draw blood too and that the (temporary) domination of the Balkan peoples would come at a steep price for the Turks.

THE NATURE OF OTTOMAN RULE

Ottoman rule, imposed over the period between 1371 and 1459, was in many ways more indirect than one might suspect. Typically, Serb regions invaded by the Ottomans did meet with significant destruction during the conquest (and anytime their Christian inhabitants rebelled), but the Ottomans preferred to rule most of their provinces by simply co-opting existing administrative structures. This practice minimized the likelihood of rebellion against the Turks, and it also made administration of the new provinces cheaper. For the conquered peoples, this practice meant that most aspects of their day-to-day lives did not change very much.

Nonetheless, many Serbian historians have lamented these centuries of Ottoman rule as a time of "de-civilization" or "re-tribalization," in political terms.[2] These concepts do capture well the sense of the Serbian polity being effectively destroyed at its highest levels. But the world of the average Serbian peasant had probably never extended much further than his or her *zadruga*, for that is how peasant life works all over the globe. Historians today disagree over just how bad Ottoman rule was for Serbs. Most would say that the traditional view that Ottoman rule was nothing but a "yoke" or a "long nightmare" of slavery, bloodshed, and cultural annihilation is exaggerated. Serbia was isolated from general European trends and politically decapitated, but its language, religion, and customs survived. Furthermore, some of its differences from Western Europe had taken shape before the Turks arrived.

Organization and Structure

The Ottoman Empire had two kinds of administrative systems. One was territorial, as the American system of states and counties is today.

There were many types of small districts and also bigger units known as *vilayets* or *pašaluks*, which referred to the area governed by one high Turkish official, or *paša*, who was something like a governor with military powers.

The other type of administrative system was based on religion. All of the religious groups of the empire (Muslims, Jews, and the various kinds of Christians) were organized into *millets*, or communities of faith. These organizations had important legal and financial functions. Within the Orthodox *millet*, taxes were collected by Christian church officials rather than by Ottomans. Nearly all legal issues—such as marriage, divorce, and inheritance disputes—involving only Christians were settled by Christian officials within the *millet*. These processes kept an important buffer between the average Serb and the Ottoman government.

The Ottomans respected Christianity and Judaism on theological grounds, as "peoples of the book." Islam recognized the others' right to exist among subject peoples and forbade, in theory and usually in practice, forcible conversion. Still, the Ottomans believed that their faith required them to conduct war against Christian governments, because they had a mission to prove the strength of Islam. So, while their goal was not to exterminate Christianity, they also could not offer equal rights to Christians within their empire. There was also a practical motivation for toleration: The Ottomans knew that a policy of massed forcible conversions in the Balkans would create fierce and unending resistance to Turkish rule. So they instituted policies that were, for the Middle Ages, tolerant. In today's terms we would say that Ottoman Christian subjects suffered discrimination, though not systematic genocide. That the relative tolerance of the Ottomans was well known at the time is attested by the fact that much of Spain's Jewish population, when expelled in the late fifteenth century, sought refuge in the Ottoman Empire.

A notorious Turkish practice was the *devširme*, which is usually translated as "child levy" or "blood tax." This involved taking Balkan children away from their parents and removing them to Istanbul, where they would be raised in Turkish and Muslim culture as intensely loyal and well-educated members of the Sultan's administration. By 1700, the practice was dying out, but perhaps 200,000 babies and young people had been "recruited" in this way.[3] This practice was doubtless unfair and subject to abuse, but it should be noted that these new Ottomans enjoyed a much more privileged (not to mention materially satisfying) life in Istanbul than would have been possible in the provinces. There are accounts of Balkan families urging the sultan's officers to take their children, in the hope that their city would then have a powerful advocate at the court in Istanbul. In fact, many of these Serb, Albanian, Greek, and Macedonian young people did in fact grow up to be powerful officials, sometimes even Grand Viziers of the Empire, such as the Bosnian Mehmed Sokolović in the 1500s. They sometimes used the power of their later offices to honor their original hometowns. The sultans, for their part, were fond of the *devširme* because it gave them a body of soldiers and officials who were intensely loyal just to them and not beholden to any factions on the Turkish domestic scene.

The World of the Serbian Peasant

Most Serbs were peasants when Ottoman rule began, and most were peasants when it ended. But their conditions of life and work changed gradually between the fifteenth and eighteenth centuries. After the disruptions of the initial Ottoman conquest, in many ways life was stable. But certain changes in economic structure, along with a decline in the sultan's ability to maintain order in the many provinces of his empire, caused the lot of Serbian peasants to deteriorate after about 1700.

The conquering Ottomans imposed a kind of feudalism on their Serbian lands known as the *timar* system, based on a hierarchical system of fiefs. In many ways, this system was similar to West European feudalism, but gradually a new kind of feudal system came to predominate in the Balkans. It was called the *chiftlik* system (based on larger holdings less subject to the sultan's or government's control) and was partly the result of changes in the world economy. The lords came to have much more independence from the sultan's power over their peasants. The peasants' lives worsened because their lords were no longer afraid of the sultan's enforcing the traditional laws or even recalling their land. Although the peasants did not become slaves, the lords ruled their estates almost as if they were plantations, driven by the desire to support their lifestyles through the export of food to Western Europe. Their demands on the peasants grew in number and in harshness. Many of the lords became very wealthy, politically powerful, and rebellious too. Sultans were tempted to turn a blind eye to abuses on the *chiftliks* because these lands often produced a lot of tax revenue.

The Serbs and the Outside World

Even though the Serbians were more or less rural, poor subjects of the sultan, their culture did not develop in total isolation in these centuries. The towns often had small colonies of merchants—often Catholics from

Dubrovnik on the Adriatic coast; in turn, some Serbs lived in or traveled to the ports along the coast. And after the 1720s, visitors to and from Russia became ever more frequent. But the most important connection to another country was with the government of the Habsburg Empire (Austria), which lay to the north and west of the Serbian lands. Many Serbs moved into Habsburg territory during these centuries, just as many had been moving westward into Bosnia and Croatia since the fifteenth century. The Habsburgs were a major military power, and they were generally in conflict with the Ottoman Empire.

Habsburg armies invaded Turkish territory numerous times after the Ottoman defeat at the second siege of Vienna in 1683. These Austrian attacks signal the beginning of what is called "the Eastern Question," the centuries-long struggle for control over Ottoman lands. As the fortunes of the Ottoman Empire ebbed, parts of its territory began to break off or be torn off by other European powers. Outside countries also began to manipulate the Ottoman government through diplomatic and financial means. The Habsburgs and the Russians would prove to be the Turks' most relentless enemies. The Treaty of Karlowitz of 1699 established Austria as a Balkan power; it awarded Vienna control over most of Hungary and Croatia, both of which had been under the sultan's control. In the 1700s, the Austrians liberated parts of Serbia, if temporarily, and organized Serbian military units to fight the Turks; this cooperation helped inspire the Serbs to regain their freedom in the great rebellion of 1804.

OTHER EFFECTS OF OTTOMAN RULE

Serbian culture under the Ottomans changed a great deal. The disappearance of the Serbian nobility had the effect of "leveling" Serbian society. Most Serbs were now simply peasants. Just about the only social differentiation was provided by priests or by locally prominent men called "notables." They were wealthier peasants or traders who often acted as intermediaries with the Ottoman government and sometimes organized militias, either for or against local rulers. These men are not called "nobles" because that term implies an aristocracy with far more inherited prestige, wealth, and power than Serbs possessed.

Other things that changed through contact with the Ottomans include popular attitudes, language, clothing, and food. Traces of the Ottoman legacy are readily apparent in the Serbian language. There are hundreds of words of Turkish origin, called *turcizmi*, in the Serbian vocabulary. Foods such as *sarma* (stuffed cabbage), *burek* (pastries made of filo dough with stuffing of meat, cheese, or apples), and *ajvar* (a vegetable paste made of red peppers and eggplant) have kept their Turkish names, as have items associated with coffee drinking and many types of traditional clothing.

Many Serbs moved during Turkish times, with effects lasting until today, into Bosnia, Dalmatia, Croatia, and southern Hungary. In some of these regions, nomadic shepherds called *vlachs* (who seem to be related originally to the Romanians) fused or became identified with the Serbian population.

In 1690, the Serbian Patriarch Arsenije III led about 30,000 families north into the Habsburg Empire. Carrying the body of Prince Lazar with them, they settled in today's Vojvodina. The Serbs had been cooperating with the Austrian invaders, whom they regarded as their potential liberators, and when the Ottomans recaptured southern Serbia, the patriarch feared reprisals. These Serbs were very useful to the Austrians. They were established as frontier soldiers in a broad belt known as the "military frontier," or *vojna krajina* in Serbian. In exchange for their promise to fight the Turks, these Serbs were given a significant degree of economic and religious autonomy. They came to be heavy majorities in regions that were traditionally Croatian. Today's disputed region of Croatia (the *Krajina*) takes its name from this historical military frontier. These conflicting claims to the region helped bring about massive bloodshed there in the 1940s and the 1990s.

The period of Ottoman rule also saw the emergence of many different Muslim communities in and around Serbia. The Turks themselves were Muslims, of course, and many of them moved into the Balkans. Although most were kicked out of Serbia by 1878, some remain; there are also small Turkish minorities in Montenegro and Macedonia. Other Muslim groups from Anatolia and the Middle East also moved into the Balkans. The Tatars and Circassians were the most important of these groups, although none remain in Serbia. Most significant, however, were the European populations who converted to Islam through contact with the Turks. The most important of these groups today is undoubtedly the Bosnian Muslims. But Albania is also a predominantly Muslim country today, and there are Bulgarian Muslims (called *Pomaks*) and Macedonian Muslims (called *Torbeši*).

During Ottoman times the phenomenon of the *hajduk* established itself. To some people, especially to the Turks, these armed Serbs were nothing but bandits or highwaymen. They roamed the countryside and, basically, robbed or lived by their wits. To Serbs, the *hajduks* represented freedom from (Ottoman) authority and, even if they sometimes robbed and harassed Serbs too, they were akin to Robin Hood figures. The many stories about Kraljević Marko are in this tradition.

The deeds of these "national bandits" were popularized and preserved in poetry and songs. By the nineteenth century, when the Serbian wars for independence took place, the legend of the *hajduks* had grown to immense proportions. These legends gave the Serbs self-confidence; they were a kind of combative ethos. The fact that more than a few Serb men were good with weapons was going to help in the coming revolutions, too.

A final area of change under the Ottomans was religion. Since St. Sava's day, Serbian Orthodox Christians had enjoyed a tradition of ecclesiastical independence. In Balkan history, strong ecclesiastical structures bring great benefits to their peoples. The Serbian Orthodox Church suffered many ups and downs during the years of Ottoman rule. It retained its traditional role as the guardian of Serbian culture, in addition to its spiritual functions. The monasteries kept the memories of Prince Lazar, Tsar Dušan, and dozens of other medieval rulers alive by tending frescoes and icons, and copying manuscripts.

After 1459 the Serbian patriarchate was placed under Greek administration. The Greeks came to form an important administrative class in the Ottoman Empire, because the sultans had traditionally greatly respected Greek Byzantine culture and because contemporary Greeks were often skilled as translators, businessmen, sea captains, and diplomats. The head of the Greek church was in Constantinople, now renamed Istanbul, and the sultan could keep a close eye on it. Serbs, like other Orthodox peoples of the Balkans, grew to resent Greek religious control. In 1557, however, the Grand Vizier, Sokolović, restored and expanded the Serbian patriarchate. But in 1766, the Turks again shut down the patriarchate.

The effects of religious oppression were blunted, though, by the fact that the great northward migrations of the 1690s and 1730s had given rise to new Serbian cultural centers in Hungary, particularly the metropolitanate at Sremski Karlovci. Indeed, the Novi Sad area was eventually home to such a large and culturally active Serbian population that it came to be known as "the Athens of the Serbs." In 1687, the bones of Prince Lazar were placed in a new monastery nearby.

Medieval Montenegro

Although small, the population of what we call Montenegro today came to be quite varied during medieval times. Italians and Croats (both

Catholic) lived along the coast, while in the interior lived Albanians, Turks, and Slavic Muslims. By the sixteenth century, the nucleus of a coherent state existed around the capital at Cetinje, but control over the far-flung clan structures was extremely difficult. The Turks claimed the region as their own, and at times they occupied parts of it, especially the valleys. In 1499, they came closest to conquering it outright. But they proved unable—or unwilling—to take it all.

The Montenegrins developed a reputation as fearsome fighters, and their traditional society lived on in proud, if impoverished, isolation. One of their greatest cultural achievements, though, was the printing press founded at Obod in 1493; it was one of the few sources of Serbian-language printed works in the world. A prominent feature of Montenegrin political life was the ability of its leaders to conduct diplomacy with the crowned heads of Europe. By the early 1700s, for instance, Montenegro enjoyed close relations with Russia. The religious and financial support given by Russia was a big boost for the ruling Njegoš family.

NOTES

1. For an excellent recent translation, see John Matthias and Vladeta Vuckovic, *The Battle of Kosovo* (Columbus: Ohio University Press, 1988).

2. These terms were popularized by the anthropologist George Vid Tomashevich.

3. Peter F. Sugar, *Southeastern Europe under Ottoman Rule, 1354–1804* (Seattle: University of Washington Press, 1977), p. 56.

4

Revived Serbia: The Wars of Independence and the Building of a New Country, 1804–1868

THE SERBIAN REVOLUTION OF 1804

The Serbs under Ottoman rule suffered discrimination, a loss of political freedom, and economic and cultural isolation. Yet, paradoxically, the very structure of the Ottoman Empire made it possible for Serbs to live together and to keep their language and national identity alive. In the late eighteenth century, however, the situation of the Serbs was growing markedly worse, because the central Ottoman government in Istanbul was gradually losing control of its far-flung provinces. Serbs were increasingly preyed upon by Ottoman elite soldiers (*janissaries*) and local warlords, who ignored Ottoman traditions and showed little restraint in pursuit of their own power and fortunes. Serbia's fate at this time was also tied to the activities of the Great Powers of Europe, who were then embroiled in the Napoleonic wars. But it was in the nineteenth century that Serbia was to become an independent country again. It developed its sense of modern nationalism and built the institutions of modern life and statehood such as an administration, a school system, railroads, and a parliament.

In the 1790s, the Serbs became the tactical allies of Sultan Selim III, who wanted to restore order in the Balkans. Selim allowed the Serbs to basically run their own affairs and even maintain an armed militia, in exchange for cooperation with the sultan's loyal governor in Belgrade, Hadji Mustafa Pasha.

In 1798, Napoleon Bonaparte invaded Egypt, which was technically still a part of the Ottoman Empire. This distracted Selim, and his rebellious subjects were able to assassinate Hadji Mustafa. By 1802, four *janissary* officers had taken control of the government in Belgrade. At the beginning of 1804, the new rulers tried to kill off as many Serbian leaders as they could, to crush the rebellion they sensed was coming. Dozens of Serbian notables were killed. The remaining leaders met at the central Serbian town of Orašac in February 1804 and proclaimed a rebellion aimed at restoring legitimate rule.

The man who quickly emerged as the leader of the rebellion was Karađorđe Petrović, who eventually became the scion of one of Serbia's competing dynastic families, the Karađorđevićs. His first name, which means "Black George," apparently referred to either his hair color or to his ferocious temper. He eventually held precarious control over forces totaling 30,000 men. By August 1804, the local *janissaries* had been unseated, but the Serb forces did not disband. The sultan was under great pressure to move against them now, since cooperating too much with armed Christian subjects was thought to be heretical. Then the Serbs sent a delegation to St. Petersburg to ask, unsuccessfully, for Russia's help.

In the summer of 1805, the sultan attacked the Serbs, but Karađorđe's forces won major victories at Ivankovac and the Plains of Mišar. Then the tumultuous events of the Napoleonic wars made themselves felt again: Russia was now at odds with Turkey. Help from St. Petersburg was promised, and Karađorđe now felt powerful enough to broaden the rebellion's goal to independence for the Serbs. They thus became the first of the Balkan peoples to begin a drive for real independence against the Turks. At this time the rebellion also became much more popular among the Serbian population. Overwhelmingly peasants, they became enthusiastic for full national independence when they realized they could take over the farmlands relinquished by the expelled Turks.

Then trouble struck. The Russian Tsar Alexander I again made peace with Napoleon in 1807, and the aid to the Serbs evaporated. The Serbs were stranded, and their declaration of independence was like a red flag to the Ottomans. They dug in and held on to their recent gains, but their situation was precarious. This kind of up-and-down pattern in Russian-Serbian relations is typical, despite the conventional wisdom that the two peoples, linked by language, ethnicity, and religion, are durable and warm allies. The American historian David MacKenzie has described the

Serbian-Russian relationship as an "unequal and sporadic partnership" in which the Serbs have been aided "considerably but not very consistently."[1] Even when Russian (and later, Soviet) officials have determined that their interests are served by helping the Serbs, or when Pan-Slavic or nationalist groups in Russia manage to drum up public support for them, the Serbs have often perceived the attitude of their great eastern neighbor to be arrogant. This was the case during the war of independence, during the wars of the 1870s, and again in the Tito era after 1945.

During this middle phase of the war of independence, Karađorđe's government took some important steps toward modernization of the country. It opened many elementary schools and created a Ministry of Education led by Serbia's greatest intellectual, Dositej Obradović. A small *Velika Škola* (Upper School) was founded so that, as Karađorđe himself urged publicly, Serbia would have the brain power to rule itself once freedom was won. These measures were only partly successful, because the government had little money and was under constant attack.

By 1809, Russia was again at war with the Ottoman Empire, and help was forthcoming to the Serbs. But Turkish attacks mounted, and there was much fierce fighting. Serbian fortunes tumbled even further as the Russian forces withdrew to defend their own homeland against Napoleon's huge invasion. The Treaty of Bucharest (May 1812) between the Russians and the Ottomans guaranteed the Serbs an amnesty and continued autonomy. The Serbs were afraid that the Turks would seek retribution; they continued to fight but were beaten steadily back.

In July 1813, Karađorđe and other prominent Serbian leaders abandoned the fight and left an exhausted Serbia for the Habsburg Empire. The Turks quickly reoccupied Belgrade. There were still many armed Serbs in the countryside, and relations between Serbs and Turks were rocky. Nonetheless, the new pasha of Belgrade tried a policy of conciliation rather than brutal suppression or retaliation, and many Serb leaders went along with it. One important Serbian leader was Miloš Obrenović. He helped the Turks put down a local uprising in early 1814, apparently believing both that conditions did not yet favor a renewal of hostilities and that his personal standing with the Turkish authorities would be improved by remaining loyal.

In 1814 Miloš ended up joining the rebels after all. Russia put pressure on the Porte (the name used by foreign diplomats to refer to the Ottoman government) to make concessions. By the time the fighting stopped in 1815, Miloš had achieved many of his goals: Serbia had some degree of territorial unity and administrative autonomy, and he had been recognized as prince for life. Miloš refused to support the Greek revolutionaries in their anti-Ottoman plots and when Karađorđe returned to Serbia, Miloš executed him.

Miloš ruled Serbia from 1816 to 1839. Although by today's standards his rule seems heavy handed and in some ways even rapacious, he is responsible for laying the foundations of the modern Serbian state. He made use of the talents of many *prečani* Serbs (a term referring to Serbs from "across the rivers" in the Habsburg Empire, where Serbs were wealthier and better educated). These men were able to serve as administrators under Miloš while the first groups of Serbs were being educated in the revived Upper School in the new country. He was also able to restore the Serbian church to independence through an agreement with the Porte. The first textbooks were commissioned. In the 1830s the first newspapers in Serbia came into existence, along with theaters and some elementary schools and libraries.

Serbia's population was now 670,000, of whom about 7,000 people lived in Belgrade. Miloš moved the capital to Kragujevac (2,000) people, partly because Belgrade was exposed to attack. By 1833 he had secured the addition of more territory to the now fully autonomous principality as well as the right to appoint his sons as successors. The prince was very popular among peasants because of his Homestead Act, which made it impossible for peasants to go totally bankrupt and lose their homes and a minimum amount of land. Opposition to his rule, though, gradually grew among a group of educated politicians and merchants who became a kind of rudimentary political party. They were called the *Ustavobranitelji* (Defenders of the Constitution), because they favored a political system that would limit the prince's power. Their political forum was the traditional congress of notables known as the *Skupština* (Assembly). In 1838, with the sultan's help, they succeeded in limiting Miloš's power in what was called the "Turkish Constitution." Important powers were now given to the members of the "State Council," who were appointed for life. An angry Miloš then abdicated and left the country. His son Milan died shortly thereafter, and power then passed to his other son Mihajlo, who was soon forced out by the Constitutionalists. They quickly called a representative of the family of would-be royals back into power.

THE REIGN OF ALEKSANDAR KARAĐORĐEVIĆ (1842–1858)

The sixteen years of Prince Aleksandar's reign were a rough-and-tumble time in which the fledgling Serbian state faced many difficulties.

The prince was not a charismatic man and did not win from the sultan the right to establish a dynasty. The Constitutionalists dominated the administration. Their style of rule was oligarchic, reflecting the amount of power they reserved for themselves.

The government opened more schools and libraries and started sending students abroad for higher education. In 1844, the first civil code (a comprehensive set of laws) was drawn up. It established a civil service and an independent judiciary. But by the end of Aleksandar's reign there were only about one quarter the number of trained judges needed. In terms of foreign policy, the prince's main goal was not to incur the anger of the sultan. Serbia was still too weak to stand up to any of its large neighbors. In 1844, Interior Minister Ilija Garašanin wrote a document called the *Načertanije*. This memorandum called upon the government to expand Serbia's borders to include areas—such as the Vojvodina, Bosnia-Hercegovina, Montenegro, and northern Albania—that had belonged to Emperor Dušan's medieval Serbian state. In addition to defining what was legitimate Serbian territory to be "redeemed" by the government, the *Načertanije* noted the necessity of Serbia's economic development. It called for cooperation with Great Powers such as Britain and France and with other Balkan peoples such as the Bulgarians. The *Načertanije* became a durable if vague blueprint for the expansion of the Serbian state. Like the linguistic ideas of the scholar Vuk Karadžić, Garašanin's document contained the potential for great conflict with Serbia's neighbors on which population groups and lands are defined as Serbian.

The other landmark event in foreign affairs during Aleksandar's reign was the period of revolutionary disturbances throughout Europe in 1848–1849. Serbia itself did not have a revolution in these years, but the one million Serbs who lived next door in the Habsburg Empire were involved in serious disturbances.

The Habsburg Empire was very diverse, with no national, ethnic, or linguistic group in the majority. The two biggest groups were the German-speaking Austrians and the Hungarians. As the Hungarians of the empire began pushing for greater self-rule, the national groups living under them began to speak up as well. These groups, including the Serbs, Croats, and Romanians, did so partly because of the inspiration of the Hungarian example and partly out of fear that if Hungary was able to secede from the empire, then their own rights might not be protected. This was a well-founded fear, since Hungarian liberals and nationalists typically showed little sympathy for the rights of the other groups living in the eastern half of the empire, areas they considered theirs by historical right.

When Hungary received a large measure of autonomy from Vienna in mid-1848, the Croats and Serbs began organizing to protect their rights. They were led by a Croatian general, Josip Jelačić; by the Serbian Metropolitan (a religious leader) of Sremski Karlovci, Josif Rajačić; and by the Serb Djordje Stratimirović, who organized the volunteer soldiers. After months of bitter battles and a huge Russian intervention to help the government in Vienna, the Hungarians surrendered. One town in the Vojvodina saw so much fighting that it was renamed "Srbobran," or "Defense of the Serbs."

The new system imposed by the Habsburg emperor, Franz Josef, did not reward the Serbs and Croats for their loyalty by giving them the territorial recognition they desired. But they were spared further Magyarization, at least for the time being. And an important arena of Croat-Serb cooperation was established.

In December 1858, Aleksandar was ousted as prince. Popular sentiment had built up against him, because of the increasing indebtedness of the peasantry and his perceived weakness in foreign policy. The aging Prince Miloš was voted back into office, largely because it was thought that his kind of direct, paternalistic but uninnovative rule would provide the security that the peasants wanted. Miloš thus returned from exile to govern for two more years before his death of natural causes.

THE REIGN OF MIHAJLO OBRENOVIĆ (1860–1868)

Prince Mihajlo returned to the throne as a well-educated man of thirty-seven. Although he was not successful in many of his endeavors, he was able to articulate a clear vision of how he wanted to rule Serbia: he would use his top-down control of the country to modernize it and prepare it for a major military confrontation with the Turks.

Mihajlo is usually associated with the political philosophy known as Enlightened Despotism, which was widespread in the rest of Europe in the late 1700s. Joseph II of Austria and Catherine the Great of Russia were famous enlightened despots (or enlightened absolutists, as they are also called). These rulers sought to transform their countries in rational, modern directions by principled, direct rule and efficient government. Mihajlo fits this definition in part because he did not believe that Serbs were educated enough to rule themselves. He wanted to turn the Skupština into a group of consultants to rubber-stamp and popularize his modernizing laws; the once-powerful state council became, in effect, simply his cabinet.

In the 1860s Belgrade's population grew considerably, although with

25,000 inhabitants it was still tiny compared to Paris, St. Petersburg, or London. Apart from Belgrade there were no major urban areas. The country as a whole had just over 1.1 million people. The prince, however, restarted the construction of an impressive national theater and founded various musical institutions. He also changed the name of the Upper School to the Academy and expanded its offerings. Law studies were especially useful in training government administrators. Mihajlo also created a government agency to make low-interest loans to peasants. The army he created supposedly numbered more than 50,000 men, but its quality was in doubt. Needless to say, all these programs cost money. The prince tried to push through new taxes and he also put much of his own money into government programs, but the financial stress on the government still lowered his popularity.

The ideas of political and economic liberalism were never adopted by Prince Mihajlo, but they spread in Serbia at the time. These ideas were famous in American, French, and English political history. Classical liberalism supports constitutions and parliaments as limits on the power of kings and princes, economic development either through laissez-faire policies or the government encouragement of commerce and industrialization, and the freedom of the individual as expressed in civil rights. These are ideas that are fundamental to most conceptions of political democracy—including the American one—and traditional capitalism. Most historians argue that classical liberalism is called into being by a rising middle class, usually under the influence of some of the political thinking of the Enlightenment, but in Serbia such a class of people barely existed. The liberals there wanted to import these ideas to serve as the catalyst for change.

Young Serbian intellectuals such as Vladimir Jovanović were exposed to liberal ideas during their studies abroad. They believed that such ideas were important for Serbia because they would help Serbia modernize. Their liberalism was opposed by the conservative, older Constitutionalists and by the princes. The liberals were never able to form an official political party, but they came to occupy important positions in government and culture.

Jovanović, whose son, Slobodan, later became Serbia's most distinguished historian, was an important popularizer of West European ideas. He linked economic and political development by arguing convincingly that what Serbia needed most was education, infrastructure, and improved government services to spark agricultural and industrial growth. This was essentially a Central or Western European model of development. Most Serbian liberals believed in these ideas, but they were eager for a system of government that would allow their party to rule, and they also wanted to copy a Western style of rule so that other European governments would accept them.[2]

Jovanović justified his ideas by asserting that Serbian culture was inherently democratic or representative, as the existence of local councils and the structure of extended families demonstrated. Liberal ideas would eventually have a profound effect on the Serbian system of government, and a much smaller effect on the economy of the country. But from today's vantage point more than a century after the peak of their influence, it is apparent that the liberals' greatest importance lay in the introduction of nationalism to Serbia. Garašanin and Karadžić, two members of the country's elite, had already circulated ideas crucial to Serbia's national identity and quest for expansion. But, properly viewed, modern nationalism is a mass phenomenon, and as long as the majority of the population was excluded or alienated from politics, there could be no nationalist "discourse": that is, the country's goals could not be expressed in nationalist terms and the population could not be mobilized through appeals to nationalism. All this would change after the 1860s.

Modern nationalism asserts the importance and the sovereignty of the people, who are collectively also called "the nation." Nationalism is secular and it stresses the commonalities of language, customs, territory, and sense of mission. In its emphasis on the people, it springs from the same impulse as classical liberal political thought. Both nationalism and liberal democracy place the people—however variously defined—at the center of a country's political life. But whereas democracy is usually concerned with how fairly a country is governed at home, nationalism can encourage expansion or even aggression by a country in foreign affairs. One of the liberals' nationalist demands was that Serbia expand its borders. Specifically, they wanted the Serbian government to defend the interests of Serbs living outside of Serbia.

In short, when the liberals imported their parliamentary ideas from Central and Western Europe, they also imported the idea of nationalism. They were very concerned about the large Serb populations (about 1.5 million in total) in Bosnia-Hercegovina and the Habsburg Empire, where a liberal movement led by the publicist and mayor of Novi Sad, Svetozar Miletić, was prominent; at this time, Novi Sad was called "the Serbian Athens" because the Serbs who lived there had an important degree of self-government and were allowed to publish books, newspapers, and religious works in Serbian. In Bosnia-Hercegovina, the Serbs lived mixed together with large numbers of Muslims and Croats, but Serb nationalists asserted historical rights to the region. They thought the time was right for Serbia to conquer Bosnia, since the Ottoman Empire was decaying and the Habsburgs were distracted and demoralized by their recent military losses to Italy and Prussia. Mihajlo knew that his country was not strong enough to annex Bosnia. Although he did have plans for Serbian expansion in other regions, the liberals chided him for his supposed lack of nationalism. This lessened Mihajlo's popularity even more.

Mihajlo wanted Serbia to follow the procedures Piedmont and Prussia had used in the respective unifications of Italy and Germany. To this end he negotiated constantly with politicians and military leaders in Montenegro, Greece, Romania, Bulgaria, and even Habsburg-occupied Croatia. Serbia established a network of propagandists, spies, and guerrilla fighters abroad. He hoped someday to lead a great Serbian army into the field and direct a multinational war to deprive the Turks of their remaining European possessions. But Austria and Russia tried to rein him in, while few non-Serbs were attracted to his autocratic style of rule. Mihajlo did manage to conclude an agreement with the sultan for removal of the last 12,000 Turks garrisoned in Serbia.

The prince's authoritarian, mistrustful personality cost him much support, as did his tumultuous personal life. His wife, Julia, was a Roman Catholic of Hungarian extraction, and this made many Serbs wary. She and Mihajlo had also had no children. But when Mihajlo sought to divorce Julia and marry his second cousin, Katarina Konstantinović, the public as well as many church and political leaders were shocked.

In the summer of 1868, the prince was shot to death while visiting Topčider Park in Belgrade with Konstantinović and her family. The way power was transferred to the next prince showed that the military would be a major political force from then on. The minister of war, Milivoje Blaznavac, bypassing the Skupština, declared Mihajlo's grand-nephew, the fourteen-year-old Milan Obrenović to be the new leader. Blaznavac made himself one of Milan's regents. When the army, under Blaznavac's command, quickly swore allegiance to Milan, the succession issue was settled and parliamentary ambitions frustrated.

SERBIAN CULTURE IN THE ERA OF REVOLUTION

One of the most important cultural developments during the late Ottoman period was the evolution of the Serbian written language. For centuries, the majority of things that had been written down in Serbian were connected with religion and church life. Of course, there were also merchants' records from the coastal trade with Dubrovnik, and among the Serbian communities of the Habsburg Empire, there was a greater variety of written documentation. But the Serbian language was yet to grow into its modern, standardized form.

The term "vernacular" refers to the spoken language, the "real" way of talking that people use in their everyday lives. Written Serbian at this time differed greatly from the way people spoke. By the mid-1700s, there were several varieties of written Serbian in use, but they were not vernaculars. Most ordinary Serbs could not read or write. The priests and scholars who did most of the writing used various complicated mixtures of Old Church Slavonic and Russian (called *Slavenosrpski*) with some Serbian words. They did this because Old Church Slavonic was the liturgical language of the Orthodox Church. Since the 1720s, there had also been many Russian visitors to the Serbian lands and they influenced the way Serbs wrote. Russian, being the language of a big country that had recently begun opening up to Western influences, had words for many new concepts that Serbian did not yet have, and Serbs also hoped that by writing in a new, blended language, their works could be read by Slavic peoples elsewhere. As the interest in popular education grew, and Serb politicians and professors saw the value in teaching more and more people to read, it became obvious that a more "genuine" written language, closer to what people used in conversation, was necessary.

The first major Serbian intellectual figure of the modern era was Dimitrije Obradović (c. 1743–1811). He is sometimes called simply Dositej, because that was the name he bore during his three and a half years in the Hopovo Monastery. Obradović's memoirs are the first major work ever printed in the modern Serbian vernacular language. Fortunately, they have been translated into English and they make fascinating reading. He also wrote other books on folklore and educational themes.

Obradović is also important because he was a cosmopolitan, secular thinker. In the tradition of the Enlightenment, he wanted his fellow Serbs to modernize their society and to jettison outdated customs and prejudices. One of the most important kinds of modernization he sought was the development of a confident Serbian identity and an independent state. In this way, he is very much a nationalist, though this is nationalism in its original Enlightenment mold, when it was believed that all the nations of the world could live in harmony together, and that it was God's will that they do so. He himself taught the young Vuk Karadžić as well as children of famous politicians. He believed that the education of young people—both boys and girls—was vital for improving humanity in general and Serbia in particular.

Another important intellectual of this era was the linguist and folklorist Vuk Stefanović Karadžić (1787–1864). Vuk was born in the Šumadija and had a minor role in the Serbian War of Independence. He too fled to Austria in 1813. He had previously studied at a Serbian school in the Habsburg city of Sremski Karlovci. Now he went to Vienna and began writing for the local Serbian press. He soon made a very important friend: the Slovene scholar Jernej Kopitar, an important government official. He encouraged Vuk to update and standardize Serbian. Today Vuk is called "the father of the Serbian language."

Through his reforms, Vuk encouraged people to "write as you speak, and read as it is written." Although conservatives—especially churchmen—bristled at Vuk's reforms, by the late nineteenth century they had taken hold. He sealed his reputation as a language reformer with the publication of a Serbian grammar (1814), a dictionary (1818), and a translation of the New Testament (1847).

Vuk was equally important, however, as a collector of folk songs. Again, encouraged by Kopitar, as well as by the great German poet Goethe and the folklorists Jacob and Wilhelm Grimm, Vuk collected hundreds of traditional Serbian poems and songs in six highly praised volumes. Some he wrote down from memory but most he got by interviewing singers and wandering bards. The best known of these songs are the heroic ballads or epics, such as the Kosovo cycle. He also collected and published what he called "women's songs," which were colorful, lyrical poems about work, love, and family.

There is a third way in which Vuk was singularly important. This is in his definition of who is a Serb and who is not. Vuk was a man of his times and had a secular worldview. Thus, he did not follow the time-honored tradition of using religion as a criterion of nationality. Nor did he use the historical standard, as had Garašanin. To Vuk, you were a Serb if you spoke like one. There is considerable overlap between many Serbian dialects and those of their neighbors, but Vuk labeled as Serbs hundreds of thousands of people in Dalmatia, Bosnia, Hercegovina, and Slavonia who did not consider themselves Serbs. This linguistic definition of Serbdom is still important—and disputed—to this day.

NOTES

1. David MacKenzie, *Serbs and Russians* (Boulder, CO: East European Monographs, 1996), pp. xi, 4.
2. The discussion of Serbian liberalism is based on the excellent work by Gale Stokes, *Legitimacy Through Liberalism: Vladimir Jovanovic and the Transformation of Serbian Politics* (Seattle: University of Washington Press, 1975) with permission of the University of Washington Press.

5

Taking Its Place in the Sun: The Revival of Serbia, 1868–1914

THE REIGN OF PRINCE MILAN OBRENOVIĆ (1868–1889)

Milan was only fourteen years old when he became prince. His regents and the administration issued an updated constitution in 1869. It was a significant step toward political democracy, since it contained important—if limited—provisions for parliamentary rule and civil rights.

Serbia's political parties continued to have a great deal of power. The Liberal Party and its leader, Jovan Ristić, followed in the footsteps of Vladimir Jovanović. Their interpretation of "people's sovereignty" included not only parliamentary government but also a nationalist foreign policy. They looked especially to Russia for assistance. The pan-Slavist movement, prominent in some Russian cultural and diplomatic circles, espoused solidarity among Europe's Slavs, especially under Russia's leadership against German power. But not all of the political parties in the country favored expansion, and Prince Milan, like Mihajlo before him, was usually cautious about Serbia's military strength.

Domestic politics under Milan were characterized by conflict. There were two rebellions against his rule; governments (defined as a slate of cabinet officers headed by a premier or prime minister) rose and fell frequently, often at the manipulation of the monarch; and scandals and controversies rocked the government and royal family. Sometimes Serbian political life was more about the ambitions and personalities of individual politicians than it was a debate on policy or political philosophy; this characteristic has been seen a great deal in fledgling democracies in the twentieth century as well.

For Ristić, however, it was not parliamentary government and economic change alone that would provide Serbia with the status it deserved. Ristić put a high priority on using military force to unite all Serbs, the way Prussia had engineered the unification of Germany in the 1860s. He also manipulated the Skupština and the laws on censorship to shore up his own position, and he passed homestead laws that seemed to protect peasants but actually discouraged innovation and competition.

In 1880 the Progressive Party came to power. Like the Liberals, they emphasized industrialization, social modernization, civil rights, and parliamentary power, but they were less tied to Russia. They are remembered most now for allowing political parties to organize and compete in a modern fashion.

After 1887, the Radical Party, led by Nikola Pašić, would hold power all the way to World War I. The Radicals were a hybrid in terms of their ideology; their early socialist and anarchist strains were transformed into a kind of peasant populism. Most of their leaders had studied abroad and were drawn to the ideas of European leftists and anarchists. One of their founders was Svetozar Marković, who is today known as the first Serbian socialist, even though his ideas for agrarian self-government were very different from Marx's concern with the urban industrial workers.

The Radicals saw themselves as the protectors of average Serbs, and this helped them get elected over and over. They were pro-Russian in foreign policy and, at home, stressed local autonomy at the expense of the central government, partly because they mistrusted the educated, urban social groups. This direct connection to "the people" also made the Radical Party the most nationalistic group in Serbian politics; they held forth constantly on the need for Serbia to liberate areas like Bosnia, Macedonia, and Kosovo where other Serbs lived under foreign rule. Besides this nationalism, the Radicals' chief contribution was that they were Serbia's first genuine, modern political party. Through their mobilization of the masses, they came to be practically a parliamentary dynasty of their own. Pašić moved away from much of the ideology of his early colleagues in the Radical movement. He became well known for his "bottom-line" or Machiavellian attitude about politics; success for the politician, his party, and the country, he believed, is the only goal. That success came to be increasingly a function of a nationalist foreign policy.

Some significant socioeconomic progress was made under Milan. Serbia began minting its own currency and compulsory elementary education was begun. A national bank was formed and railroads connecting Belgrade to Zagreb, Sarajevo, and Niš were constructed. Bright students were still being sent abroad to study, but the nucleus of the University of Belgrade was being expanded at home.

The years 1874 to 1878 are called the "Great Eastern Crisis." These years form a very important chapter in the Eastern Question, the events surrounding the Ottoman Empire's gradual loss of territory and power after about 1700. During this crisis, Serbia would expand in territory and power and be recognized internationally as a kingdom, even though its battlefield performance was mediocre.

Rebellions in Hercegovina, Bosnia, and Bulgaria in 1874–1875 called forth a harsh and partly uncontrolled Turkish reaction. Supplies, money, and volunteers made their way into Turkish territory to fight the forces of Sultan Abdul Hamid. In June 1876, Serbia and Montenegro declared war on the Ottoman Empire and attacked Bosnia, hoping to annex it. The better-armed Turks, however, routed the Serbs' camp at the Battle of Djunis, in central Serbia. Russia threatened to attack the Turks if they did not leave the Serbs alone. The fighting stopped temporarily because restive minority groups, constitutional debates, and huge financial problems made the Ottoman Empire especially weak. Russia and Romania declared war on the Ottomans in April 1877, and the next year the Turks asked for an armistice. The fighting was very costly to Serbia in terms of human life and government finances. More than 16,000 Serbs died, about 13,000 were wounded, and thousands of refugees were created.

The Great Powers then held a peace conference. Eventually the Treaty of Berlin was signed on July 13, 1878. Serbia was accepted as independent and gained territory around Niš. But Serbia had to accept the Austrian occupation of Bosnia. To keep Serbia landlocked, the Austrians also occupied a small district called the Sandžak of Novi Pazar, between Serbia and Montenegro. It was also apparent now that Bulgaria was going to act as the Tsar's close ally and protégé. Russophiles in Serbia were gravely disappointed.

After being thus disappointed by the Russians, King Milan forged a very close alliance with Austria-Hungary, a move that was unpopular at home. Serbs now turned their desires for nationalist expansion southward; Macedonia and Kosovo would occupy the Serbs' attention for the next three decades.

These regions, while of indisputable historic and ethnic importance to Serbs, were major international bones of contention and would only be annexed with a great deal of bloodshed. A foreshadowing of the conflict, which would eventually bring about the debacle of the Balkan wars in 1912–1913, was the founding of the Society of St. Sava. This Serbian "cultural organization" used education, religion, and propaganda to advance Serbia's interests among the very mixed population of Macedonia. The Bulgarians and Greeks formed similar organizations. Some Macedonians insisted that they were neither Serbian, Bulgarian, nor Greek, and they formed the Internal Macedonian Revolutionary Organization in 1893. Such organizational work among groups, both secret and public, greatly sharpened the tensions in the region. But the cataclysm there would come after Milan's time.

Milan, who declared Serbia a kingdom on March 6, 1882, faced his other main foreign policy challenge shortly before the end of his reign. He attacked Bulgaria out of resentment over its successes and in order to distract his own population. Once again, in the disastrous Battle of Slivnica, the Serbian army failed to carry the day.

Milan's poor record in foreign policy and his scandalous private life made it virtually impossible for him to govern. He abdicated in March 1889. Just before he left the throne, Milan approved a new constitution, Serbia's fourth. An embittered Milan may have believed that this liberal document would unleash chaos in the country that had rejected him, or he may have wanted to pacify the country's leading politicians so that his son would not have a rough start as ruler.

THE REIGN OF ALEKSANDAR OBRENOVIĆ (1889–1903)

King Aleksandar began his reign at age thirteen, again under the guidance of regents. The young king seemed to have inherited a lot of his parents' worst characteristics and was also hectored by them for much of his life. During his reign, little progress was made on important issues facing the country. In some ways, Serbia even became a pariah among the very European countries that earlier rulers had been trying to imitate and impress.

Aleksandar's reign is known for his crude and cynical manipulation of the political system. He played politicians and parties off against each other and toyed with the constitution at will. The Radical Party remained powerful, but the king caused twelve different cabinets to fall. His father, the ex-king, meddled in political and military issues, and the royal family's reputation sank even lower when Aleksandar chose an enormously unpopular woman, Draga Mašin, to be his wife. There were also several conspiracies and an assassination attempt against the king in the 1890s.

Popular opinion continued to grow more nationalistic. Aleksandar himself came to the throne in the year that marked the 500th anniversary of the Battle of Kosovo, and there were important celebrations among Serbs throughout the Balkans. Many Serbs were growing increasingly disenchanted with their northern neighbor, Austria-Hungary, which was in possession of Bosnia and seemed to enjoy toying with the Serbs. King Aleksandar, for his part, was criticized for failing to capitalize on the Greco-Turkish war over Crete in 1896–1897 and for squandering Russia's good will.

On June 11, 1903, King Aleksandar's reign came to its ignominious end. A large conspiracy of about 120 politicians and military officers, had taken shape against him. A group of these men broke into the royal residence and brutally murdered the still-young king, queen, and five of their associates and family members. The mutilated bodies were then unceremoniously dumped into the courtyard of the palace. This grotesque regicide completed the recent growth of a very negative image of Serbia in many quarters of Europe. The military emerged as a major factor in Serbian politics.

At this time, about 87 percent of Serbia's population of 1.9 million still lived in the countryside. The only cities of any size were Belgrade and Niš, but even these cities were still small as compared to many other European countries. Belgrade, for instance, had fewer than 55,000 inhabitants, although most of them could read, and the city was developing the infrastructure of a modern capital. Most important for Serbian politicians, however, were the facts that many Serbs still lived under foreign rule and that the country did not have an outlet to the sea.

THE REIGN OF PETAR KARAĐJORĐJEVIĆ (1903–1921)

In contrast to the previous regimes, King Petar's reign has been called the "golden age" of Serbian politics. Two aspects of Petar's political philosophy stand out above all others: his intense patriotism and nationalism on the one hand, and his commitment to liberal governance on the other. Before taking the throne, he had already done many things that gave Serbs a good idea of the depth of his commitment on these issues. His family credentials were impressive—after all, he was the grandson of the original Karađjorđjé, leader of the 1804 uprising. And he had married Princess Zorka of the Montenegrin ruling family, thus opening up the possibility of a dynastic union between these two historical "branches" of the Serbian family. During the Great Eastern Crisis he had led soldiers into Bosnia and fought against the Turks. He was pro-Russian, had been trained at the French military academy, and had translated John Stuart Mill's *On Liberty* into Serbian. There were no scandals in his private life, and he inspired confidence. Because he was able to rally the Serbian people and administration behind him, the country was able to mount the major military campaigns necessary to achieve national expansion.

In domestic policy, the first major act of King Petar's rule was to restore the 1888 constitution, which was then quickly strengthened by the Skupština with Petar's approval. Most of the old political parties had faded from view, but Nikola Pašić and the Radicals were still the main parliamentary force to be reckoned with. In the early 1900s, opposition to Pašić's style of rule had led to the emergence of a splinter group of Radicals, called the Independents. The Social Democratic Party also appeared, led by Dimitrije Tucović and Vasa Pelagić; the number of industrial workers in the country, though still small, was growing rapidly. No vigorous legal steps were taken against the conspirators who had killed the last king, causing some domestic and international controversy. The lack of subordination of the military to civilian power was a serious flaw in Serbia's golden age of democracy. The Belgrade University was expanded in 1905, and it was now possible for students to study a wide range of humanities and professions, from philosophy to pharmacy, without leaving the country. Also, an ethnographic museum and a school for actors were founded.

The foreign policy of King Petar's rule was dominated by the wars of 1912–1918. This period included the two Balkan wars (1912–1913) and World War I (1914–1918). The wars are linked in Serbian historical writing because all three revolved around the liberation or occupation of *irredenta*, a term signifiying "unredeemed lands" that the Serbs hoped to "redeem" (in historical or ethnic terms). Serbia was to emerge victorious and grow massively as a result of these wars. But there were sobering effects as well: The Balkan wars were a bloody nightmare for civilian populations, and World War I brought great suffering to Serbs and radically changed the dynamic of Serbian politics by creating the country of Yugoslavia.

THE BALKAN WARS

The Balkan wars were fought over some of the last Turkish territories left in Europe: Macedonia and Kosovo. They marked the end of the Ottoman Empire in Europe and the rise of Serbia as a significant regional power. Indeed, they represent the greatest military victories ever won by Serbia.

Russia sponsored the creation of a Balkan League that linked Montenegro, Bulgaria, Greece, and Serbia. This alliance provoked a war with the Turks in October 1912. Sometimes this First Balkan War (October 1912 to May 1913) is simplistically termed a "war of liberation," aimed at pushing the Ottomans out of Europe. Likewise, the Second Balkan War (June to August 1913) is often simplistically regarded as a typically petty, bloody Balkan squabble over the spoils, since in it the erstwhile allies fought over the disposition of "liberated" Macedonia. These catchphrases, however, miss two important points. First, expansion took on a momentum of its own as each of the league's members took over territory to which it had no clear ethnic claim. This imperialism was, indeed, a pan-European phenomenon, and not just a Balkan one, but it was decidedly un-idealistic. Second, the plunder, slaughter, and expulsion of civilians was a deliberate, significant, and sobering aspect of both wars. Thus, these wars were far more representative of "total war" and mass nationalist conflicts than they were of traditional ethnic rivalries.

The Serbs contributed a significant amount to the severe Turkish defeat in the First Balkan War. The Balkan League had about 700,000 troops, of which half were Serbian, while the Ottomans could only put about 320,000 soldiers into the field. The irregular forces of the league (including Serbian Chetniks) pillaged and depopulated hundreds of villages; thousands of Muslim civilians—mostly Turks but also other nationalities—were killed, and at least 200,000 ended up in perilously squalid refugee camps. A commission from the Carnegie Endowment for International Peace visited the area and compiled a massive report on the murders, robbery, rape, and forced expulsions that we might today call "ethnic cleansing."

Bulgaria started the Second Balkan War by attacking Serbia, because it felt cheated of its claims in Macedonia. Montenegro, Romania, and the Ottoman Empire entered the war and Bulgaria was quickly defeated. About 150,000 Bulgarian civilians were violently uprooted by the new victors. The allies made significant territorial gains. Militarily the wars had the greatest impact on Serbia, which now had an experienced military but a society weakened by the cost and bloodshed of the wars. Exact casualty figures are elusive for wars such as these, but the best estimates are that the two wars left the following numbers of dead and wounded: 61,000 in Serbia; 9,000 in Montenegro; and 150,000 in Bulgaria. The Serbian military was now confident of its powers, but it had a new enemy

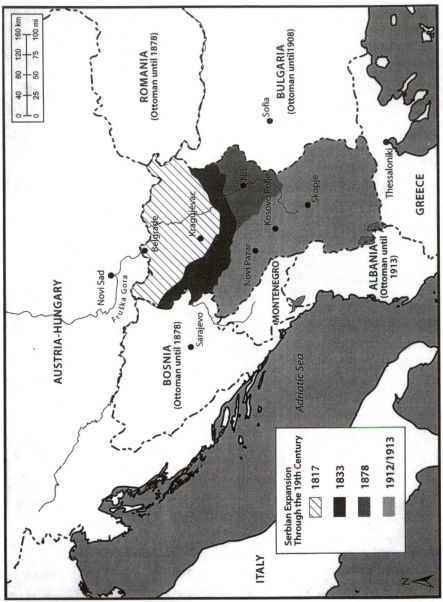

Christopher Ferro

in Bulgaria. The wars also had significant effects on the Ottoman Empire. Convinced of the desperate need for military reform, the Turks rushed to ally with the Great Power most willing to assist them: Germany. This alliance provided for the empire's fateful entry into World War I.

Serbia doubled its territory, but by becoming the most important regional power, the Serbs hardened Austria-Hungary's mistrust and animosity. The Serbs were also unable to assimilate Macedonia, which was a welter of rival national groups. Serbia reoccupied but could not pacify its old heartland of Kosovo, which even by 1913 had an Albanian majority. The country of Albania was created in 1913 by the Great Powers, who wanted to block Serbia's advance to the sea in the regions vacated by the defeated Ottomans.

ECONOMICS

As isolated and agrarian as the Serbian economy might have been under the Ottomans, it did not improve drastically after independence was won. Most historians and economists who have studied Serbia used to conclude that the years from 1804 to 1914 represented a success story of gradual economic improvement against tough odds; although most Serbs remained peasants, the country was seen as gradually clawing its way up from its backwardness, developing foreign trade, railroads, and industry as soon as conditions permitted. But other evidence suggests that Serbian agricultural productivity fell after liberation and that the government pursued many policies that prevented most Serbs from increasing their productivity and improving their standard of living. These new findings cast Serbia's governments up to World War I in a less favorable light.[1] These governments were uniformly preoccupied with the national question and military expansion, but such political and military concerns are no substitute for careful economic policies that stimulate growth. In turn, the lack of social change, which economic transformation would have brought, made the Serbian population even more susceptible to the appeal of ethnic nationalism.

Homestead laws, while popular, preserved inefficiency in farming. Inheritance patterns resulted in rural overpopulation and "dwarf plots" too small to support families. Enterprising peasants were also held back by the lack of "incentive goods" in shops and by laws that rewarded the mismanagement of forests. Technical training for peasants was woefully inadequate. Railroad building came late, because Serbian companies feared competition from outside producers, and the government spent too much on weapons to be able to afford railroads.

MONTENEGRO IN THE NINETEENTH CENTURY

In the 1800s, Montenegrins renewed their reputation as skillful soldiers. They defeated several Turkish attempts to shave off parts of their
country or cut it in two. The famous battle of Grahovo (in the western
part of the country) in 1858 was a resounding victory for the Montenegrins. During these decades, the cultural and political modernization of
Montenegro also began. Making their appearance were the first law
codes, schools, a printing press, and a judiciary. But the central government still lacked many powers and only a tiny part of the population
was urban. A strong pattern of immigration for economic reasons appeared. Many of the writings of Milovan Djilas are vivid explorations of
this era.

In the 1850s, the positions of bishop and prince were separated. In
1910, Prince Nikola declared the country a kingdom. Now there were,
in effect, two Serb kingdoms. Some Montenegrins were attracted to the
Yugoslav movement, but for the most part Montenegro was bent on
expansion in the same way that Serbia was at this time. On the eve of
the Balkan wars, Montenegro had fewer than 200,000 inhabitants; its con-
quests in those wars pushed the population up to 500,000 and gave it a
common border with Serbia.

The *vladika* (prince-bishop) Petar II Petrović (r. 1830–1851), known as
Njegoš, is considered Montenegro's national poet and first modern
writer. His best-known work is *Gorski vijenac* (*The Mountain Wreath*,
1847), which quickly came to enjoy almost iconic status among Montenegrins and Serbs. This poem is a dramatic evocation of a fratricidal
religious struggle between Orthodox Christians and Slavic-speaking
Muslims.

For Montenegrins, *The Mountain Wreath* has become a kind of national
epic because it reaffirms their connections to the Serbian and Christian
world and it celebrates their military skill. For other Serbs, the poem had
great resonance because it evoked themes similar to those in their own
Kosovo epics and it reminded them that the Montenegrins were their
allies. There is an increasing amount of debate today, however, about
how to reconcile the poem's vices with its virtues. All countries have
national epics and "foundation myths," and *The Mountain Wreath* contains a great number of important observations about social conditions,
customs, and the freedom-loving nature of the people. But the religious
and political leaders in the poem are almost literally swimming in blood
and they seem to revel in it. How should Montenegro's neighbors—or
its minorities—feel about a national epic in which "the poet hails the

massacre as the road to national rebirth"?[2] Curiously enough, both communists and nationalists have interpreted *The Mountain Wreath* in positive ways, and their analyses also make for interesting reading. They both tend to focus on the progressive nature of Montenegro's leaders in the struggle against feudalism and imperialism. Taken in sum, Njegoš's literary work has had two other lasting effects: he reaffirmed the links of history and identity between the Serbs and their Montenegrin kin, and he proved the Serbian language capable of expressing important philosophical ideas. As a ruler, he took important steps toward the creation of stable frontiers and modern, centralized government for Montenegro; his travels helped introduce Montenegro to the outside world; and he promoted education. He is buried in an elaborate tomb on the top of Mount Lovćen outside Cetinje.

NOTES

1. This section is based on Michael Palairet's *The Balkan Economies, c. 1800–1914: Evolution Without Development* (New York: Cambridge University Press, 1997), with permission of Cambridge University Press.

2. Branimir Anzulovic, *Heavenly Serbia: From Myth to Genocide* (New York: New York University Press, 1999), p. 60.

6

Serbia in the Great War

THE DEATH OF THE AUSTRIAN ARCHDUKE

The "shots heard round the world" rang out in Sarajevo on June 28, 1914. In this well-known event, the heir to the throne of the Habsburg Empire, Franz Ferdinand, was assassinated as he visited the recently annexed province of Bosnia. Austria-Hungary and Serbia had been on increasingly bad terms for more than a decade because of economic conflicts, Serbian national claims on Bosnia, and the Austrian desire to stop Serbia's growth as a regional power. The assassination pushed the two countries into war but it also sparked the great conflagration known as World War I, or the Great War. This war, in turn, was the most enormous bloodbath the world had ever seen, causing over 10 million deaths and bringing enormous social, political, and cultural changes in its wake.

Members of a nationalist group called *Mlada Bosna* ("Young Bosnia") planned and carried out the assassinations. A young Bosnian Serb named Gavrilo Princip pulled the trigger. Historians have argued long and vehemently about the share of responsibility for the murders borne by Pašić's government. The starting point for grasping this issue is the fact that Serbia had for decades coveted the territory of Bosnia and Hercegovina, which it considered ethnically and historically Serbian. Once

Macedonia had been annexed in the Balkan wars, Bosnia remained the biggest piece of Serbian irredenta. Austria-Hungary had occupied Bosnia in 1878 and annexed it in 1908. Then two controversial trials took place inside the Habsburg Empire, which adversely affected Serbian honor and interests. Inside Serbia, an organization called *Narodna Odbrana* ("The National Defense") was formed in 1908. Its goal was to arouse opposition to Austrian control of Bosnia. The group was putting pressure on Serbian politicians and organizing volunteers to carry out guerrilla activities across the border.

In 1911, though, another similar group was formed, this time called *Ujedinjenje ili Smrt* ("Union or Death"). It was popularly known as the Black Hand, and its methods and goals were steeped in the romantic, conspiratorial nationalism that young revolutionaries across Europe had indulged in for much of the nineteenth century. The Black Hand decreed fake identities for its members, the use of elaborate codes to set up meetings, oaths of total loyalty, a secret network of "cells" of members, and an elaborate and eerie initiation ritual. The members of this group included some civilians but mostly Serbian military officers, including the chief of military intelligence, Dragutin Dimitrijević. This man, known also by his nickname of Apis (The Bull), had been one of the main conspirators in the shocking regicide of 1903. The ideology of most of the Black Hand's members was to create a greater Serbia by whatever means necessary.

SERBIA IN WORLD WAR I

World War I is a watershed event of an importance in world history that is hard to exaggerate. It is often, and properly, credited with marking the thematic beginning of the twentieth century. For most students, the Great War stands in the shadows of World War II. But with the Great War the concepts of "total war" and "world war" entered our vocabulary, and it had an enormous cultural effect in the fostering of pacifism, irony, and alienation. Many countries like Great Britain and France actually suffered far more casualties in World War I than in World War II, and the war saw the collapse of four major European powers (the Habsburg and Ottoman Empires, Imperial Germany, and Tsarist Russia) and the creation of a plethora of new countries.

For Serbia, too, the Great War is of particular importance. The Serbian army fought well, even though it was eventually defeated by the overwhelming combined forces of the Central Powers. The Serbian people suffered immense losses and the country was razed, but the idea of cre-

ating Yugoslavia as a common South Slavic state took concrete shape.
The birth of Yugoslavia effectively linked Serbia's fate to that of the
Croats and other peoples with whom the Serbs lived (and sometimes
clashed) from 1918 to 1999.

After a month-long diplomatic crisis following the assassination, the
shooting between Austria-Hungary and Serbia began across the Danube.
The fighting on the Western Front commenced on August 4, 1914, with
the German invasion of Belgium, while Russian success at mobilization
on the Eastern Front was evident by the second week in August. On
August 12, 1914, the Habsburg army crossed the Drina River from Bosnia. They managed to capture the important city of Šabac, but little more.
To the surprise of outside observers, the Serbian forces, ably led by Vojvode (Commander) Radomir Putnik and by Vojvode Živojin Mišić,
quickly repulsed the Austrian assault around Cer Mountain. By the end
of August, the Serbs had liberated their territory and even pushed into
Bosnia; the Habsburgs feared that they would capture Sarajevo to free
the jailed assassins, so they moved Princip to the Theresienstadt Prison
in Bohemia, where he later died. The Serbs held Bosnian territory for
almost six weeks before they were beaten back.

The Austrian forces were unable to overrun Serbia because the Serbs
were seasoned and enthusiastic soldiers. They were exhausted and underequipped, but they had large reserves and were determined to defend
their homes. Their draft could put a higher percentage of the male population into uniform than any other European country.[1] Some pressure
on Serbia (as on France) was also relieved because of the speed of Russian mobilization; thus the Serbian and Habsburg forces were of approximately equal strength at first, numbering around 180,000 each. The
Habsburg commander, General Oskar Potiorek, was also an overly cautious general, who assigned many soldiers to police duty behind the lines
and was thus unable to muster decisive force.

For more than three months, fierce fighting raged in western Serbia.
The Austrians brought in large numbers of reinforcements and managed
to take Belgrade in December. King Petar at this point told his troops
that they were free to return to their homes with honor, but he also
joined them at the front lines with a rifle in his hands. The Serbs soon
mounted a major counterattack. Austria suffered a massive loss of prestige by being repulsed twice by "little" Serbia, a poor Balkan state only
about one-tenth its size. General Potiorek lost his job, and German officers now grumbled that their country was "shackled to a corpse."[2]

The year 1915 did not bring Serbia any relief from hardship. Austrian
gunboats on the Danube bombarded Belgrade. Serbia had lost about

100,000 soldiers already, and then a horrible typhus epidemic swept the country and killed between 100,000 and 150,000 people. The flow of supplies to Serbia from the Allies was slight. The government of Greece was obliged by treaty to help the Serbs. The premier, Eleutherios Venizelos, eventually allowed the Allies to land their "Army of the Orient" at Thessaloniki. But his political and personal conflicts with King Constantine paralyzed Greece and turned the Army of the Orient into "the gardeners of Salonika," since they were confined to their bases.

The Allies were also putting an enormous amount of pressure on the Serbian government to make territorial concessions to Bulgaria. This policy of "courting" potential allies was carried out by both sets of Great Powers during the war. The Allies' blandishments to Italy (Habsburg territory in Dalmatia and the Alps) are the most famous of these. Pašić had agreed to some concessions, since Serbia was starving for food, medicine, and fresh soldiers. But it was to be the Central Powers who won over the Bulgarian King Ferdinand. They promised him all of Serbian-held Macedonia, and he attacked. Serbs were rightfully resentful that their allies, the British and French, were helping to carve their country up. Macedonians, in turn, were also pawns in the international diplomatic equation.

Germany sent new forces to Serbia now, too, because of the Allied landing at Gallipoli, near Istanbul, in April 1915; Turkish forces needed assistance that could best go along Serbia's rail system. This time the forces of Field Marshall August von Mackensen, the German hero of the Eastern Front, were overwhelming. Belgrade fell in October, and the Bulgarians captured Niš and Skopje. The Serbian government first relocated to Kragujevac and then decided to flee across Albania rather than surrender or continue a suicidal war. In harsh weather, mercilessly pursued by their attackers, short of food and medicine, more than 120,000 Serb soldiers and civilians escaped. Thousands died of exposure, disease, and Austrian attacks. The Albanians whose territory they crossed were largely unsympathetic. The Italians—supposedly the Serbs' allies—whom they encountered on the coast were also indifferent. Eventually French ships took these Serbs to the nearby island of Corfu. This was a massive defeat and also a haunting spectacle of exodus. Montenegro was also overwhelmed by January 1916.

During 1916, more than 110,000 Serbian troops were transferred to Salonika, where they joined the Allied army. This large collection of soldiers—including English veterans of the Gallipoli campaign, French units of Moroccan and Vietnamese troops, and even small numbers of Russians and Albanians—was finally allowed to kick into gear in September 1916. The six reconstituted Serbian divisions—named after regions and rivers in their homeland such as Drina, Šumadija, and Timok—fought admirably well. By November, Serbian troops had stormed Kajmakćalan Peak and liberated Bitola; they were again on their home turf (albeit in newly acquired Macedonia). The most important political actions of the Serbian government in the summer of 1917 were the Salonika Trial and the execution of some of the Black Hand (including Apis) and the Corfu Declaration (of the new country of Yugoslavia).

It would take two more years to liberate the rest of Serbia, but for many people inside the country, the fighting to clear out the occupiers had resumed not a moment too soon. Both the Austrian and the Bulgarian occupation regimes were very harsh. Plunder, ruthless exploitation of natural resources, forced labor, concentration camps for political opponents, and starvation characterized the war for many Serb civilians, even though some of the cruelties were the result of neglect and chaos.

Milutin Bojić is the most famous of the many Serbian writers and artists to die in the war. In his brief life he wrote works that reflect two major themes: the Serbs' powerful national pride and their agony during the disastrous war. Even more so than his plays and epics, the war lyrics in *Poems of Pain and Pride*, published in 1917 in Thessaloniki, made him enormously popular. His personal suffering seemed to embody Serbian history at the crossroads of greatness and disaster.

YUGOSLAVISM

The Declaration of Corfu, signed by Prime Minister Pašić and a group of Croat and Slovene politicians called the Yugoslav Committee, is seen as the crowning achievement of political Yugoslavism. The declaration was vaguely worded in many controversial areas and it was assumed by all parties that mutually satisfactory details would be worked out after the war. But a certain political structure was agreed upon: a union (meaning a common postwar state of some sort) of Serbs, Croats, and Slovenes under the rule of the Karađorđević dynasty, with equality for the Orthodox and Catholic faiths and for the Cyrillic and Latin alphabets. To understand how such an arrangement could work, it is necessary to examine the multifaceted concept known as Yugoslavism.

Yugoslavism is the promotion of solidarity among South Slavic peoples. It was believed that these groups have a great deal in common and are natural allies in politics and natural partners in culture. The name of the country "Yugoslavia" did not refer to any one specific ethnic group, nationality, or language. Before World War I, there was no ethnic or national group called "Yugoslavs." Yugoslavia actually means "Land of the South Slavs." It refers to a cluster of distinct peoples (national groups) who speak similar languages. If the term Yugoslav refers to a group of related peoples, and not to the Serbs alone, then how did Serbia come to be involved in Yugoslavia? Why did the Serbs give up their own, independent state to be part of a new, multinational country first formed in 1918? Especially just as Europe's big multinational empires like those of the Habsburgs and Ottomans were finally collapsing?

The answers to these important questions are found in the idea of Yugoslavism, which existed in both a cultural and a political form.[3] Cultural Yugoslavism, which has medieval roots but rose to prominence with the work of the Croatian linguist and publicist Ljudevit Gaj (1809–1872), stressed the similarities between the languages, literature, and customs of the South Slavs. Another important figure in Yugoslavism was the Croatian Bishop of Djakovo, Josip Juraj Strossmayer (1815–1905). He founded an important scholarly organization in Zagreb called the Yugoslav (not Croatian!) Academy of Arts and Sciences. He also hoped to promote a reconciliation between the Roman Catholic and Eastern Orthodox churches. Many Croatian writers extolled the heroic virtues of Serbs and Montenegrins. Croats were most attracted to Yugoslavism early on because of their precarious position in the Habsburg Empire, where both the German-speaking Austrians and the Hungarians threatened them with assimilation. Thus Croatian intellectuals and political leaders envisioned various kinds of cooperation with related Slavic groups, both within and outside the empire, because they needed allies to help preserve Croatia's language and territorial integrity.

Political Yugoslavism was sometimes indistinguishable from cultural Yugoslavism. The government in Vienna found it very threatening. Politically, some Yugoslav proponents wanted to band together just long enough to carry out a struggle against their common foes, such as the Turks or Hungarians; others wanted to create a joint country.

Yugoslavism is a supranational ideology. That means that it looks beyond the individual nation and focuses on the links between nations. This kind of loyalty seems illogical to most people today. We see the "nation-state" as the logical subdivision of the world and the ideal (or at least unavoidable) basic unit in international relations. But when Yugoslav ideas were gaining strength, many Balkan peoples did not yet have firmly established national identities.

Old loyalties of religion, dynasty, and regionalism had only recently begun to break down. Nations are created, even though common languages and cultural affinities might have long existed on their territories.

Nations are mass, secular phenomena, and they were born in most of Europe as a result of the cultivation by intellectual and political elites of a mixture of ideas from both the Enlightenment and Romanticism. Educated South Slavs noticed many connections between their cultures. This was especially true in the case of language, which in the 1800s was thought to be the single most important defining characteristics of a nation. The languages of the various Slavic peoples in the Balkans were obviously closely related. In these early years of the national idea, no one was quite sure just how big their nation was going to turn out to be. Labeling a neighboring people a "related tribe" was not an insult; it was part of the slow process of self-identification.

Both cultural and political Yugoslavism split into various branches. An important bone of contention was the issue of integralism. Were the South Slavic peoples becoming *one*, or were they just working together? In political terms, this led to the conflict of centralists versus federalists; people favoring a strong central government (usually Serbs) had many disagreements with people (usually Croats and Slovenes) favoring much local autonomy. In the cultural realm, some favored what one might call "coordinated" Yugoslavism (the growth of a new, unified culture) and others espoused "parallel" Yugoslavism (to enrich the related cultures that already existed).

Thus we see that Yugoslavism was a very elastic concept. The cooperation envisioned ranged from cultural exchanges and confederal political ideas, through the creation of a common literary or government language, all the way to the formation of a blended, mono-ethnic state based on a new Yugoslav nationality. Some of its practitioners, indeed, simply believed that the South Slavs were really one people, separated by historical accident. Two themes unite all the views, though: These peoples are related, and it would be beneficial for them to cooperate.

WHY WERE THE SERBS ATTRACTED TO YUGOSLAVISM?

Serbian responses to Yugoslavism were varied but also seldom enthusiastic. Basically, few Serbs saw a compelling reason to join a supranational or internationalist movement when their own nationalism was deeply rooted and proving successful. Not until the early 1900s was there an outburst of popular support for the idea of a common South Slavic state, even though Serbian intellectuals and political leaders, as we have seen, often cooperated with Croats and Slovenes. The basic ambition of the Serbian state was still the liberation of all territories considered ethnically or historically Serbian. This drive, reinforced by Serbia's obvious success in building a large, independent state by 1913, distracted the Serbs from too much cooperation in Yugoslav movements; it also promised to bring the Serbs into conflict with the other South Slavs over territories claimed by more than one party. Indeed, Serbia's national ambition had already led it into bloody disputes over Macedonia.

Yugoslavism was made attractive to the Serbian government by the events of World War I. In the fall of 1914, when the country was under attack by the Austro-Hungarian army, the government of Premier Pašić issued the Niš Declaration. It declared that the goal of Serbia was officially to defeat the invading forces, preserve its current borders in the south, and then create a South Slav state covering all the northern Balkans. The northern boundaries would run as far as Szeged (today in Hungary) and Klagenfurt (today in Austria) and over to the Adriatic, thus including the territory of the Croats, Slovenes, and Bosnian Muslims. Pašić issued this sort of "maximum demand" at the outset of the war because, like most people in 1914, he believed that World War I would be brief. He wanted to get his country's maximum aims into circulation—and more important, to get Serbian troops into these regions and present the world with a fait accompli—before the fighting ceased and the Great Powers arranged the peace settlement to suit themselves.

Specifically, Pašić was propelled by the desire to get all Serbs into one state. This had been—and would continue to be—the basic plank of the "Serbian national program" for decades. To do this, Serbia would need to take control over the Habsburg territories of Vojvodina, Croatia, and Bosnia, where so many Serbs lived. That other South Slavs—whose existence and even basic rights Pašić did not want to deny—would be brought under Serbian control was acceptable, as long as the world recognized that Serbia had graciously liberated them from foreign rule. The idea of Serbia as the "Balkan Piedmont" was still strong, and it took Serbian aspirations well beyond the recreation of Tsar Dušan's medieval empire as envisioned in the previous century by Garašanin. Further momentum was added by geographic studies showing the northern Balkans to be one logical economic unit.

Although some Serbs, such as the conspirators in the Black Hand and others who spoke of the South Slav peoples as *jednoplemeni*, or "of one tribe," denied that Croats were a separate people and wanted to assimilate them by whatever means necessary, most Serbian leaders by 1914 were envisioning a greater Serbia with entrenched minorities. Thus, for all his wiliness and expansionism, one should not accuse Pašić of wanting to create an ethnically "pure" Serbia. If we remember, though, that Vuk Karadžić's definition of who was a Serb included everybody living in Bosnia and many people in Croatia, as well as the Macedonians and the Montenegrins, we see that the minorities would have been few. The Serbs would be in an incontestably dominant position within the new country. If it had come to pass in this manner, the new Yugoslavia would, in fact, have been almost a Serbian empire, although probably one with a constitutional form of government.

Why Yugoslavia?

In the face of all the problems that the new Yugoslavia was going to have in the interwar period and then again in the 1990s, many students at this point ask, "Why did Yugoslavia come into being at all? Was it doomed to fail right from the start?" Some of our pessimism in looking back at the first Yugoslavia comes from our having watched the collapse of the second Yugoslavia in the 1990s. With the virtue of hindsight, it seems as if many of the problems were insurmountable. But many historians say that Yugoslavia was not an impossible project. Its demise, whenever it was to come, also need not have been as bloody as it was. But it is a healthy exercise in historical thinking to consider the reasons why the country came into existence in 1918.

Idealism, especially on national issues, is not popular nowadays. But it did have a certain hold over certain groups in society in the early part of the century. The similarities between the South Slavs, and the successful instances of cooperation in the past (the revolutions of 1848, the Serb-Croat coalition after 1900, and the ongoing educational and artistic movements), and the good government (and Yugoslavist stance) brought to Serbia by the reinstatement of the Karađorđević family kept the Yugoslav ideals alive. As we have repeatedly seen, the slipperiness of the term "Yugoslav" also meant that people could promise to cooperate without reaching agreement on important details. That helped the country get born, but it made governing it later very difficult.

Marxist historians have elaborated a second important factor: the desire of the wealthier classes among the various national groups for security. Right after World War I, there was a great deal of unrest throughout Europe, as soldiers returned home—often with their rifles but without jobs. In some places, especially Croatia, these soldiers turned into renegades or bandits, attacking estates, settling old scores, and sometimes acting like "Robin Hoods" and building up small peasant followings. Estimates are that at one point there were as many as 60,000 such soldiers on the loose. This so-called "Green Terror" (a color often used to indicate the political loyalties of peasants in European history) might have been responsible for making some of the wealthy landowners and merchants amenable to the idea of joining Yugoslavia, where the Serbian gendarmerie could bring order to the countryside.

Another explanation focuses on the role of Great Britain and the United States, both of which, by the spring of 1918, came to support the idea of carving up the Habsburg Empire, after its new kaiser, Karl, refused to break his alliance with Germany and sign a separate peace. These Great Powers put pressure on the Yugoslav Committee and the Serbian government in exile to come to an agreement. Popular opinion in Great Britain also supported the Yugoslav idea, because of the publicity work for the cause done by Wickham Steed of the London *Times* and Professor Robert W. Seton-Watson.

Another factor also relates to international relations, though this time in a negative sense. The South Slav lands were bordered mostly by countries that were hostile. Austria, Hungary, and Bulgaria had been on the losing side in World War I. They had lost territory (and suffered humiliation and reparations). Yugoslavs could expect irredentist claims to be leveled at them in the future, as the "revisionist powers" (as the former Central Powers were called after the war) sought to restore their pride and power. Groups like the Croats and Slovenes feared they would be too weak on their own to resist this irredentist pressure. Strength in unity—or at least in numbers—was also important in the northwest, where the Yugoslav lands bordered Italy. Despite being a winner in the war, the Italians felt slighted by not being granted their maximum territorial desires. The lot of Slovenes and Croats in Italy (and in Austria) was not particularly enviable, and Slovenes especially looked to the Serbian army for protection right at the end of the war. Once the Serbs arrived and secured the border, of course, the political unification began.

NOTES

1. John Keegan, *The First World War* (New York: Knopf, 1999), p. 153.
2. Cyril Falls, *The Great War* (New York: Putnam, 1959), p. 54.
3. Excellent discussions of Yugoslavism can be found in the general histories listed in the bibliographical essay. An outstanding recent treatment is in Andrew Wachtel, *Making a Nation, Breaking a Nation: Literature and Cultural Politics in Yugoslavia* (Stanford, CA: Stanford University Press, 1998).

7

The Troubled Creation: The First Decades of Yugoslavia, 1918–1941

After the victory in World War I, the interwar period (1918–1941) turned out unsuccessfully, and it gave both Serbs and non-Serbs plenty to complain about. This period, also called "the first Yugoslavia" or "Royal Yugoslavia," runs from the end of World War I to the Axis invasion of 1941. Unfortunately the Yugoslavs never resolved their basic disagreements over government structure and power sharing between national groups. This huge and fundamental issue, along with severe economic problems, had plagued the country from the beginning. While neither was unsolvable, the government's failure to tackle them successfully meant that Yugoslavia was too weak to stand up to German pressure by the time World War II hit the Balkans. Severe economic stagnation in these years was caused only in part by the Great Depression; agricultural programs such as technical training and loans received just a minuscule slice of the budget, while military and police expenditures soared. This stagnation undercut the government's popularity and enhanced regional and ethnic resentments, which in turn made the country even less stable.

POLITICAL HISTORY IN THE INTERWAR ERA

The Royal Yugoslav government carried out its censuses in 1921 and 1931, and estimates have been made for 1940. The population grew considerably in this time: from a total of 11.9 million to 13.9 million to 15.9 million. The percentage of the population dependent on agriculture for a living remained remarkably high throughout: it went from 79 percent in 1921 to about 75 percent in 1940. Although these censuses did not include specific questions about nationality or ethnicity, the category of "Serbo-Croatian speakers" netted 74.4 percent of the respondents in 1921 and 77 percent in 1931. This is a confusing designation, not least because it does not let us distinguish between the two main rival nationalities in the new country, the Serbs and the Croats. This linguistic category also included Bosnians, Montenegrins, and Macedonians, many of whom considered themselves neither Serbs nor Croats.

Using a combination of the linguistic categories and the religious categories used in the two censuses, the American historian Joseph Rothschild has worked out the following ethnic or national breakdown for interwar Yugoslavia. It is more accurate and important than the actual census results:

Serbs 43 percent (of whom about one-fifth lived in the former Habsburg territories of Vojvodina, Bosnia, and Croatia)

Croats 23 percent

Slovenes 8.5 percent

Bosniaks (Bosnian Muslims) 6 percent

Macedonians 5 percent

Others (Albanians, Germans, Hungarians, Gypsies, Turks, Ruthenians, Czechs, Slovaks, Jews) 14.5 percent[1]

These statistics show us two things: no group had a majority in the country, yet Serbs were far and away the biggest single group. This would continue to be the case in Yugoslavia right up until 1991. Some sort of common political ideology or ability to hammer out an acceptable modus vivendi was essential here, because Yugoslavs tended to vote almost exclusively along ethnic lines. It was also going to be very important that Serbs and Croats feel secure and prosperous, because either of these groups had the power to wreck the entire country.

The elections for the constituent assembly that was to draft the first Yugoslav constitution made the government nervous because of the strength of the Croatian Peasant Party (headed by Stjepan Radić and usually called by the Croatian acronym HSS) and the Communist Party (founded in 1919 as a spin-off from the Social Democrats). The two strongest parties, not surprisingly, were Serbian. The veteran Radical Party was as nationalistic as ever and even more closely tied to businessmen and bureaucrats than before the war. Pašić would return to the office of premier—this time of all of Yugoslavia, and not just of Serbia—at the end of 1920. The Serbian Democratic Party was a mixture of former Radicals and former Habsburg Serbs, led by Ljubomir Davidović and Svetozar Pribićević. Medium-sized parties included the Slovene Populists (or Clericals), headed by Monsignor Anton Korošec; two Muslim parties, one for the Bosnians and the other for the Turks and Albanians; and the Agrarians, with branches in Serbia and Slovenia. Even smaller were the parties representing various other minorities and the Social Democrats.

To protest Serbian heavy-handedness, most Croatian delegates boycotted federal proceedings from 1920 to 1924. In a clever political move (though one that his critics disparage as "buying" his majority), Pašić traded guarantees of diplomatic posts and local self-rule to Slovene and Bosnian delegates for their support of the constitution. It passed. Two hundred twenty-three delegates voted for the constitution; 193 were either opposed or boycotting. The date of the vote—June 28, 1921—was St. Vitus's Day, or *Vidovdan* in Serbian. That was a day already doubly momentous for Serbs, since it was the date of the Battle of Kosovo in 1389 and of the assassination of the Habsburg Archduke Franz Ferdinand in 1914. The constitution seemed quite favorable to Serbian interests. It was centralist in essence, but it did guarantee basic civil rights to individuals. But if a country's laws are only as good as the administration that carries them out, then here was the rub: the government apparatus inherited from Serbia was not efficient, sensitive, or even particularly welcome in many parts of the country. These administrative problems were partly due to the horrific damage from the world war and partly to the fast-and-loose style of rule of the Radical Party and the smaller groups' fear of domination. There was only one non-Serbian premier (Korošec) in the whole twenty-three years of interwar Yugoslavia. The HSS and Radić were already feared—and persecuted—by the government, fond as he was of exposing the differing interpretations of the Corfu arrangement. He even sought outside diplomatic support, from sources as unlike as Fascist Italy and Soviet Russia, for the Croats. One wonders how the Croat members of the Yugoslav Committee during the war might have fared had they possessed Radić's ability to "play hardball"; the Serbs might have been forced to accept a looser federation. But Radić also missed bargaining opportunities as a result of his penchant for vitriolic speeches and bluster.

King Aleksandar was not totally unpopular in the rest of the country, and he had named his second son Tomislav, after the first great Croatian king. (The king's third son would be given a Slovene name, Andrej.) But after 1927, Radić had joined forces with his old arch-foe, Pribićević, to oppose what they viewed as the crass and counterproductive "Balkan-style" rule from Belgrade. This alliance increased the power of both groups, but it angered the government by holding up legislation in the Skupština. Throughout 1928, the ethnic name-calling in the Skupština—much of it by Radić—continued; tempers rose and the unrest spilled over into the streets of the country. Some angry Serbs began calling privately for Radić's head. Events in Parliament climaxed in a tragic way on June 20, 1928. A highly nationalistic—and personally insulted—Montenegrin delegate named Puniša Račić took out a revolver and shot down five Croats.

Two of his victims died on the spot, and Radić, the third, died seven weeks later. The unrepentant Račić got a twenty-year sentence, but he didn't serve it all. When Tito's Partisans found him during World War II, they executed him. In general, though, the government reaction was blasé. Croats were at first shocked and then even more grievously insulted when it became apparent that this outrage was not enough to prompt more conciliatory policies.

King Aleksandar then rescinded the constitution, renamed the country "Yugoslavia," and set out to save it from regionalism, separatism, and ethnic politics. He shut down the free press, arrested political opponents, and ruled directly for two years; he wanted nothing, as he put it, to come between him and the people. He abolished the historical boundaries within the country and set up a new administrative system to break up regional loyalties.

In 1931 Aleksandar issued a new constitution based only on his own authority. Authoritarian rule was common in Europe in this decade of economic depression and political unrest, but in countries like Yugoslavia, where national conflicts poisoned the atmosphere, leaders like Aleksandar aroused great resentment. New election laws made it very hard for small parties to get into Parliament, and the king formed his own party.

In 1932, a group of Croatian fascists, known as Ustaše, filtered into the Dalmatian hinterland. They attacked government installations and escaped back to Italian territory. It was a jolting reminder that the Croatian national issue was not resolved. The movement's leader, a former lawyer named Ante Pavelić, hailed from rural Hercegovina. He had fled Yugoslavia and organized the Ustaše abroad with the aim of using violence to achieve a separate Croatia.

Two years later, while on a state visit to France, King Aleksandar was assassinated by members of a Croatian-Macedonian conspiracy. Pavelić and his fellow Ustaše had made contacts with the Internal Macedonian Revolutionary Organization (IMRO), who also resented the Serbian domination within Yugoslavia. These groups had contacts with and received support in varying degrees from Italy, Germany, and Hungary. The murder of the king on October 10, 1934, was a dark day in Serbian history. Even though the king was resented for depriving Serbs of their democratic rights, he had succeeded in restoring some sense of order. More important over the long run, he had helped create the first modern state that contained all Serbs, hence his recently burnished reputation as the Serbian "King-Unifier." It was not a purely Serbian state, but as we have seen, the term "Yugoslav" permitted a variety of interpretations. For many Serbs it was simply the umbrella concept for a South Slav state in which they were unified and dominant.

Aleksandar's successor was to be his oldest son, Petar. Since he was not yet eighteen, it was determined that Prince Paul, a cousin of Aleksandar's, and two other Serbs should act as regents. Yugoslavia would not really have a functioning king again until Petar Karađorđević assumed his throne (a bit early) in 1941. But Prince Paul, known as the prince regent, played a large and positive role in Serbian and Yugoslav politics. The electoral process was resumed, but the shifting sands of coalition politics made the governments short-lived; public enthusiasm and policy continuity were victims of this unstable system, which reminds one of Italy in the decades after World War II. One of these small parties that appeared on the scene, however, had a portentous meaning for Serbia: it was a fascist movement, led by the former minister of justice, Dimitrije Ljotić. There were far right-wing political groups all across Europe by this time, and Ljotić's election appearance heralded the arrival of a pure and violent Greater Serbianism that would help make Yugoslavia during World War II so complicated and bloody a place.

From 1935 to early 1939, the premier was Milan Stojadinović. He tried to calm the country's political scene, but he gradually drifted toward the far right, flirting heavily with fascism and cozying up to Mussolini and Hitler. Elections in December 1938, showed that hundreds of thousands of Serbs were fed up with the authoritarian government. There seemed to be a mandate to put the country on a sounder footing by meeting some Croatian demands for autonomy.

Prince Paul pushed hard, and on August 26, 1939, an agreement called the *Sporazum* ("Understanding") was ratified by the Skupština. This agreement gave autonomy to Croatia in education, taxation, and economics. In general, though, the politics of interwar Yugoslavia are properly seen as chaotic, divisive, and inconclusive. The country lacked the stability to modernize, and the *Sporazum* did not come in time to heal the wounds of the 1920s before the outbreak of World War II.

SERBIAN AND YUGOSLAV CULTURE IN THE INTERWAR ERA

As controversy ridden as the political scene in the new country was, the realm of culture displayed few of the same nationalist disagreements. For one thing, King Aleksandar's government basically left culture to the artists and writers, who had been more pro-Yugoslav than the general population. Through the mediation of respected literary journals in Zagreb and Belgrade, a core set of South Slav writers emerged as the new Yugoslav "canon." Writers whose works were appreciated, discussed, and spread by the Yugoslavists included the Slovene Ivan Cankar; the Croat Mažuranić, the Serb Aleksa Šantić, and, perhaps most important, the Montenegrin Njegoš. In addition, Ivo Andrić was a Serb, and as a Bosnian Serb he had a profound and pervasive feel for the difficulties—but also, many would say, for the possibilities—of multiethnic coexistence. The Croatian sculptor Ivan Meštrović designed Njegoš's tomb and many other Serbian monuments by blending and updating elements from the various South Slav traditions.

ANALYSIS OF THE PROBLEMS OF ROYAL YUGOSLAVIA

Whatever problems the Serbian population had with Royal Yugoslavia, it is hard to avoid the conclusion that they enjoyed a level of security and a pride of ownership that the other groups did not have. There were of course times when there was no effective government in the country, or when supranationalism reigned, as in Aleksandar's dictatorship. But the Serbs, by dint of their numerical superiority and influence, can safely be said to have dominated interwar Yugoslavia. Serbs did not pose a full-blown assimilationist threat to the closely related Slovenes and Croats. But Serbs' power over certain ethnic groups more vaguely defined Slavic groups such as Macedonians and Bosnians was more problematic, and Serbian calls for running the Albanians out of Kosovo created great tension.

Non-Serbs had many grievances. Some groups resented their lack of territorial or legal status and language. Slovenes and Croats were upset that Italy and Austria still controlled some of their irredenta, while they also never felt at home in Yugoslavia, dominated as it was by Serbia's police, military, legal system, and royal family. They also felt that Serbian business cliques wielded undue (and often corrupt) influence and that the relatively industrialized former Habsburg territories were being drained of their wealth to benefit the country's south. The urgency of creating a new country out of the war-damaged shards of old ones justifies some of these measures, and Serbia had a framework on which to build. But Serbs were not used to living with minorities. Some of what the Croats and others perceived as hegemonism was simply Serbian insensitivity and bluster.

MONTENEGRO IN THE NEW YUGOSLAVIA

In the interwar period, the government counted Montenegrins as Serbs. There was no cultivation of a separate Montenegrin identity, even though there were unpleasant memories of the way Pašić had sent the royal family packing in 1918. Montenegrins who agitated for cultural or political autonomy were called "Greens," but their views were not welcome under King Aleksandar, who favored the pro-Serbian "Whites." The country had been devastated by World War I and economic growth was slow. During the royal dictatorship, Montenegro became part of the new district called Zetska. To be sure, this name reflects the history and geography of Montenegro, but this impact was deliberately diluted by including within Zetska much territory from Bosnia-Hercegovina, Serbia, and Kosovo. King Aleksandar wanted to increase the power of the central government, not to encourage ethnic or historical particularism. Meanwhile, there was popular pressure on Muslims to leave Montenegro.

NOTE

1. Joseph Rothschild, *East Central Europe Between the Two World Wars* (Seattle: University of Washington Press, 1977), pp. 202–203.

8

Nazis, Partisans, Chetniks, and Ustaše: The Maelstrom of World War II

World War II in Yugoslavia was without doubt one of the most complicated periods of fighting in European history, but its significance for *contemporary* Serbia cannot be underestimated. Its entanglements might have been edging toward oblivion by now, except that memories of the war were revived in the 1990s with disastrous results. A thumbnail sketch of the years 1941 to 1945 in Yugoslavia is as follows: the Germans and their Italian, Hungarian, and Bulgarian allies invaded and quickly carved up Yugoslavia, where various kinds of occupation regimes, puppet governments, and resistance groups emerged.[1] The Allies began supporting guerrilla operations against the Axis. At first they supported Serbian insurgents called Chetniks, but then support swung to the multinational, communist-led Partisans. Great numbers of civilians and soldiers alike were killed as the Axis extracted all the wealth they could from the country and as various Yugoslav nationalities fought cruel, exhausting civil wars with each other. By the middle of 1945, the numerous and well-organized Partisans, led by the Communist Party chief Josip Broz (called Tito), had driven out the Germans and crushed domestic opposition. Tito was intent upon creating a different kind of Yugoslavia than the royal version. Socialism of course brought both changes in property relations and a rapid increase in industrialization. But Yugoslavia was also reconstructed on a federal basis that established a balance of power among the national groups. Tito allowed only one political party, however, his own Communist Party.

THE COURSE OF THE WAR

When the Axis forces attacked on April 6, 1941, they did not expect to have an easy time of it, given the rugged terrain and the size of Yugoslavia's army. But surprisingly many Yugoslav soldiers deserted, and the country surrendered quickly on April 17. Belgrade had been pulverized by Nazi bombers; about 8,000 Serbs had died in all, while German losses were under 200. Hitler then partitioned the country. He rewarded his Hungarian allies with parts of Slovenia, Croatia, and the Vojvodina. To Bulgaria he gave most of Macedonia. Italy, already in possession of Istria since 1918, expanded its holdings in Dalmatia and occupied Montenegro and the entire southern half of Slovenia, including the capital city of Ljubljana. The Germans annexed two regions: the region called the Banat, in the eastern Vojvodina, where there were populations of *Volksdeutsche* (ethnic Germans), and all of northern Slovenia, which had belonged to the Habsburg Empire before 1918. A puppet Serbian government was established over a reduced Serbian territory, south of the Danube. Lastly, Albania—now an Italian puppet state—was given control over the Kosovo region.

The Independent State of Croatia was also set up as a German satellite state. It is often referred to as the NDH after its initials in Serbo-Croatian. This large country represented the maximum national program of the Croatian fascist party, the Ustaše, led by Ante Pavelić. It included not only the traditional central and Slavonian Croatian areas, and all of Dalmatia that was not taken by the Italians, but also all of Bosnia and Hercegovina. The NDH had over 6 million people, nearly 2 million of whom were Serbs! A further three quarters of a million were Bosnian Muslims. (By contrast, the satellite state of Serbia had just under 4 million people but few minorities.) But the Ustaše, considered fanatical even by the Germans, set about "cleansing" their new country and trying to make it ethnically homogeneous. The Ustaše were obsessed with reminding the world that Croats and Serbs were distinct peoples, a point in and of itself that is true. They were also deeply embittered over the policies of Royal Yugoslavia, claiming that the murder of Radić in 1928 showed the bottom-line Serbian goal of doing away with Croats altogether. This exaggeration does not even come close to providing a justification for the murderous policies the Ustaše pursued when they got their own country, although it is important to remember that many Croats suffered under Ustaša rule, too, and most of them did not support the Pavelić government. It was never, for instance, even as popular as Hitler's government was in Germany.

The Serbo-Croatian word "Ustaša" (plural: "Ustaše") means "insurgent." The group was both anti-Serbian and anti-Yugoslav and agitated for an independent (and expanded) Croatia aligned with the Axis powers. There were never terribly many Ustaše, perhaps 600 with Pavelić in Italy, and smaller groups at home in Yugoslavia and in Germany, though the ranks were swelled by opportunists when Pavelić was handed control of the NDH by his allies.

Pavelić adopted propaganda techniques and self-glorification familiar to us from his Nazi and Italian neighbors. Much of his political thought is traceable to an earlier Croatian politician, Ante Starčević, who founded the nationalistic Party of Rights in 1861. Starčević believed that Serbs were simply Croats who had wandered away from their Catholic Christianity and that Slovenes were just "mountain Croats" who spoke a western variant of the Croat language. Furthermore, the Muslims of Bosnia had been so determined to keep their land and power after the Turkish invasion that they became Muslim.

Pavelić's government planned on killing one-third of its Serbs, converting one-third to Catholicism, and expelling the remainder. The NDH was to become a pure Croatian state with two religions: Roman Catholicism and Islam. Pavelić elaborated upon Starčević's ideas considerably, demonizing Jews and leftists as well as Serbs.

The Ustaša government was not popular even with Croats. Many Croats were appalled by the atrocities and resentful of all the land that Pavelić "gave away" to Italy. To the sophisticated citizens of Zagreb, the Ustaše—many of whom came from poor, rural areas—seemed crude and untrustworthy. Still, by using several military formations, establishing labor and death camps at places like Jasenovac and Stara Gradiška, and enjoying the blessing or at least acquiescence of a significant number of Catholic priests, the regime killed several hundred thousand Serbs, most of Croatia's and Bosnia's Jews, and large numbers of political opponents. Not even the Bosnian Muslims, supposedly Pavelić's allies, were immune from Ustaša attacks.

This violence began just a few weeks after the Ustaše took over. Most of the Serbs in the NDH were concentrated in the old Habsburg military frontier zone, which included the regions of Lika, Kordun, and Banija; there were also large numbers in Hercegovina. The names of the villages, ravines, and fields where the Ustaše slaughtered Serbs in these areas have been recorded in numerous eyewitness accounts. The massacres at the village of Glina in May and August of 1941 are especially notorious. The Croatians, and sometimes their Bosnian Muslim allies, killed Serbs in primitive, face-to-face ways that represent a different aspect of the process of genocide in World War II. There were no gas chambers or crematoria, as in Poland. Soldiers bashed in the heads of prisoners, women, children, and old men with clubs and maces, hacked them up with axes and knives, threw them off cliffs, buried them alive, burned them in churches, and worked them to death in labor camps. Today these form a kind of litany of horror in Serbian history. Their echo resonates strongly in the background of Serbian-Croatian relations to this day.

Well over 150,000 Serbs fled or were deported from Croatia, and as many as 200,000 Serbs were forced, often literally at gunpoint, to convert to Roman Catholicism. Many Orthodox priests were singled out for death or deportations, and Pavelić even created a small (and ultimately ineffective) "Croatian Orthodox Church" to try to strip Serbs of their culture. The participation of some Catholic priests in these undertakings is especially inflammatory. The Archbishop of Croatia, Alojzije Stepinac, denounced the forced conversions and eventually protested other Ustaša excesses, although critics continue to claim that he never took a firm enough stand against Pavelić.

Inside Serbia itself, the Germans were looking around for Serbs to help them run the country. As in Croatia, the chief German goals were economic exploitation and the suppression of any resistance movements, although, as recent scholarship has pointed out, Serbia also became a testing ground for Holocaust techniques aimed at exterminating the Jews of Europe. They set up General Milan Nedić in a "Government of National Salvation." Nedić had a small, ineffective military force at his disposal, the Serbian State Guard, with which the Germans wanted him to help put down the various revolts that were starting to crop up. Ljotić's small Serbian fascist movement, called Zbor, also had a small "party army," called the "Serbian Volunteer Corps"; it assisted the Nazis and Nedić. So did a unit of anticommunist Russian immigrants (called "Whites," because they were against the communist "Reds") and one of the various groupings of Chetniks, those under the direction of the aging veteran Kosta Pećanac. These groups are called "collaborators," because they worked with the Nazis and helped them carry out their policies. Other terms used to describe forces like Nedić's are "quislings" or "fifth column." True fascism barely existed in Serbia, as the small size of Ljotić's movement shows, but the term "fascist" can be used for his movement, as for the Croatian Ustaše. The Germans, Hungarians, Albanians, and Bulgarians, all of whom took over parts of Serbia during the war, are usually called "occupiers."

After the collapse of the country in April, there had been only local and uncoordinated uprisings, mostly against the Ustaše in Bosnia-Hercegovina. The Communist Party, which was small and had been driven underground but was well organized and had many seasoned leaders who had just fought in the Spanish Civil War, did not start operations against the Nazis until after the Nazi-Soviet Pact of 1939 was broken in June 1941, when Hitler invaded the USSR. The first massive uprising was against the Italians in Montenegro on July 13. Milovan Djilas and the communists there ended up conducting a brief reign of terror, which taught the Partisans the important lesson of avoiding indiscriminate reprisals against civilians, lest that make it harder to get supplies, recruit new troops, and find safe hideouts.

The two main resistance groups in Serbia proper, however, both had their first headquarters in the Šumadija. A career officer of the Royal Yugoslav Army, Draža Mihailović (often spelled Mihailovich in English-language sources), was determined to carry out an underground war against the occupiers. Starting with a tiny band of followers, he established himself temporarily at Ravna Gora in Western Serbia. During the war, he would be constantly on the move through the Serbian and Bosnian countryside. His followers were called Chetniks. This Serbian word literally means "guerrilla fighter," and it had been used in many wars previously. Mihailović was continuing the tradition of fighting an "irregular war" behind enemy lines, as it were, in the service of the exiled Serbian government. When the fighting stopped in April, the Germans let most non-Serb prisoners of war go home. But they interned about about 170,000 Serbian soldiers, and later sent many of them off to forced labor inside the Third Reich. Still, Mihailović's forces grew and grew. By the summer of 1941, he had 10,000 men with him, ready to continue the war against the invader. In October 1941, the British government recognized Mihailović as the official and main resistance leader in Yugoslavia. It is ironic, but within a few short months, Mihailović had arrived at a decision on strategy that would eventually turn the British completely against him: he wanted to wait out the war and then restore the old Yugoslavia.

The Chetniks did not have much of a strategy, except to wait for the German defeat, conserving their strength for the ultimate battle with the Partisans, after which they planned to restore Petar to the throne. They supported a Greater Serbia, or Serbian domination of Yugoslavia, not a federal state. Today Mihailović has the status of a hero for many Serbs.

His deeds during the war are often exaggerated and his fall is often blamed—erroneously—on the British and American intelligence services, who withdrew support from him halfway through the war. The Chetniks were actually fighting an unwinnable war, as we will see shortly.

Mihailović's personal political views, besides being very pro-Karađorđvić, were very anti-German. He is usually characterized as a moderate because he approved of representative government and opposed fascism. Still, Mihailović gathered around himself other Serbian leaders with more extreme nationalist views, such as Stevan Moljević. Some of the other famous commanders were Pavle Djurisić, Zaharije Ostojić, and Ilija Trifunović-Birćanin. The Chetnik movement did not appeal to any group but the Serbs, and not even to all of them.

The ideas of the other main resistance group, however, were radically different in content and had much greater appeal across the country. It was well organized by the highly trained Communist Party of Yugoslavia and its fighters were known as "the Partisans." This group called immediately for the equality of all the nationalities within Yugoslavia, and thus many non-Serbs were immediately attracted to its ranks. They were joined also by many intellectuals and people on the left of the political spectrum. They organized quickly among the persecuted Serbian communities of Bosnia and Croatia. For most of the war, especially in Slovenia, the Communists allowed noncommunists to join their army. This tactic allowed them to raise bigger armies than the Chetniks.

The Partisans were led by Josip Broz, known as Tito. By ethnicity he was half-Slovene, half-Croat; he became the secretary-general of the Yugoslav Communist Party in 1937. Tito knew that the Yugoslav Communist Party, established in 1919, had been dominated by Serbs in the past but that its chances for driving out the occupiers and taking power were much greater if it promised a federalist solution to the nationalities problem.

Like the Chetniks, the Partisans too were first based primarily in Serbia. Both groups carried out hit-and-run operations against the Germans and their allies. But in the fall of 1941, the Nazis began carrying out brutal reprisals against Serbian civilians. For every German soldier wounded in Serbia, fifty civilians would be executed. The number of civilians to be murdered for every German killed was one hundred. This draconian German policy led to mass executions of civilians in Kraljevo on October 18 and in Kragujevac on October 21. This latter massacre, which had 7,000 victims, many of them schoolchildren, was memorialized by the great Serbian poet Desanka Maksimović in her work "A

Bloody Tale." In all, the Germans executed something like 25,000 Serbian civilians in 1941 alone. The Germans also cracked down on the Serbian Orthodox church, fearing that it would be a source of support for the Chetniks. They sent two of its leaders, Bishop Velimirović and Patriarch Gavrilo himself, to the concentration camp at Dachau.

Meanwhile, relations between the Chetniks and Partisans soured. The biggest difference of opinion was over tactics. The Chetniks decided to taper off their resistance activities against the Germans because the horrific reprisals were causing so much suffering among Serbs. The Partisans decided to continue attacking the occupiers.

In the rest of Yugoslavia, this parting of ways of the two groups in Serbia became a great propaganda tool for the Partisans. They were not very popular, it is true, in Serbia, but in the rest of the country they were regarded as the group that actually had the means and the will to take the fight to the Germans. The Partisans did not carry out negotiations with any of the Axis until later in the war, when their reputation was already made. Their success built upon itself; as the tide turned, they attracted more and more recruits from all parts of the country, including deserters from other forces. The Partisans also welcomed tens of thousands of women into their army, including into combat units.

By September of 1941, Tito had a force of 10,000 and had captured the Serbian city of Užice. Brimming with confidence, the Partisans called this their "liberated territory" or the "Republic of Užice." It was indeed an important city, as it contained an arms factory that was of great use to the Partisans, but their optimism was premature. The German army brought in reinforcements and crushed the communist stronghold. By the end of 1941, Tito had made his way to Bosnia, where the Partisans would be strongest for the rest of the war. The rugged terrain was well suited for a guerrilla war. The German and Chetnik presence was not strong there and Pavelić really never exercised effective control.

The year 1941 also brought the arrival of a British intelligence officer in Serbia and the first outright clashes between Chetniks and Partisans. The British, and later Americans, would eventually send about twenty missions each into the country, funneling supplies and information to the anti-Nazi forces and trying to decide whether to throw their weight behind Mihailović or Tito. Other resistance groups included Christian Socialists in Slovenia, the conservative (but secessionist) Balli Kombëtar in Kosovo, and the Bulgarian Communist Party in Macedonia.

The Partisans, hiding in the Bosnian mountains, hoped that the Soviets would airdrop supplies and weapons to them. But the Soviet planes were not to come until 1944. The main reason at this point was that Stalin, in a life-or-death struggle with Axis armies, had no weapons to spare. The Soviets were also cautious about supporting Tito because they did not want to endanger their alliance with Britain and, later, the United States. Stalin worried that Tito's plans for a social revolution in Yugoslavia would anger the Western Allies. They might suspect that Stalin was encouraging Tito's revolution and withdraw the vital support they were giving the Soviet Union. Thus, ironically, the British and Americans would end up being much more supportive of Tito than were the Soviets during the war.

The Partisans disrupted enemy transportation and communication lines, occasionally making arduous "long marches" and fighting some bitter battles against the Axis forces. In September 1942, they captured the Bosnian city of Bihać. The Partisans then held an important political meeting. On November 26, 1942, Tito convened a session of what he called the Anti-Fascist Council for the National Liberation of Yugoslavia (AVNOJ in Serbo-Croatian). The Partisans intended for this meeting to give political legitimacy to their struggle. They wanted official Allied recognition, which the Chetniks currently had, and they wanted to rally more forces to support them. Tito sought to allay outsiders' fears of his planned socialist revolution by promising free elections, a just federal structure, and the protection of private property. Shortly thereafter the Partisans held another important meeting to found the Antifascist Front of Women of Yugoslavia, which heightened the important role women played in the liberation movement.

In 1942 Mihailović was promoted from colonel to general and chief of staff of the Royal Army. He was also made minister of war—an odd move, since the exiled government was in London. Expectations for him were high but his resources were few. In Serbia, his men continued to develop covert links with the Nedić administration, not to help the Germans but to steal weapons and make sure that the Chetniks would be in control of the machinery of government and police when the Germans left. But controversy was beginning to develop around the various Chetnik forces, as some of them joined in Axis attacks on Partisans; others allowed themselves to be disarmed or were "legalized" and started openly supporting the Nedić government in Serbia. Furthermore, thousands of Chetniks in Croatia went on the Italians' payrolls and promised to cooperate with the Pavelić government. That might not be so odd, because if one considers the Chetniks collaborationist, then all three of those groups were allies. But when we recall the destruction that the Ustaše were visiting upon Serbian communities in Croatia, this cooperation is astonishing. Later, when Italian-Croatian relations grew strained, the Chetniks would attack their Croatian "allies."

In occupied Serbia, the harshness of Axis rule continued unabated. In the Hungarian-occupied Vojvodina, more than 16,000 people were executed by the authorities between the invasion and the end of January 1942. The victims were Jews and Serbs, some of whom were suspected of opposing the Axis invasion. More than 3,000 of these people were civilians from Novi Sad who were rounded up by the Hungarian army and militia and killed between January 21 and 23.[2] Many of their bodies were dumped into the ice-covered Danube. News of these massacres fired the zeal of Tito's Partisans to liberate the Vojvodina, in the process of which new atrocities were committed. The Hungarian Holocaust figures prominently in the writing of the great novelist Danilo Kiš, who was born in the Vojvodina but lived out the war in Budapest. The Hungarian prime minister, László Bardossy, who helped organize the massacres, wanted to convince Hitler that Hungary could rule conquered territory with a firm hand and should be given more of it; the soldiers involved seemed to fear being sent to the Eastern Front and wanted to prove that there was still a threat of insurgency at home, so they should be kept there; both the government and the soldiers were anti-Semitic and feared the Partisans, whom they suspected the Jews might turn to for protection.

The pivotal year in the internal struggles in all of Yugoslavia was 1943. The Partisans won—or at least survived—two huge battles in Bosnia, the Italians withdrew from the war, and the United States and the United Kingdom switched their support from Mihailović to Tito. It was now apparent that the Nazis and their allies were going to lose the whole European war, but in January the Germans assembled the largest force yet used against the Partisans. This "Operation Weiss," also known as the "Fourth Offensive," used well over 50,000 Italians, Chetniks, Ustaše, and Germans. They attacked the Partisans in Bihać and drove them southeast to the Neretva River. Again trying to keep their sick and wounded from falling into enemy hands, the Partisans narrowly escaped across the rugged terrain. The decisive action came in early March when the Partisans broke through the encircling Axis forces by attacking the Chetniks head on. The Chetniks caved in, suffering both great losses and humiliation. It was dawning on the Western Allies that the Partisans were effective anti-Nazi fighters.

British Prime Minister Churchill decided to send another intelligence-gathering mission to Yugoslavia in May. This one included Captain William Deakin, who later became an important historian, and it linked up with Tito's forces. The Germans, bolstered by Bulgarian troops, attacked the 20,000 remaining Partisans in the massive "Operation Schwarz," or "Fifth Offensive." At the epic Battle of Sutjeska River, more than 7,000 Partisans were killed, but with most of their leaders still alive, the Partisans escaped again through the rugged mountains.

Italy surrendered in September and its troops left the Balkans en masse. Some of them surrendered to the Partisans and ended up fighting their former German allies in a unit named the "Garibaldi Brigade" after the nineteenth-century Italian revolutionary. The Italians left behind enormous stocks of weapons, ammunition, food, vehicles, and even ships, most of which were confiscated by the Partisans. Now their growing prestige as fighters was attracting ever more recruits. Tito now had enough weapons to outfit them, and he had access to the Adriatic coastline, for receiving Allied supplies. As strong as Tito's forces were, they still only had about 1,200 combatants in Serbia.

A high-ranking British soldier, Fitzroy Maclean, visited the Partisans and impressed Churchill with their successes. It seems that information about the Chetniks and Partisans was caught up in the interdepartmental rivalries and personal politics of the various branches of the British government. So, the Partisans' accomplishments were sometimes exaggerated and sometimes understated, depending on who was processing the intelligence information. But the British began supplying both Mihailović's and Tito's forces in equal amounts.

On November 29, the Partisans held another meeting of AVNOJ, this time in the Bosnian town of Jajce. Now increasingly confident of victory, Tito had himself named prime minister of the embryonic government of liberated Yugoslavia. Federalism was accepted in principle, and, over the objections of Moša Pijade and some other Serbian delegates, the Bosnian Muslims, Macedonians, and Albanians were specifically promised increased autonomy. King Petar's government which set up in London was declared illegitimate, and he was banned from the country until a referendum was held. In December, after the Nazi invasion, Roosevelt, Churchill, and Stalin concluded their war summit in Teheran. Among the many decisions they made there was the joint recognition of the Partisans as an Allied force. Mihailović's chances were growing ever slimmer.

In 1944, the Chetniks made a last-ditch effort to stem the diplomatic tide that was shifting against them. At the "St. Sava Congress" in the Serbian village of Ba, they adopted proposals about recreating Royal Yugoslavia with more rights for Croats and Slovenes, and a new political party was formed. But these efforts came too late. In May, the British had Mihailović removed as Yugoslav minister of war. That same month a surprise German paratroop attack almost resulted in Tito's capture; the Partisan headquarters moved to the Mediterranean island of Vis, where they had substantial Allied protection. King Petar publicly endorsed Tito's war effort in September.

By late summer, the Partisans headed east to attack the Germans in Serbia. They outnumbered the demoralized and underequipped Chetniks by at least two to one, and the Germans were being pushed back steadily by Soviet forces. Belgrade was freed from German rule on October 20, by a cooperative venture of Partisans and Soviet troops. Tito had wisely arranged for the Soviets to exit the country almost immediately, so that he would have a free hand to arrange the postwar government as he saw fit. The Partisans then attacked westward into the NDH. The Chetniks were avoiding head-on battles with the Partisans, and Hitler was only continuing to prop up the Ustaša government because Croatia lay on the escape route north for German forces.

By May of 1945, some of the Chetniks were fleeing north, trying to reach Italy or Austria. Some of them imagined the Western Allies would welcome them as partners in a postwar fight against communism. Others wanted to escape from Europe altogether. Others simply wanted to surrender to the Americans or British, rather than to the Partisans or Russians, who they feared would execute them. The Ustaše fled north as well, though their fratricidal anti-Serbian campaign continued. British, New Zealand, and American forces were moving into Yugoslavia from the west as Zagreb fell to the Partisans on May 9, a day after the war had ended in the rest of Europe. Conflicts loomed with the Allies over border regions where a lot of Yugoslavs lived, like Trieste in Italy and the Austrian province of Carinthia. But the war was over. Sadly, in Yugoslavia, though, the killing was not.

SERBIA AND THE HOLOCAUST

It took more than forty years for scholars to arrive at a reasonable consensus on the nationality and number of Yugoslav deaths resulting from the multilateral fighting and shifting alliances in the war. An even more recent subject of investigation has been the fate of Jews in Yugoslavia, especially in Serbia. The Ustaša government in Croatia was very anti-Semitic, although it sometimes "bent the rules" for prominent Jews. Historians are still working to pinpoint how much German influence there was in Pavelić's adoption of extermination measures against the

Jews, but one point is undeniable. Although they had long regarded Jews as an alien, unpatriotic, and even "parasitic" element in Croatian society, the Ustaše were also obsessed with anti-Serbianism. Within Croatia, Serbs were the largest minority, and in the Balkans as a whole, it was the more numerous Serbs who threatened the Croats' identity.

Serbia's relationship with its small Jewish population was even more complex. Historians have traditionally been comfortable with classifying Serbia as one of the less anti-Semitic countries in Eastern Europe, along with Bulgaria (in contrast to Romania, Slovakia, or Poland). This idea is not unfounded. Anti-Semitism had almost always been pervasive across Europe, resulting in discrimination, expropriation, pogroms, and expulsion over the centuries. Despite the legal restrictions and occasional outbreaks of vitriolic rhetoric that Serbian Jews suffered in the nineteenth century, things were worse in many other places. It is a sad comment on the human condition, but Serbian anti-Semitism in its traditional forms was "par for the course"—that is, certainly not excusable but representative of a pervasive and persistent problem in Western society.

Another complicating factor in studying the role of Serbia in the Holocaust is the fact that many historians have blamed only Croatia for wartime anti-Semitic atrocities. Because the Ustaše killed so many Serbs, some people have emphasized similarities between the Serbs and the Jews: two groups on friendly terms with each other, and both of them mercilessly persecuted by their neighbors. Some Serbs press the comparison further by maintaining that Serbs were also a "Chosen People," singled out by God for a special mission in history.

In fact, what is really important is the question of how Serbian Jews fared during World War II. The answer is simple and sad: 94 percent of Serbia's Jews were killed.[3] This amounts to about 15,000 or 16,000. The question that follows is: Who killed them? The short answer here is that it was, for the most part, the German occupiers. Scholars take this conclusion in two different directions.

Some are now studying how the German military and the Nazi party worked together to turn Serbia into a testing ground for the techniques of mass experimentation later used at Auschwitz and elsewhere. The mass atrocity compaigns carried out at the initiative of army commanders and other local functionaries might have even encouraged the higher-ups in the Nazi party to pursue the "Final Solution" across Europe.[4] After all, large-scale murder of Jews and other groups did not begin at Auschwitz until the spring of 1942; by then, the majority of Serbia's Jews were already dead. In August, the chief of the military occupation forces in Serbia, Harald Turner, declared that the Jewish problem in Serbia had been "liquidated" and that Serbia was *judenfrei* ("free of Jews"). Some historians even insist that the atrocities in Serbia were an integral part of the Final Solution, and not just the preparations for it.[5] From the start Turner was interested in eliminating potential resistance in Serbia. This was far more than just a brutal military measure; it was a convenient mechanism for singling out Jews for annihilation as a group. The Germans conveniently judged the entire Jewish community to be a potential threat. Starting in October 1941, Turner and the overall military commander in Yugoslavia, General Franz Böhme, issued orders to kill all Jews.

The other direction the research goes is into studies of Serbian collaboration with the Nazis. Individuals and governments across Europe collaborated with the Nazis by helping round up Jews, by confiscating Jewish property, and by acting as police and guards in ghettos and camps. Serbia was no different, as it turns out. The part of the issue that is most hotly debated is *how much* Serbian collaboration with the Germans took place. Recent research has brought to light the ways in which some Serbs cooperated with the Nazis. In August 1941, for instance, more than five hundred Serbs, many of them well-known persons, signed "The Appeal to the Serbian Nation," which was then published in newspapers. The appeal did not stress collaborating with the Germans in particular, but rather with "the authorities." The alternative was to help the insurgents, who were said to be communist, criminal, and foreign elements; their uprising would destroy the country (either because of their own depradations or the German reprisals) and so Serbs should work to preserve their nation by shunning the Partisans. This appeal is based on the desire to survive. Serbs were not alone in feeling this way in the Europe of that day. But in late 1941 there was a bizarre "Grand Anti-Masonic Exhibition" in Belgrade. It was organized by members of the Nedić government and it contained inflammatory "evidence" that Jews were part of an international communist conspiracy directed at Serbia. Thousands visited the exhibition, the praises of which were sung in the local media. The government even issued postage stamps with anti-Jewish themes.

More damning is the evidence that Serb soldiers, police, and militiamen helped round up Jews and send them to concentration camps. Most Serbian Jews were executed in the camp at Šabac and at two in the greater Belgrade area: Sajmište and Banjica. The Sajmište camp even used mobile gassing vans brought in from Germany. Members of armed bodies affiliated with the Nedić government also executed captured Partisans (mostly non-Jews) and turned over Serbian civilians for execution by the Germans (Jews and non-Jews). There is also some evidence that there was a small group of Serbs that functioned as a branch of the Gestapo.[6] General Nedić, perhaps eager to please his Nazi patrons or to gain from them more territory or independence of action, declared himself for a racially "pure" Serbian state; some Orthodox officials also expressed their sympathy for Nazi ideas.

These manifestations of Serbian collaboration with the Nazis were not huge in extent, nor were they unusual in occupied Europe. But they are an important, and tragic, part of the historical record, and it was not in Croatia alone that Jews (and Roma, and other groups) were victimized. The Ustaše probably acted much more on their own than did the Serbs, but with similarly devastating results: 75 percent of Croatia's Jews—30,000 or 40,000—died at this time. The study of Serbian participation in the Holocaust is important because it helps keep the fratricidal Yugoslav fighting of the war years in proper perspective. It also reinforces an emerging consensus in the rapidly growing field of Holocaust studies in general: the Nazi campaign against the Jews was more than just an elite Nazi phenomenon. The Holocaust was pushed by varying strata of the German government; it was not carried out just by the Schutzstaffel, elite Nazi forces (SS). It did not begin with the establishment of the large extermination camps in Poland, nor could it have happened without significant cooperation from the non-Jewish population.

THE CONTROVERSY SURROUNDING MIHAILOVIĆ

As a result of the suffering of Serbs in World War II, and the unpopular federal policies of the communist regime that followed, the figure of Draža Mihailović looms very large in many Serbian histories of the twentieth century. His status approaches that of an icon, or at least a martyr, in many accounts of the war. Adding to his aura is the persistent belief, now largely discounted by most Western historians, that Mihailović would have defeated the Partisans had it not been for the trickery of the British and American intelligence services. Mihailović's story is indeed a sad one, and his legacy is important in helping get a grasp on the confusing years of war and revolution in Serbia. But his life, work, and death need to be examined in full.

Mihailović's legacy contains positive and negative elements. The positive ones have already been elaborated. But there were three negative elements. First, he did fail as a military leader. Granted, he had powerful enemies and insufficient supplies. He also seems to have been a decent and brave man in personal terms and was not a fascist. But Mihailović was not a brilliant military thinker, a political innovator, or even a great organizer. He did not succeed in assembling a talented and loyal staff. He relied too much on personal friendships and family ties to select his commanders. His soldiers' *hajduk* image contrasted with the more modern and professional appearance of Tito's army. Probably Mihailović's most telling failing was his inability to overcome the territorial loyalties of his units. Since most Chetniks only wanted to fight close to their homes, a mobile army that could carry out sustained campaigns under central command never developed.

A second unpleasant, but important, part of Mihailović's legacy is the Chetnik collaboration with the Axis forces. Since Mihailović did not have control over all Serbian resistance fighters, he is not accountable for the activities of all Chetniks. But some cooperation with the Nazis took place in the fall of 1941, and by 1943 some of his commanders were regularly working out cease-fires with the Germans. Both groups hoped to marshal their forces to fight the Partisans. The Chetniks also fought side by side with the Germans against the Partisans in 1943. They cooperated even more with the Italians. The Chetnik leader Jezdimir Dangić was the best-known collaborator with the Italians; in addition to the various Chetniks loyal to Pećanac and "legalized" by Nedić, Fr. Momčilo Djujić led a group which was linked with Ljotić's fascists. The Germans were never fully convinced of the Chetniks' loyalty and planned to disarm them in the event of an Allied invasion or when the Partisans were subdued. It should be noted that the Partisans also reached certain tactical arrangements with the Germans, such as the exchange of prisoners and cease-fires to allow them to concentrate on other enemies.

The final negative legacy is atrocities. The Chetniks sometimes victimized civilians who supported the Partisans or who were simply Croatian by nationality or Muslim by faith. In terms of scale, nobody committed more atrocities in wartime Yugoslavia than the Ustaše. The Germans displayed a chilling and consistent savagery. In contrast, the Partisans themselves usually left civilian populations alone (except for requisitioning supplies). They were also popular because they allowed many deserting enemy soldiers to join their ranks.

But the Chetniks killed thousands of Muslim civilians around Foča in Bosnia in 1941 and 1942 and in the Sandžak in southern Serbia in 1943. They claimed to be avenging atrocities wrought by Muslim Ustaše units. Such massacres by Muslim forces did take place, and they have provided the material for some of the most lurid writing in recent Serbian literature, such as the novel (and now film) *The Knife* by Vuk Drašković. Most Muslim units who cooperated with the Axis did so under duress, but to brutalized civilians it does not matter much who their attackers are or what motivated them. The frustration of the Chetnik fighters at their inability to protect Serbian populations from the Ustaša is understandable, but this does not justify their own killings then, or the ones undertaken in the name of revenge in the 1990s by a new generation of warriors. Most Yugoslavs in the 1940s also feared that had the Chetniks won the war, they would have launched a massive pogrom against actual and potential Croatian opponents; in one document, the Chetnik leadership indicated that it planned to kill a number of Croats equal to how many Serbs died in the NDH; later Chetnik claims were that between 600,000 and 800,000 Serbs were killed there, conjuring up images of a vast potential bloodbath if the Partisans were to have lost.

Things turned out to be gruesome enough as it was. The Partisans won, of course, and they hunted down and executed at least 10,000 Chetniks after the war. Near the towns of Bleiburg and Kočevje, along the Austrian-Slovene border, they also killed about 30,000 or more Ustaše, other Axis supporters, and anticommunist civilians. Mihailović and his handful of final followers were captured near Višegrad along the Serbian-Bosnian border on March 12, 1946. He was executed on July 17 of that same year.

OVERVIEW OF CASUALTIES IN THE WAR

The total casualty figures for Yugoslavia are important not just because they show the extent of the fighting there, although that certainly helps to explain the lingering and recently inflamed animosities among Serbs, Croats, and Bosnian Muslims. But these figures have also been subjected to great manipulation for propaganda purposes in the decades since World War II, and that tells us something about the politicization of history. Tito's government long circulated the figure of 1.7 million deaths in Yugoslavia during World War II. Everyone knew the fighting there had been fierce, and this astronomical figure, equivalent to 11 percent of the prewar population, confirmed that impression. The Communist Party of Yugoslavia (CPY) seems to have substantially inflated this figure, though, to make its struggle, sacrifices, and ultimate triumph seem all the more awe inspiring; perhaps it wanted to strengthen its case for the defeated Axis powers to pay war reparations. It also wanted to drum up support for its new policies of "brotherhood and unity" by reminding Yugoslavs what had happened when they had failed to work together to fend off the German invasion and by pointing out the dangers of aggressive nationalism at home.

It turns out that the figure was off by a substantial degree. The new, increasingly accepted figure is about 1 million, which still represents a staggering amount of bloodshed, amounting to 6.4 percent of Yugoslavia's prewar population. Two scholars, working carefully and independently, recently arrived at these numbers. One, Bogoljub Kočović, was a Serb, and the other was a Croatian, Vladimir Žerjavić. Serbs turned out to have been the biggest group of victims in numerical terms, with 487,000 deaths. Of those, well over 300,000 occurred on the territory of Pavelić's NDH. In relative terms, 6.9 percent of the country's Serbs died (that figure was around 17 percent for Serbs in Croatia and Bosnia). For Croats, the number is 207,000 deaths. Every nationality in the country suffered atrocities as well as war losses, but the highest losses relative to number were among Jews, of whom 77.9 percent (60,000) were killed.[7]

It is sad to report, but the appearance of these solid figures has not halted the misuse of wartime suffering by irresponsible nationalists in Croatia and Serbia. Some Serbs continue to claim that their losses in Croatia were double the new figures, or even that one million Serbs died at the Jasenovac concentration camp alone. This heightening of the Ustaša terror is presumably done to show that Croats are cutthroats and can never be trusted to protect their minorities. The best figures now available put the Jasenovac death toll at about 85,000, of whom 50,000 were Serbs. But some Croatian nationalists and historians continue to put the figure far lower than that in an effort to rehabilitate the Ustaša regime.

CONCLUSION

World War II brought the death of the first Yugoslavia and the creation of the second. The Serbian dynasty was no more, and hundreds of thousands of Serbs died on all sides of the conflicts. The fitful historical relationship between Serbs and Croats turned very bitter only during this time; previously, there had been periods of both rivalry and cooperation between the two groups, with some deterioration in the interwar period. But an astronomically larger degree of animosity and mistrust had now sprouted. Serbian-Muslim relations were much embittered. After the war, exhaustion from the war and optimism about the early years of the socialist experiment would distract Serbs and Croats from these problems, but only for a while.

Some Serbs felt that the tragedy of their situation went well beyond deaths. By bravely resisting Nazi pressure in March of 1941, this argument proceeds, Serbs had brought an invasion down on their heads; as a result of that German invasion, the resistance struggle brought the communist Partisans to power, who then created huge new problems for Serbs, especially by allowing areas with Serbs to be, in effect, ruled by Croats, Albanians, Hungarians, and Bosnian Muslims (see next chapter). If one pushes this argument even further, it took until the rise of Milošević in the late 1980s for Serbs to begin righting the wrongs of the 1940s.

Tito and the Communists were determined to keep any pro-Serbian interpretations of Yugoslavism under wraps. Yugoslavism now meant federalism, and although Serbs continued to be the leading presence in the military and in the party, in terms of formal government structure Serbian power was going to be much diluted. In fact, many Serbs see World War II as the start of the period of the partial submergence of the Serbian nation in a sea of one-party rule, socialist economics, and privileges granted to other national groups.

NOTES

1. The following chart gives the approximate maximum strength of the various military forces in Yugoslavia. These force levels were not consistent throughout the war, nor did all of the groups reach their peak levels simultaneously.

Partisans under Tito	100,000*
Chetniks under Mihailović	50,000
Serbian State Guard under Nedić	20,000
Serbian Volunteer Corps (fascists) under Ljotić	4,000
Pro-German Chetniks under Pećanac	8,000
Royal Yugoslav Army (at start of war)	700,000
Germans	24 divisions (approx. 55,000)
Italians	23 divisions (approx. 53,000)
Italian-controlled Chetniks (*Milizia voluntaria anticomunista*)	40,000
Croatian Ustaše (fascists)	20,000
Croatian Domobrani (Home Guards)	70,000
Croatian gendarmes (rural militia)	20,000
Bosnian Muslim SS Division *Handžar*	12,000
Sandžak Muslim Defense League	1,000

| Hungarian army (Nazi ally) | five divisions |
| Bulgarian army (Nazi ally) | three divisions |

*This number is somewhat misleading because for much of the war, Partisan strength was around 20,000 to 30,000. After the surrender of Italy in September 1943, the figure grew rapidly as it became more and more apparent who would win the war. By the end of the war, the number of persons cooperating with the Partisans was much higher.

2. Branko Petranović, *Srbija u drugom svetskom ratu, 1939–1945* (Beograd: Vojnoizdavač ki i novinski centar, 1992), p. 261.

3. Philip J. Cohen, *Serbia's Secret War: Propaganda and the Deceit of History* (College Station: Texas A&M University Press, 1996), p. 83.

4. This conclusion is that of the "functionalist" school of historians of the Nazi period. For a presentation of some of its approaches, see the works of Christopher R. Browning, including *The Path to Genocide: Essays on Launching the Final Solution* (New York: Cambridge University Press, 1992).

5. Walter Manoschek, *"Serbien ist judenfrei": Militärische Besatzungspolitik und Judenvernichtung in Serbien 1941/42* (München: Oldenbourg, 1995), p. 194.

6. Cohen, *Serbia's Secret War*, pp. 50–52.

7. Christopher Bennett, *Yugoslavia's Bloody Collapse: Causes, Course and Consequences* (New York: New York University Press, 1995), p. 45.

9

Serbia in Tito's Yugoslavia, 1945–1980

INTRODUCTION

In a nutshell, Serbian history after World War II was bound up with the history of the other Yugoslav peoples even more tightly than after World War I. There was no longer a Serbian king over the whole multiethnic country, and Tito's communists were at first eager to suppress all nationalism—especially among Serbs and Croats—for both practical and ideological reasons. Therefore, the history of Serbia from 1945 through the 1980s is in many respects the history of Yugoslavia as a whole. Historians often study and teach about a certain era by "periodizing" it, or breaking it down into smaller time periods based around central trends. A periodization of postwar Yugoslavia usually looks like this:

1945–1952: dominance of the Stalinist model

1953–1971: experimentation and liberalization

1972–1980: political and economic decentralization; growth of greater unifying role of the military; "negative selection" among leaders; economic stagnation

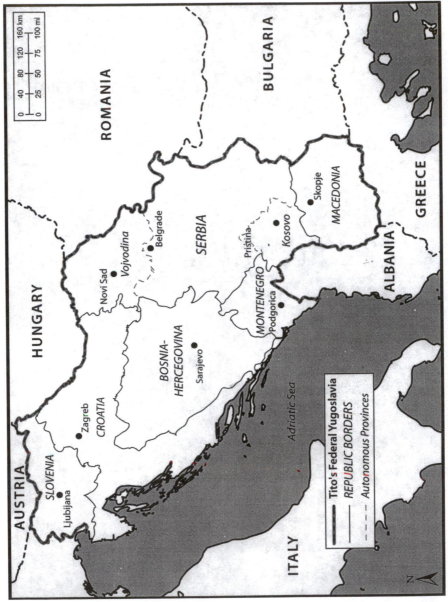

Christopher Ferro

1981–1991: post-Tito period with raging economic problems and increasing nationalist unrest in the absence of effective central leadership

While it is possible to single out certain events and trends that had special meaning for the government of Serbia, for its population, and for Serbs living across the rest of Yugoslavia, one cannot trace a typical textbook pattern of history for these decades, simply because Serbia was not an independent country. By foregrounding conditions in the new Republic of Serbia (as the Serbian administrative unit inside Tito's Yugoslavia was called) against a backdrop of general Yugoslav history, we will get a sense of how life changed for Serbs in the postwar decades and what issues were important to them.

POLITICS

With the war won by mid-1945, the Partisans were interested in converting AVNOJ into a permanent government. They now needed to administer the entire country, not just their "liberated zones," and they had to reach some agreement with King Petar's government-in-exile in London. They also needed international recognition and help in rebuilding their war-mangled country. Eyewitness accounts of the first ten years of this new, second Yugoslavia (also called socialist or Titoist Yugoslavia) stress the enormous confidence, even cockiness of the Communist Party. Its large number of members and success in the anti-Nazi war had given them enough confidence to clash openly with the other Allies over Trieste and south Austria, and with the Soviets over relations with Bulgaria and Greece. Tito's armed forces even shot down two American C-47 transport planes over Slovenia in 1946. No one knew where Yugoslavia—which, after all, had been so rickety before the war—was headed, but one thing was apparent: for Serbs, this new socialist and multiethnic government was going to bring immediate and sweeping changes.

Elections for a constituent assembly were held on November 11, 1945. The voting age was now eighteen for men *and* women, but younger people could vote if they had fought as Partisans. Some 250,000 Yugoslavs accused of collaboration (the ones who had not already been killed, although most of them had not been convicted by any court) were not allowed to vote. The CPY selected and supported candidates under the name of the "Popular Front," and the election result was never in serious doubt. Serbian politicians were determined to contest the elections, however. The communists did not make this easy. Some of the old interwar politicians were still around and not compromised in communist eyes. Milan Grol of the Democratic Party and Misa Trifunovi of the Radicals led the effort. But plans to cooperate with the Croatian politicians Šubašić and Juraj Šutej came to nought, and the Popular Front garnered 90 percent of the votes.

By the end of January 1946, the country was renamed the Federal People's Republic of Yugoslavia and a new constitution was in place. It was modeled on a Soviet constitution from the 1930s. Tito was declared prime minister, a position he would keep until he was made president in 1953. An older Serbian politician, Ivan Ribar, was made president, but this was just an honorary position. Until 1947, some other noncommunist Serbs held important positions, but they were soon sidelined by Tito's communists. CPY influence became pervasive at all levels of government. This was also the case in the other communist countries of Eastern Europe. With the transformation of Yugoslavia into a one-party state (though not a totalitarian one), more and more aspects of citizens' daily lives would become politicized and subject to government control. The potential for labeling all opposition and noncooperation as disloyalty grew. Civil society was more or less submerged in Serbia.

The idea of civil society, which many political scientists, philosophers, and historians believe is fundamental to the functioning of democracy, is that politics is largely kept out of peoples' economic and social lives; sometimes this ideal is also described as citizens being actively involved in voluntary associations with each other (horizontal connectedness) rather than being forced to participate in government-controlled professional and leisure-time organizations (vertical regimentation). When civil society is destroyed or underdeveloped, authoritarian leaders—whether nationalist, fascist, or communist—have an easier time controlling their countries.

Many Serbs were arrested for supposedly collaborating with the Nazis or for supporting the Chetnik forces of Draža Mihailovič, who was himself condemned as a traitor. Some people were even denounced for not being sufficiently pro-Partisan. Homes and businesses were confiscated, and the wealth redistributed or kept for the use of communist officials and veterans. Macabre lists of executed persons were published in the newspapers as communists tried to break the back of all potential opposition, be it in the form of business leaders, the Serbian Orthodox Church, or noncommunist intellectuals. The important Serbian novelist Svetlana Velmar-Janković has described this atmosphere of terror, made doubly traumatic because it came on the heels of an atrocious war, in her famous novel *The Dungeon*; it also figures prominently in the novel

Premeditated Murder by another very highly regarded Serbian author, Slobodan Selenić.

Tito reinstated the historically based administrative units based on Yugoslavia's six main national groups. The exception to this generalization was Bosnia-Hercegovina, which had no one dominant national group. Bosnian Muslims would complete the process of official nation building in 1968, by which time they were considered one of Yugoslavia's nations rather than just a religious or regional group. Of course, Croatia, Serbia, and Macedonia also contained lots of "minorities," or residents who were not members of the titular nationality. Some of these minorities were from other main nations and others were from what Tito called "nationalities" (generally smaller and non-South Slavic groups). Slovenes and Croats were generally pleased with the new territorial arrangements. Croats no longer had control over Bosnia (as the NDH did during the war), but they did have Istria, Dalmatia, and Slavonia, as well as the old military frontier and the area around Zagreb. Slovenia had its narrow bit of Adriatic coast back and many of its co-nationals who had languished under Italian rule before World War II.

Serbs, on the other hand, were patently unhappy with the new republics. True, Vojvodina had been slightly increased in size, but both that region and Kosovo were given a slightly different status from central Serbia, now often referred to as "Serbia proper." This central area, which did include the major cities of Belgrade, Niš, Smederevo, and Kragujevac, corresponds roughly to the lands controlled by the Serbian monarchy before the Balkan wars of 1912–1913. Vojvodina, site of the Serbian cultural renaissance in the late eighteenth century, and Kosovo, the cradle of Serbian culture, were still ruled from Belgrade but both areas had some degree of autonomy. The status and titles of Vojvodina and Kosovo would change over the decades, and they remained technically a part of Serbia until their autonomy was revoked by Slobodan Milošević in 1988, but Belgrade found it ever harder to impose its will on the regions, where many Serbs continued to live. Coupled with the fact that many Serb communities were now on the other side of internal borders in Croatia and Bosnia, Serbs felt rising frustration as a nation. There was the additional consideration that more Serbs than any other group had died in World War II, many at the hands of the Croats and the Partisans. Frustration was joined by insecurity as Serbs entered the communist era.

The new federal system had a new kind of Skupština. It was bicameral (having two houses, or branches, like the House of Representatives and the Senate in the United States). One of them was the Federal Council (*Savezno Veće*), which was elected directly by the citizens of the republics;

the other was the Council of Nationalities (*Veće Naroda*), whose members were chosen by the local skupštinas in the six republics and two autonomous regions. Only one party was allowed to run for or hold office: the Communist Party, which renamed itself the League of Communists of Yugoslavia (LCY) at its sixth party congress in 1952, reflecting its desire to shed its Stalinist legacy.

The Seventh Party Congress of the LCY, meeting in Ljubljana in 1958, firmed up the new practices of workers' self-management; the LCY was now committed, at least in theory, to renouncing its use of overt administrative control over society in an effort to guide and influence it. Still, no other parties were permitted; censorship, though loose by East European standards, also continued to exist. Controversial issues relating to nationalism and, especially World War II, were taboo. The party hoped to "influence" society by keeping control over government appointments and by corralling unions, student groups, and veterans' organizations into the Socialist Alliance of the Working People of Yugoslavia, an ideologically friendly but somewhat depoliticized umbrella group for all sorts of professional and interest groups. That said, the LCY did struggle against most vestiges of Stalinism (often called "bureaucratism") in its ranks in an effort to mobilize public support and to distinguish Yugoslavia from its Soviet-controlled communist neighbors. In 1954, the Novi Sad Agreements were signed, declaring that Serbo-Croatian was one language with two alphabets. (A similar agreement between Vuk Karadžić and many other scholars had been signed in Vienna in 1850.)

It was also in the 1950s that Yugoslav foreign policy began to develop its unique profile. Tito began visiting the leaders of newly decolonized countries such as India, Indonesia, and Egypt to explore the potential for cooperation with countries that were neither American nor Soviet satellites. In 1961, this grouping coalesced into the Nonaligned Movement, which held its first conference in Belgrade. For the next nineteen years, Tito was one of the leaders of this movement; it brought him a lot of world attention and legitimacy at home, especially because nonalignment meshed well with Yugoslavs' sense of pride and independence. It also buffered Tito from the imperial ambitions of both Washington and Moscow. Economic ties with developing countries did develop but not to the extent that the LCY probably hoped. Serb scientists and engineers often worked in nonaligned countries, especially in the oil industry and construction of power plants and dams. Still, by the 1970s, many Yugoslavs thought that the government should be focusing more on developing trade with European countries, which had always been Yugoslavia's chief trading partners.

The Constitution of 1953 replaced the Stalin-style original constitution of 1946, but by 1963, Yugoslavia's experiments required the drafting of yet another constitution. The Slovene party leader Edvard Kardelj was the LCY's chief ideologist and, as such, played the chief role in the designing of all the country's constitutions. In 1966, the most important Serb communist, Aleksandar Ranković, was dismissed from his posts and forced out of public life. He had been vice-president of the country and the chief of the secret police and had also controlled much of the party's personnel policy. Ranković was a powerful man, and his fondness for a strong central government earned him the mistrust of non-Serbs, especially the Albanians of Kosovo, who saw him not just as an old-style communist but also as a Serbian nationalist. He was standing in the way of Yugoslavia's economic and political reforms and was also accused of bugging Tito's quarters!

In 1968, Serbia witnessed two major episodes of unrest. The bigger of these was student demonstrations. From Mexico to France to Japan, 1968 was a year of tremendous student activism and social upheaval. The United States saw not only huge protests against the Vietnam War but also the assassinations of Martin Luther King, Jr., and Robert Kennedy, while in Czechoslovakia a reform movement called the "Prague Spring" was put down by a brutal Soviet invasion.

In April 1968, about 4,000 students marched through Belgrade to protest an incident of police brutality. (In France, by comparison, about 800,000 students took to the streets in May of 1968.) They were dissatisfied with the educational process of which they were a part. Too few classes, run-down buildings, cramped dorms, outdated textbooks—these were some of the students' complaints, which were echoed in the Paris demonstrations and, ironically, in the Albanian demonstrations in Kosovo in 1981. The demonstration brought a strong police response and more than 150 students were injured. Sit-ins and occupations of buildings at the Belgrade University ensued. Students in other major Yugoslav cities, such as Ljubljana, Sarajevo, and Zagreb held demonstrations in solidarity with the Belgrade students. There were some further clashes with police. Students failed to rally workers to their cause, unlike in France, where about 10 million workers—half the work force—went on strike, to some extent in support of the student demonstrations.

In that decade of "student power," however, challenges went out to much more than just the conditions of study. The students felt a generation gap keenly—not just in terms of style but also of substance. Students were worried, for instance, about unemployment in Yugoslavia, which should have been almost nil in a socialist country. They saw the system failing them, and they resented the World War II generation for being out of touch and smug in their secure jobs.

The students also had more theoretical political concerns. Many of them were influenced by neo-Marxist thinking, based on Marx's humanistic early writings from the 1840s that emphasized the concepts of "alienation" and "contestation" (challenging all authority). These students placed little value on party unity, bureaucratic procedures, or violent revolution. Neo-Marxists wanted the country's politicians to stay "honest" and to continue their own ideological development. The students believed that the League of Communists had no monopoly on truth, and they wanted more freedom of discussion and debate on campus. They also resented the growth of what they called "dinar socialism" with its fixation on materialism.

Finally, Tito used his personal prestige to bring the student crisis to an end. He met with them and promised to improve campus conditions. Still, the demonstrations had an important legacy. They were a rite of passage for many of today's Serbian politicians and academics, and they signaled a new sense of unease as the country entered the final decade of Tito's rule.

The other scene of unrest in 1968 was Kosovo. The demographic tensions caused by an increase in the Albanian share of the population in this "cradle of Serbian civilization" were heightened by the fact that Kosovo was the poorest part of the entire country of Yugoslavia. In 1968 its unemployment rate was 20 percent (twice the national average) and the per capita share of the gross national product was one-quarter that of Slovenia.

The Albanian Kosovars were demanding their own university, more textbooks in Albanian, and even the augmentation of their own teaching cadre by teachers from Albania proper. But political factors outweighed educational ones. With the Serb nationalist Ranković out of power, Albanians were emboldened to seek more self-rule. The year 1968 marked the beginning of the contemporary Albanian nationalist movement in Kosovo.

Another event of huge importance in 1968 was the invasion of Czechoslovakia by the Soviet Union and its allies in August. President Tito had just visited Prague to show his support for the reformers there who were sweeping away the Stalinist legacy in Czechoslovakia and replacing it with "socialism with a human face." Many Yugoslavs found in the "Prague Spring" an echo of their own evolution away from the Soviet model since 1948. The Brezhnev Doctrine, as the Soviet justification for their suppression of the Czechoslovak experiment was called, stated that the Soviet Union had the right to intervene in any country where socialism was threatened. Naturally many Yugoslavs, aware of how they had been branded as heretics by the Soviets in the late 1940s, and of how different their version of socialism continued to be from that of the USSR, feared that this doctrine might be turned on them.

Unlike in the case of the crushed Hungarian revolution of 1956, Tito publicly condemned the Soviet invasion. Fear of a possible Soviet invasion led to a surge in membership in the LCY; Tito also established the Territorial Defense Forces in each republic. The new Law on National Defense, built on the Partisans' successful experiences with guerrilla warfare during World War II, borrowed some of the rhetoric of economic self-management to form an auxiliary military force. Although they were never used to repel a foreign invasion, in the 1990s they would become the nuclei of the armed forces of the breakaway republics of Slovenia, Croatia, and Bosnia-Hercegovina.

The period from 1967 to 1971 is often called the "Croatian Spring." It was an assertion of Croatian nationalism that made both LCY centralizers and many rank-and-file Serbs nervous. The leading Croatian cultural organization, known as the *Matica Hrvatska*, rejected the 1954 Novi Sad Agreement and pressed for recognition of Croatian as a separate and fully equal language. There were student demonstrations against the government and party, and within the Croatian branch of the LCY, there were calls for an even more extensive devolution of federal economic and political power. Tito decided that this Croatian activism went too far in undercutting his power and that it evoked too many bad memories among non-Croats related to the Ustaše atrocities of World War II. In 1971, then, he expelled from the LCY leaders such as Mika Tripalo, Savka Dabčević-Kučar, and Pero Pirker. This cleared the way for a settling of accounts with the younger generation of Serbian communists, too, whom he suspected of being too liberal, too nationalist, or both.

In 1974 another constitution was issued. This completed Kardelj's experimental vision of the totally "self-managing society," but the LCY never retreated all the way off the scene and it never transformed into a purely social democratic party. The lengthy 1974 document gave even more economic and political power to the republics, upsetting many old-line LCY and military leaders. It also made the Serbian autonomous units of Kosovo and Vojvodina basically equal to the six original republics at the federal level, a move that angered Serbs who began to voice support for self-rule for the Serbs in Croatia, where they made up 60 percent or more of most districts. The Bosnian Muslims received official federal recognition as a national group in the 1960s. The move to split off a separate Macedonian Orthodox Church from the Serbian one began in the late 1960s, and by the 1970s, the Slavic-speaking Muslims of the Sandžak were also declared an ethnic group. These developments heightened Serbian suspicions that their territory and ethnic unity were being sacrificed more and more to maintain a kind of balance of power within Yugoslavia during Tito's twilight years. The stage was also set for a serious vacuum of power at the top after Tito's death. There was to be a rotating system of presidencies within the party, the government (equivalent to a prime ministership), and the Parliament, based on the eight ethno-territorial units (the six republics plus Kosovo and Vojvodina). Many major decisions were going to have to be made unanimously or not at all, while any recentralization of power to meet the grave national and economic crises that were just around the corner would be decried as either too pro-Croatian or too pro-Serbian, depending on who was in charge. The League of Communists had already been split into separate republic-based organizations in 1969, but now these branches were strengthened further. Tito and the military were the only two countrywide institutions left; one of them was mortal, while the other was increasingly seen as a bastion of Serb influence. Neither was interested in the growth of civil society, alternative political movements, or a frank discussion of the country's past and present problems.

ECONOMICS

Wartime destruction in Yugoslavia was colossal. In addition to the massive numbers of casualties and refugees, about 40 percent of its industry and 50 percent of its agricultural capacity had been destroyed. Tens of thousands of people were homeless. But much of the war damage was repaired quickly, as the result of the mobilization of voluntary youth work brigades, some forced labor, and a huge volume of food, clothes, medicine, and vehicles donated by the United Nations Relief and Rehabilitation Agency. After the Tito-Stalin break, direct American aid flowed into the country. This aid totaled over $500 million by mid-decade; it included but was not limited to food and weaponry.

Recovery was only one goal of the Communist Party; carrying out a social revolution and completely reordering society was another. Thus, the party tried to impose various kinds of collectivization on the Serbian countryside in the period from 1945 to 1953. It did so, in fact, across all of Yugoslavia, believing that the country's peasants were too poor to produce efficiently and that individual ownership would breed "petty-bourgeois" political attitudes. This was a huge political issue for the government, because the peasantry comprised about 75 percent of the overall population of Yugoslavia. The CPY did not follow a linear path in implementing its agrarian strategy, and many peasants did not acquiesce in party dictates.[1]

At first large estates, religious holdings, and especially the property of enemies of the Partisans and of expelled Germans were nationalized. This move was generally popular. More than 50 percent of this land was given to individual peasant families. Much of the land was in the northern Serbian region of Vojvodina. By 1948, nearly 250,000 people had settled there. The CPY hoped that these settlers, some of whom were placed on collective farms, would become "model peasants," filled with a new socialist consciousness; they were supposed to exude a sense of "Yugoslav" nationality, too, since they were being recruited from all over and since Vojvodina was already home to a great deal of ethnic diversity. What actually happened, though, was that few Croats and Muslims moved and 72 percent of the colonists were Serbs. Most of them came from Serbian regions of Bosnia, Croatia, and Macedonia, where they no longer felt comfortable or where the countryside was ravaged; others were veterans who were promised good land in the Vojvodina as a reward for loyal service. Also undercutting government hopes was the peasants' disillusionment at living standards in the Vojvodina, which had sustained much war damage.

Other laws were even less popular. The communists instituted the controversial *otkup*, or compulsory delivery of foodstuffs, so that peasants would not hoard scarce items needed in the cities. A Five-Year Plan was launched in 1946, calling for industrial output to increase nearly fivefold and agricultural production by 1.5 times. Unlike the Soviet model that it generally followed, however, it did not enforce rapid collectivization. Intermediate forms of socialized agriculture, called cooperatives, were presented as modern versions of the the traditional peasant *zadrugas*; their use was supposed to accustom peasants to working together and with the state. By 1948, over 3 million Yugoslav peasants worked together in cooperatives, but they were still technically independent owners; by contrast, there were only about 300,000 people living on collectives.

These policies underwent rapid change, though, after the Tito-Stalin split of June 1948. The Union of Soviet Socialist Republics (USSR) and its allies blockaded Yugoslavia, and food could no longer be imported. Yugoslavia also needed even more produce so that it would have something to export to earn foreign currency, since its industry was mostly still in ruins. It was decided to collectivize rapidly, though with as little brute force as possible. The Communist Party may have also wanted to deflect the stinging Soviet criticism that Yugoslavia's largely independent peasantry meant that their society was actually capitalist at heart.

By the end of 1949, 18 percent of the country was collectivized. The figure for Serbia was 17 percent, while Montenegro was 63 percent collectivized. Within Serbia, there were huge differences, though: the figure for Vojvodina was 40 percent, Kosovo 22 percent, and "narrow" Serbia just 6 percent. This rate for central Serbia, or the Šumadija, where most Serbs lived, was by far the lowest for the whole country, indicating that Serbian officials and peasants had little enthusiasm for collectivization.

The peak for this policy was hit in 1951, when 24 percent of the arable land in Yugoslavia was included in collective farms. By 1953, however, drought and resistance by peasants had produced a fall in output, and the KPJ, showing its ideological flexibility, ended its heavy-handed experiment. Membership in collectives became voluntary, and Serbian agriculture became once again overwhelmingly private. Only Poland had a share of government-controlled agriculture as small as that of Yugoslavia. Furthermore, the party "ended the long struggle for control of the countryside and the hearts and minds of the Yugoslav peasants."[2] Tito and company would have to look elsewhere for a successful ideological experiment to define Yugoslavia's "third path." This inability to overcome traditional thinking among the population would end up plaguing the government in other important areas, too—such as nationalities policy.

Like all of the Yugoslav republics, Serbia experienced significant economic progress from the 1950s through the early 1980s. Critics of the Tito-era policies argue that the growth would have been much greater if conflicts with other republics over resources had not taken place, or if market principles had come into play earlier. But industrial growth was significant, often over 10 percent a year, and the society left its traditional agrarian roots and became much more urbanized and secular. Even for the people living in Serbia's myriad small towns and villages, agriculture gradually became more of an "occupation" than a "way of life."[3]

In the 1950s, the Yugoslav government embraced the principles of a new economic system called "workers' self-management." This system, which was based on "socially owned property" rather than private means of production (as in capitalism) or state property (as in the Soviet system), was a foundation of Yugoslavia's "separate path to socialism" made necessary by the break with Stalin in 1948. Milovan Djilas and the Slovenes Edvard Kardelj and Boris Kidrić (Tito's chief economic planner) developed these policies. At first workers' councils were set up to exercise "grassroots" control over certain political and economic functions. But in the 1974 constitution Kardelj expanded this "vision" and called for a "self-managing economy." All enterprises with more than two hundred and fifty employees were broken down, on paper anyway, into subunits called Basic Organizations of Associated Labor (BOALs) that were supposed to make production decisions, set prices, and invest or disburse profits. The LCY wanted to avoid the two extremes of administrative fiat and rule of the market. Kardelj even claimed that workers' self-management actually provided for a type of pluralism. A multiplicity of parties was supposedly not necessary, because the pluralism of self-managing interests served this function for society as a whole.

To say that the last Kardelj constitution made the system less workable would be an understatement. In the years from 1970 to 1978, the federal Yugoslav government grew in size by 73 percent and the republican governments by an average of 35 percent. The net result of this fragmentation on the one hand, and bureaucratization on the other, was that it became easier for the republics to go their own ways. Workers were often mystified by the new arrangements, central planning still played an important role, and the economic need for companies to earn their keep was constantly mitigated by the political dangers of rising unemployment.

In the late 1970s, the Yugoslav economy began to run out of steam. Industrial growth rates slowed dramatically, as the basic expansion that resulted from mobilizing peasants and building heavy industries and transportation reached a plateau. The world oil crisis created many problems, and the government was borrowing heavily to keep popular consumption high so that discontent with the government would be kept low. By 1985, individual productivity, net income, and personal spending were falling sharply, and the national debt passed $18 billion in hard currency. Such economic conditions doubtless added to the sense of disillusion and anxiety that many Serbs and others felt as communism was discredited in the rest of Eastern Europe and national conflicts began to rattle the foundations of Yugoslavia; the creation of a kind of vacuum of belief aided political leaders in manipulating their populations with nationalist propaganda which, in turn, added greatly to the ferocity of the fighting.

There had also been some major mistakes in industrial planning. A phenomenon known as "political factories" led to the duplication of industrial facilities in various republics. Since investment funds were controlled by the party and administration, often at the republican level where self-sufficiency seemed desirable and consultation with other federal units was not usually required, all the republics sometimes built superfluous industry for themselves instead of making use of an already existing, and usually underused, factory somewhere else in the country. In Serbia, the giant steel plant at Smederevo, the cement factory at Golubac, and the lead and zinc works at Trepča were inefficient enterprises that consumed a disproportionate share of government subsidies.

Another controversial aspect of economic life was the Federal Fund for the Accelerated Development of the Underdeveloped Republics and Kosovo, known by the acronym FADURK. This program was designed to help Montenegro, Macedonia, Bosnia, and southern Serbia (Kosovo) develop their industry and close the gaps between their standards of living and those in the rest of the country. FADURK was created in 1963 and fell apart in the late 1980s. It was funded by federal taxes, and it seems to have improved the absolute and relative economic standing of Montenegro, while Macedonia basically kept pace with the growth in the rest of the country. Bosnia and Kosovo experienced important economic growth but they did not keep pace with changes in the rest of the country; thus, FADURK failed its objective of reducing socioeconomic differentiation across Yugoslavia. It also generated resentment among those republics who paid for most of it (Slovenia and Croatia) or who were declared ineligible to reap its benefits (most of Serbia).

A study of the basic indicators of economic development and of the standard of living across the decades of socialist Yugoslavia give a good indication of the kinds of change Serbia was experiencing. Social and demographic issues are tied in with economics, so they will be included together in this section. First, let us look at the ways in which Serbia changed during the communist decades. In 1953, the population of Serbia (all nationalities) was 6.9 million; by 1988, 9.8 million people lived in Serbia. The number of Serbs (in all republics) as a percentage of the total population of Yugoslavia had fallen in that same time, however, from over 40 percent to 36 percent. Most alarming for Serbs, however, was certainly the fact that in Kosovo, Serbs had fallen from 24 percent of the population in 1948 to 10 percent in 1991; in that time, the Albanian population there had more than tripled in absolute terms, to 1.6 million. There were actually more Serbs in the province by the 1990s (almost 200,000) than in 1948, but their growth had been much slower than the Albanians' and their numbers had decreased, in absolute terms, since a peak in the early 1970s.

Most socioeconomic indicators for Serbia indicate improvements in the standard of living in these decades. Between the 1940s and the 1980s, for instance, the number of infant deaths per 1,000 live births decreased from 107 to 31, and illiteracy decreased from 27 percent to 11 percent.[4] The number of inhabitants per doctor was lowered from 2,440 to 515, while male life expectancy rose from fifty-seven to sixty-eight and female from fifty-nine to seventy-three. Spending devoted to consumption increased significantly, as did ownership of durable goods such as televisions, washing machines, cars, and refrigerators.

How Serbia and its various regions fared in comparison to the rest of Yugoslavia in these decades, however, is more problematic. The differential between Kosovo, the poorest part of Serbia and of all of Yugoslavia, and the wealthiest part of Yugoslavia, Slovenia, continued to grow despite the government's investment strategies. By the 1980s, the average Slovene was seven times as productive in economic terms as the average Kosovar, with wide gaps in their respective educations, health care, and real income. Most of "narrow Serbia" was close to or just below the national average in such indicators, with Vojvodina following Croatia and Slovenia at the top of most lists. At the time of Yugoslavia's breakup in 1991, the average resident of Serbia generated $2,238 of the gross national product (GNP), whereas the average Croat produced $3,230 and the average Slovene nearly $6,000; the figures for Bosnia and Macedonia were quite a bit below Serbia, while the national average was $3,060. Tito's redistributive investment strategy, carried out through FADURK, left every republic or region with grounds for complaint. The wealthy areas resented the drain on their own development (even though their growth continued to outstrip that of the rest of the country); the poor areas never thought they got enough help, and "narrow Serbia" resented being left off the list of recipients, especially since much of the defense industry had been relocated into Bosnia to make it less vulnerable in the event of a Soviet (or even NATO) invasion.

RELIGION

The Serbian Orthodox Church survived the Communist era, but it was brutalized immediately after the war. After about 1950, its main hardships in the country were financial and legal. The Yugoslav government did not carry out large-scale purges of believers. For the most part, Tito's goals were to punish alleged or real religious collaborators with the Axis, to cripple the Catholic and Orthodox churches' ability to foster nationalism, and to make sure religious leaders confined their influence over their parishioners to spiritual matters. In other words, the churches should belong to the private sphere and should stay out of politics. It is unclear just what role the church will play in the future of Serbian politics, although in most periods in the past it has been, in the tradition of most of the Eastern Orthodox churches, closely linked to the government. The majority of Serbs still profess belief in Orthodox Christianity, although formal membership and regular attendance tend to decrease over time in all industrialized societies.

After World War II, the Catholic Church in Croatia was treated more harshly than the Serbian Church. As many as 400 Croatian priests were executed after the war, while about one hundred Serbian priests were killed. The communists maintained that there had been more outright collaboration by Catholic priests than by Orthodox; they also feared the Vatican's influence in the country; and Catholic bishops protested bitterly against many communist policies. The relationship with the Vatican and with many Croatian Catholics was embittered by the trial and conviction of Archbishop Alojzije Stepinac for collaboration with the Ustaše. Tito was eager to placate the Orthodox Church because Serbs were the largest population group in the country.

In the first few years after the war, most of the church's property and investments were nationalized. These losses included over one thousand buildings and 90 percent of church lands, which included many agricultural tracts. Government subsidies to the church—a common practice in Europe—were cut off. Churches and monasteries damaged during the war were left unrepaired; others were abandoned or put to use as hospitals or orphanages. Money from Serbian communities in the United State and Canada helped to restore some of these buildings, however.

The patriarch, or head of the church, Gavrilo Dozić, returned from his confinement in Germany in November 1946. He opposed communism but avoided confrontation with Tito. He refused to compromise on certain key issues, like government-sponsored priests' associations and the proposed splitting off of the Macedonian Orthodox Church. Another leading churchman, Bishop Nikolaj Velimirović, chose not to return to Yugoslavia. He emigrated to the United States, where he died in 1956. He left behind many writings on Serbian culture and on spiritual issues such as pietism.

By 1952, all religious instruction in schools had ceased; government harassment and a shortage of priests made teaching the catechism on church property difficult. The government also made civil marriage and divorce take legal precedence over church-sponsored procedures. This practice, too, is common even in noncommunist countries, and religious ceremonies were not forbidden. The government ended up creating "priests' associations," which most Orthodox clergymen joined; these groups limited the priests' freedom of speech but also gave them access to politics and to financial resources that could be used for relief and reconstruction projects.[5] The upper hierarchy of the church disapproved.

Patriarch Gavrilo died in 1950. The next patriarch, Vikentije Prodanov (1950–1958), negotiated with the government on several important legal issues. German Djorić (b. 1958) was the first patriarch to recognize the controversial priests' associations. Holding the church together was his main goal, but government pressure and political disagreements among the faithful resulted in two major splits. By 1967, the Macedonian Orthodox Church had declared its independence from the Serbian church. Its leader, Dositej, was not recognized in this role by Patriarch German, but Tito's government, eager to foster a distinct Macedonian culture (thereby keeping the region safer from both Bulgarian and Serbian irredentism) supported him.

Just three years before that bitter split, the Serbian bishop in North America, Dionisije Milivojević, had been defrocked by the home church. A dispute had arisen between Bishop Dionisije, based in Libertyville, Illinois, just north of Chicago, and Patriarch German and the Synod (church council) in Yugoslavia. The reasons for the conflict are complex, involving personality, politics, and administrative issues. As a result, two different Serbian Orthodox churches came into existence in North America. The Serbian Orthodox Church in the United States of America and Canada has eighty-six churches and is based in Serbia; the Serbian Orthodox Diocese for the United States and Canada has fifty-five churches and is based in Libertyville, where the St. Sava Monastery is located and where King Petar Karađorđević was buried on November 14, 1970. Patriarch German resisted pressure to create an autocephalous Montenegrin Orthodox Church, although that too came into existence in 1993.

In 1968, the remains of the great medieval emperor, Dušan, were reburied to great fanfare at St. Mark's Church in Belgrade. In 1989, another even more symbolic reburial took place: the remains of Prince Lazar, martyr of the Battle of Kosovo, were moved from Belgrade to the Gračanica Monastery, not far from where he died. This act was accompanied by the huge outpourings of Serbian nationalism described in the next chapter. Serbia was reclaiming Kosovo as its own. A group of twenty-one priests had already expressed great concern over the growing Albanian-Serbian rift in Kosovo. They issued the "Appeal for the Protection of the Serbian Inhabitants and Their Holy Places in Kosovo" in 1981, after Albanian riots there had spurred some Serbs to flee the province and resulted in damage to ancient church buildings in Peć. This was actually a criticism of government policy in the area, which many

Serbs saw as prejudiced in favor of the Albanians. They reminded the Yugoslav government that Kosovo was the Serbs' "Jerusalem," an indispensible part of their identity that they will never relinquish. Church officials were now virtually free to speak their minds. In 1984, work on the huge Church of St. Sava in Belgrade was resumed; it had been interrupted by the German invasion in 1941 and was not restarted under Tito. The largest functioning Orthodox church building in use in the world, St. Sava's is built on the spot where the remains of its namesake were burned by the Turks in the Middle Ages. It was recently rededicated, with tens of thousands of people watching the ceremonies and taking part in the mass.

Since 1990 the patriarch of the Serbian Church has been Pavle Stojčević. In 1991, as Yugoslavia was breaking apart, the church entered stormy waters. Pavle has repeatedly protested against the historical victimization of the Serbs and has "patriotically" supported Serbian claims in Bosnia. Tempers flared as Serbian historians and church officials, frequently irresponsibly, published new works exaggerating the Serbian losses in World War II (which were already, in truth, grave enough) and linking the Vatican to a perennial Croatian plot to crush Serbia. But as the war worsened, Pavle entered into a dialogue with the head of the Catholic Church in Croatia, Franjo Cardinal Kuharić, condemned atrocities, and campaigned for the Dayton peace process. Many church leaders ended up urging Milošević to resign.

INTELLECTUAL LIFE

Following World War II, the Communist Party kept Yugoslav academics, publishers, and media on a short leash. As Tito, Kardelj, and the other leaders steered the country onto an anti-Stalinist course, or "third path," in the 1950s, however, intellectual life gradually thawed. Soon there was more leeway to discuss and publish about controversial issues in Serbian history, although there was never complete academic or press freedom. In the 1960s debates about World War II reemerged, and in 1983, the book *Party Pluralism or Monism* appeared. Its authors, Vojislav Koštunica and Kosta Čavoški, would both become political figures in the 1990s, but their scholarly work focused on (and implicitly criticized) the way in which the CPY created a political monopoly for itself in the 1940s. Another scholarly issue sparking debate among Yugoslavs was the ethnic composition of medieval Dubrovnik.

Among the best-known Serbian historians of the century were Branko Petranović, Andrej Mitrović, Dragoslav Janković, Vaso Čubrilović, and

Sima Ćirković. An older history of the Serbian people by Vladimir Ćorović (d. 1941) was also expanded and reissued. Four leading literary historians were Jovan Deretić, Svetozar Koljević, Sveta Lukić, Predrag Palavestra, and Radovan Popović. Vladimir Dedijer (d. 1991) was a journalist and party organizer who went from being an enthusiastic official biographer of Tito in the 1940s to a radical Serbian nationalist by the late 1980s. He published a massive diary of Partisan activities in World War II; later he held political positions and was a visiting professor at a number of prestigious American universities. English-language versions of his work, such as *The Battle Stalin Lost*, were very well received and remain popular reading. He embarked on a more controversial path in the early 1980s, however, when he published a new and very unflattering biography of Tito. He then took up the purported Vatican-Croatian conspiracy against Serbia in the 1940s. Although the quality of some of his scholarship is disputed today, he edited many important document collections, raised Serbia's and Yugoslavia's profile in the outside world, and captured the mood of his country at mid-century.

THE ARTS

Literature, which is arguably the arena of the greatest Serbian cultural achievements in the modern era, flourished after World War II. Ivo Andrić (1892–1975), who grew up in Bosnia, is the only Yugoslav writer to win the Nobel Prize for Literature (1961). Andrić's work realistically depicted individual people's problems and the conflicts between cultures and governments. His most famous novels are *The Bridge on the Drina* and *The Damned Yard*. He was a prolific writer of excellent short stories such as "In the Guest House." Andrić was also a supporter, albeit a cautious one, of Yugoslav ideals; within his generally pessimistic works there are definitely hopeful elements and symbols.

Miloš Crnjanski (1893–1977) is also in the front rank of twentieth-century Serbian writers. A poet and a novelist, he was long out of favor among Yugoslav communists. But he was a foremost representative of modernism, and by the late 1950s his work was again both popular and influential in Yugoslavia. His novel *Diary about Čarnojević* (1921) has unfortunately not yet been translated into English, but in Europe it is considered a classic depiction both of the last years of the Habsburg Empire and of the negative effects of World War I. In 1929, the novel *Migrations* was published. It is the story of a family of Serbs in the Habsburg Empire. They are the descendants of the families who moved north in the Great Migration of 1690. Fighting in the emperor's army in Western

Europe, they are exposed to all sorts of pressure to assimilate and compromise their Serbian identity. Like all of Crnjanski's fiction, these novels are written in a beautiful lyrical style that is at once lush and simple. Crnjanski is also remembered fondly as the author of some of the most famous poems in the Serbian language, including the avant-garde "Sumatra" and the nostalgic and patriotic "Lament for Belgrade" and "Stražilovo."[6]

Another magnificent Serbian prose writer was Danilo Kiš, who was born in Subotica in 1935 and died in Paris in 1989. Kiš was classified by many as a postmodernist, but his novels have very recognizable backdrops in the great political nightmares of the twentieth-century: World War II, the Holocaust, and Stalin's terror. *A Tomb for Boris Davidovich* is often compared to the political classics *1984* and *Darkness at Noon* in its treatment of Stalinism. Kiš also proved to be no friend to nationalist extremists of any stripe, and, like the eminent Czech novelist Milan Kundera, he staunchly defended the right of Serbian and East European authors to be regarded as artists and storytellers first and as political figures or dissidents second.

Desanka Maksimović (1898–1993) is probably the most beloved poet in twentieth-century Serbian literature. In her long career she wrote novels, short stories, essays, and children's stories, but it is on her poetry that her enormous reputation chiefly rests. Favorite themes include nature, religion, love, and childhood, but she also memorialized the suffering of Serbs under the brutal Nazi occupation. Chief among her later postwar works was the highly acclaimed *I Seek Clemency* (1964). In this poetic dialogue with Emperor Dušan, author of the important Law Code (*Zakonik*), which points out crimes and sins and prescribes harsh punishments for them, Maksimović reflects on human weaknesses and attempts to soften the harshness of the Code. *I Seek Clemency* was published in various languages across Yugoslavia. By promoting her work in this way, the LCY might have been encouraging a humanistic and inclusive understanding of Serbian history, something that could only reassure Serbia's smaller neighboring republics. The noted English scholar and translator Celia Hawkesworth has pointed out that feminist readings of some of Maksimović's work are possible. Most Yugoslav critics, however, placed her in the "tradition of 'patriotic' writing by women, whose role was to express grief and compassion as a counterweight to heroic action and suffering."[7]

The wars, dictatorship, and sanctions have preoccupied writers in the 1990s. So far, three significant works of this era of Serbian literature that have appeared in English are by Slobodan Selenić, *Premeditated Murder*;

Vladimir Arsenijević, *In the Hold*; and Vladimir Jokanović, *Made in Yu-goslavia*. These novels examine the responses of everyday Serbs, especially young people, to the brutality and rhetoric of war.

Since the mid-1800s, Serbia has produced painters who are representative of general European artistic trends. Realists such as Uroš Predić and Paja Jovanović were famous for their treatment of Serbian historical themes. Djura Jakšić was an accomplished Romanticist while Vladimir Veličković was famous for surrealism. Until the 1920s, classical music in Serbia was far less developed than it was in the neighboring South Slavic regions of Croatia and Slovenia, which had benefited culturally from the rule of the Austrian Habsburg family with its great capital city, Vienna. The most outstanding early figure was Stevan Mokranjac, a conductor and composer who toured at home and abroad with various Serbian choral societies. In the postwar period, one of the major composers was Dušan Radić, who created cantatas using the poetry of the world-famous Serbian writer Vasko Popa.

Serbia has had a number of philosophers who were important within the country, though for the most part they have had little international influence, except for the Praxis group discussed in this chapter. Some other intellectual figures from recent Serbian life are Slobodan Jovanović, a prolific historian who also became a government official during World War II; the archaelogist Dušan Srejović; the internationally famous grand master of chess, Svetozar Gligorić; the geographer Jovan Cvijić (1865–1927); and the inventors Nikola Tesla and Michael Pupin, both of whom emigrated to the United States.

DISSENT

All regions of Yugoslavia manifested various kinds of academic, religious, or journalistic resistance to the Titoist government. Eventually, most Serbian dissidents became nationalists, and today scholars are trying to determine at what point in time the goals of these Serbs calling for more freedom under Tito mutated from civic to ethnic nationalists. In Croatia, national and economic concerns were dominant, while Slovene dissent showed the strongest dose of counterculture such as environmental, feminist, gay, and punk movements.

The most famous individual dissident in Yugoslavia was Milovan Djilas (d. 1995), a Montenegrin who spent most of his adult life in Belgrade. A member of Tito's inner circle, he had been a prominent communist since before World War II and he helped chart Yugoslavia's "new course" after 1948. In 1954, Djilas was expelled from the LCY for criticizing the LCY's monopoly of power and criticizing the USSR. He was in and out of trouble with Tito for the next two decades, publishing many of his books abroad, (*The New Class* in 1957 and *Conversations with Stalin* in 1961) but continuing to live in Belgrade.

Djilas underwent an ideological transformation from hard-core communist to social democrat, and although he understood the power of nationalism in Serbian society, for the most part he rejected its extreme manifestations. He has been called "the Yugoslav Trotsky," a reference to Stalin's rival who was banished for his alternative political ideas which many people think might have transformed the USSR into a more humane and less authoritarian country. To the Yugoslav communists, though, Djilas simply went too far in questioning the party's hold on power. Djilas is one of the great figures of twentieth-century European intellectual history, and his life and writings make fascinating, and valuable, objects of study.

Another salient dissident movement was the Praxis group of philosophers and sociologists, which was centered on the universities of Zagreb and Belgrade. The group derived its name from the neo-Marxist use of the Greek word meaning roughly "learning by doing" (as opposed to doing things according to a dogma). They published the widely-read *Praxis* journal but denied that they had any desire to challenge the LCY for political power.[8] They did speak out, though, against limitations on academic freedom, nationalism, and the government's market-based economic reforms, which they blamed for "selling out" leftist ideals.

The LCY, especially its chief theoretician and Tito's heir apparent, Edvard Kardelj (1910–1979), considered the Praxis group pessimistic and obstructionist. The philosophers just claimed that they were using the same arguments against the LCY's monopoly on power that Tito and Kardelj themselves had used against Stalin in 1948 and more recently against the Chinese. In January 1975, however, the "Belgrade 8" were fired from their university jobs. They included the well-known figures Svetozar Stojanović, Miladin Životić, Nebojša Popov, and Mihailo Marković as well as Trivo Indjić, Dragoljub Mićunović, Zagorka Pešić-Golubović, and Ljubomir Tadić. Many eventually found work in specialized research institutes, at a safe distance from the students they were accused of corrupting. But several of them reemerged as important figures on the Serbian political scene a decade or two later. Marković helped create the draft of the incendiary Serbian Academy of Sciences & Art Memorandum of 1986, and he went on to become a close ally of Milošević. Stojanović and Tadić also supported the Serbian national revival in the late 1980s, while Životić kept up his consistent critique of nationalism as a form of bureaucratic manipulation right up to his death in 1996. In 1989 Mićunović became one of the founders of the Democratic Party (which also included the post-Milošević leaders Zoran Djindjić and Vojislav Koštunica).

Another form of dissent in Serbia was based on a critique of communist rule from the point of view of Serbian nationalism. This stream of thought and activity began in the late 1960s but would crescendo during the Kosovo crisis in the 1980s. The historical novelist Dobrica Ćosić gave vent to—and helped to create—the nationalist concerns of many Serbs in major public addresses he delivered in 1968 and 1977. He left the LCY but stayed in the limelight as an increasingly ardent proponent of reforming Yugoslavia in a way that would, depending on one's point of view, restore Serbs either to their rightful status within it or to a position of intolerable domination over it.[9]

A final and very different type of dissent in Serbia took place within the ranks of the party itself. In the early 1970s a new generation of leaders was rising up within the ranks of the League of Communists of Serbia, as the local branch of the LCY was called. Unlike traditional Serbian communists, who believed that centralized rule was necessary to foster the kind of modernization that would overcome nationalism and regionalism, these younger "technocrats" believed that decentralization and economic liberalism were the right recipe. In this way, they were like the new generation of communists in Slovenia and Croatia. The chief figures in this movement were the chairman of the LCS, Marko Nikezić, a former ambassador to Egypt and foreign minister and the LCS's secretary, Latinka Perović, who was a professor.

They had the misfortune of rising to power just after the tumult of the Croatian Spring. Tito was determined to run nationalists out of all branches of the party, and he swept away the Serbian liberals. This purge enshrined a process known as "negative selection" whereby these younger, flexible, and more liberal communists in various republics were demoted or forced into retirement; their places were taken by *apparatchiks*, who were colorless bureaucrats or party yes-men who lacked the intellect and spirit of innovation necessary to deal with the country's mounting problems. The same system also took hold in the military, where Tito also came to value loyalty above talent and pragmatic or humane vision. This "clearing of the decks" might have solved some short-term problems for Tito, but it was also a huge career boost for a generation of second-string politicians who would inherit the country after his death. There were some exceptions, of course, but in general, the purges of the early 1970s woefully degraded Yugoslavia's long-term ability to adapt and survive.

MONTENEGRO IN TITO'S YUGOSLAVIA

After World War II, Montenegro was established as a republic within the new Yugoslavia. It was the smallest, and poorest, republic. Its economic profile was improved by the influx of federal money for transportation, education, and industrial projects, especially in the metallurgical sector; it also had some earnings from tourism and the excellent harbor at Bar. That port city was connected to Belgrade by railway in 1976, an engineering feat through rugged mountains that also produced a stunningly beautiful ride for passenger trains. After World War II, industrial production accounted for 6 percent of Montenegro's economy; by 1974 the figure was 33 percent.

Montenegrins had fairly smooth relations with the rest of Yugoslavia and the Communist Party, although a high percentage of Montenegrins supported Stalin during the Cominform dispute of 1948; many of them were arrested and sent to Tito's concentration camp at Goli Otok in Dalmatia. Occasionally voices in Montenegro were heard that criticized Serbian domination of their culture, but the biggest political problems for Montenegro arose after the death of Tito. The small size of the republic—just over 600,000 by 1991, of whom only 62 percent were of Montenegrin "nationality"—led some other Yugoslavs to accuse it of being over-privileged. It was the Albanians of neighboring Kosovo, most notably, who came to wonder why a group as small as the Montenegrins should have its own republic and a great deal of power at the federal level while they, who were three times as numerous, had to remain part of Serbia. The answer, of course, lay in the fact that Montenegrins were Slavs who were part of the original Yugoslav idea.

Montenegrin writers and artists have been a strong presence on the Serbian cultural scene since World War II. The important political figure Milovan Djilas wrote short stories, novels, and a study of the importance of Njegoš, in addition to his voluminous memoirs and political studies. The most important literary figure was Miodrag Bulatović (1930–1991), whose "experimental" fiction was widely translated in the United States and Western Europe. Another fascinating writer, known for rich detail and exciting plots, was Ćamil Sijarić (b. 1913). His characters are common folk from all over Montenegro, especially the rugged, traditional-minded highlanders of both the Orthodox and Muslim faiths. His novel *Bihorci*

(*The People of Bihor*, 1955) is a study of rural religion and of the cultural restrictions on women's freedom.

NOTES

1. The information on agricultural policy is drawn from *Peasants and Communists: Politics and Ideology in the Yugoslav Countryside, 1941–1953*, by Melissa K. Bokovoy, © 1998 by University of Pittsburgh Press. Used by permission of the University of Pittsburgh Press.

2. Bokovoy, *Peasants and Communists*, p. 153.

3. Joel M. Halpern, *A Serbian Village: Social and Cultural Change in a Yugoslav Community*, rev. ed. (New York: Harper and Row, 1967), p. 339.

4. Dijana Pleština, *Regional Development in Communist Yugoslavia: Success, Failure, and Consequences* (Boulder, CO: Westview Press, 1993), pp. 180–181.

5. Stella Alexander, *Church and State in Yugoslavia Since 1945* (Cambridge: Cambridge University Press, 1979), p. 189.

6. Thomas Eekman, *Thirty Years of Yugoslav Literature* (1945–1975) (Ann Arbor: Michigan Slavic Publications, 1978), p. 18.

7. Celia Hawkesworth, *Voices in the Shadows: Women and Verbal Art in Serbia and Bosnia* (New York: Central European University Press, 2000), p. 211.

8. For a detailed treatment of these ideas and movements, see James H. Satterwhite, *Varieties of Marxist Humanism: Philosophical Revisionism in Postwar Eastern Europe* (Pittsburgh: University of Pittsburgh Press, 1991) and Gerson S. Sher, *Praxis: Marxist Criticism and Dissent in Socialist Yugoslavia* (Bloomington: Indiana University Press, 1977).

9. See Nicholas J. Miller, "The Nonconformists: Dobrica Ćosić and Mića Popović Envision Serbia" in *Slavic Review* 58:3, (fall 1999): 515–536. Although Ćosić's novels have not had the highest critical reception in the West, *Into the Battle* is an exciting novel of ideas about Serbs in World War I.

10

What Price Independence? The Breakup of Yugoslavia, 1989–1995

INTRODUCTION

The 1980s were a time of great political and social change across Eastern Europe. Yugoslavia, because it was fully independent of the USSR and already had a liberal communist government, was well positioned to be in the vanguard of the democratization movements that ended up sweeping away the Berlin Wall, bringing the Solidarity movement to power in Poland, and eliminating the tyranny of the Ceauşescu family in Romania.

Many journalists and commentators observed in the 1980s that two Yugoslav republics, Serbia and Slovenia, were moving the fastest toward freedom of expression, the construction of a civil society, and the birth of a multiparty system. We have already seen how "liberal" or "progressive" Yugoslavia itself was, compared to the rest of Eastern Europe. By the 1980s, the cultural (and counter-cultural) establishments in Belgrade and Ljubljana were making a name for themselves, bucking the party line on many issues. These two republics' dissident movements developed in very different directions, however. The Slovenes were engaged in individualistic and humanistic concerns such as political pluralism, antimilitarism, civil rights for marginalized groups (women, pacifists, gays, ethnic minorities) and alternative culture (punk rock and avant garde art). Most dissident Serbs were engaged in disputes over nationalism. These two oppositions found common ground only in their desire to end the one-party system and censorship.

With good reason, most scholars date the beginning of the end of Yugoslavia with the death of its often popular, always powerful leader, Josip Broz Tito. As he aged, Tito had of course left more and more of the day-to-day governance of the country to officials under him. He had also ruled, for the most part, with a lighter hand after the early 1950s. The Tito regime tended to work more according to the principle of "he who is not against me is with me." Personality aside, Yugoslavia also had ideological reasons for allowing a certain cultural, economic, and political openness; in the years after the rupture with Stalin in 1948, as we have seen, the Yugoslavs struck off on their own "third path" of development, based on nonalignment and workers' self-management. Avoiding Stalinist methods was part of this new identity.

Tito's prestige, power, and determination to maintain balance among the national groups is one key to the country's survival. Yugoslavia was also arguably the most liberal communist country ever, so popular resentment at the government was not overwhelming. Yugoslavia's open borders and heavy international borrowing meant that people were free to travel, work abroad, and distract themselves with the temptations of a consumer society. Despite various complaints, all the nationalities in the country saw certain benefits in the system. Much patriotism was built into propaganda phrases such as "Tito, Party, Army" and "Brotherhood and Unity" This latter phrase even worked somewhat at the personal level, since the percentage of ethnically mixed marriages in the country was over 10 percent in the 1980s, and almost 10 percent of the population chose to identify itself on the last two censuses as simply "Yugoslav," dropping more specific national labels. In the Warsaw Pact, countries of Eastern Europe, anti-Russian or anti-Soviet nationalism fueled opposition movements; but Yugoslavia was fully independent, so its communists could not be labeled as Soviet stooges.

When Tito died on May 4, 1980, many people in Yugoslavia expressed genuine grief. Undoubtedly many were also feeling bewilderment over the country's future. Not wanting to be surpassed in the history books— or to be shunted aside prematurely—Tito had set up no real "heir apparent" to follow him. The system of rotating leadership positions, separate republican communist parties, and economic fragmentation quickly proved unequal to the task of governing. Unfortunately, there were also almost no civic movements that cut across national lines and that could have formed the basis for a federalist, democratic political party.

YUGOSLAV SOCIETY AND POLITICS IN THE 1980s

Less than a year after Tito died, major unrest broke out in Kosovo. This was very much a harbinger of things to come. Population trends in Kosovo set Serbs very much on edge, while the Albanians' grievances started with standard-of-living issues and then merged with dissatisfaction with the province's legal status. The Serbian population in the province was dropping, both in absolute and proportional terms. The source—as well as the scope—of the absolute drop is hotly disputed today: Albanian scholars and most Westerners attribute it to a voluntary outmigration of Serbs in search of better living conditions, while many Serbs claim their co-nationals left the province because of calculated harassment and discrimination by Albanians. The source of the biggest increase in the Albanian population, however, is not disputed: a high birth rate. The topic of legal Muslim and Albanian immigration into Kosovo from other parts of Yugoslavia and of illegal immigration from Albania has not yet been fully explored. Suffice it to say that many Serbs believe in a conspiracy theory that the Tito government encouraged an influx of Albanians in order to undercut Serbia's claim to the area. By 1981, the Serbs only formed about 13 percent of the population.

Kosovo was the poorest part of the former Yugoslavia. Despite the investment of considerable federal funding since the 1960s, the gap in economic indicators and standard of living between Kosovo and Slovenia (the most developed republic) had widened. But in 1963, Kosovo was raised from the status of "Autonomous Region" to "Autonomous Province." The sidelining of Interior Minister Ranković, a strong Serbian nationalist, in 1966 made more concessions to the Albanians possible. One of these was the founding of the University of Priština as an Albanian-language institution. Albanian success fueled new political demands. Tito was sympathetic to these demands, partly in order to keep relations with Albania positive and deny the Soviet Union or other imperialist powers a foothold along Yugoslavia's southern flank. More important, he was doing with the Albanians what he had already done with (or for) the Macedonians, Bosnians, and Montenegrins: establish them as part of a cultural and political fence around Serbia, to limit that republic's power.

Kosovo was never made a republic outright, but the 1974 constitution upgraded the status of both Autonomous Provinces, so that by the early 1980s, Kosovo was functioning politically much like a de facto republic. Serbs were incensed. The Kosovo riots of March and April 1981 started as student protests over living conditions. Yugoslavia's late-blooming development policy in the province had opened a Pandora's box of enfranchisement: It created more demands than it could satisfy and, thanks to the openness of the border with Albanian proper and the long-standing Serbian cultural attachment to the region, every issue became politicized. At least twelve people died in the riots, and possibly many more, as army units were rushed in. Police then made considerable numbers of arrests under martial law, and quick trials brought long sentences; hundreds of Albanians were booted out of the League of Communists. The scale of these demonstrations and the harsh government reaction to them shocked many observers.

As tensions within the country rose throughout the 1980s, the increasingly contentious mood in Serbia was stoked further by the broadening freedom to discuss Kosovo's historical importance in traditionally nationalist terms. Books, many of them neither balanced in scholarship nor conciliatory in intention, were joined by television reportage and petitions circulated by clergy from Kosovo to raise the public's consciousness. The heart of the matter was the feeling that Kosovo was being ripped away from Serbia, and that this was intolerable. That Kosovo was indispensible to any Serbian state formation was stressed again and again by prominent Serbs. At first, the Serbian communists opposed the nationalist wave, but it eventually swamped them. Slobodan Milošević even rode that wave to great power. Two key aspects of the increasing "Albanization" of Kosovo that did not make headlines then were that Serbs had not been a demographic majority in the province since 1700 and that Kosovars might well not have been determined to secede and could have been satisfied with the status of a republic in within Yugoslavia.

The Serbian attachment to Kosovo need not have translated into hatred and violence. More specific factors in the 1980s and 1990s accounted for those phenomena. The two other main factors heightening Serbs' anxieties and making them susceptible to manipulation by their leaders and media were the geographical dispersion of their co-nationals throughout the rest of Yugoslavia and the country's plummeting economic fortune. Many commentators and scholars have noted that the memory of historical grievances and potential for violence were indeed present in Serbian culture but that their manifestation in the atrocities and aggression of the 1990s was brought about by elites who threw gasoline, if you will, on dimly glowing coals.[1] Such ideas are now widely used by modern scholars who do not accept stereotypes about wildly homicidal European nations or "ancient ethnic hatreds" and violent folklore that turn twentieth-century peoples into automatic killing machines.

After 1981 Serbian writers and intellectuals took up the Kosovo issue with a vengeance. Most prominent among them was the historical novelist Dobrica Ćosić, who had been kicked out of the League of Communists for "nationalist" views in the 1960s. Many novelists and philosophers (and for that matter economists and managers), in Serbia and elsewhere, ran afoul of the communist government from the late 1960s on. Since they often lost their jobs or were sometimes imprisoned or emigrated, they became known in the West as dissidents. But in Serbia's case, most of the dissidents were as anti-Yugoslav as they were anticommunist. Again, nationalism need not be viewed as inherently violent or intolerant, but the 1990s were to prove that many of Serbia's earlier nationalist dissidents were unconcerned with human rights improvements in general or were ignorant of the ramifications of their actions. In short, as Russian history also shows, being an anticommunist dissident does not make one necessarily a democrat.

Ćosić was a vocal public figure within the Serbian Academy of Arts and Sciences (SANU) and the Serbian branch of the Yugoslav Association of Writers. A preoccupation with national concerns and a crescendo of rhetoric in the freer post-Tito media environment made these institutions combative. In 1985, a committee of SANU, which included members of the famous Praxis school of dissident philosophers, drafted a now famous Memorandum in which Serbia's grievances with the rest of Yugoslavia were put down in highly inflammatory terms. The members of SANU never officially adopted the Memorandum, and it was never officially released to the public, but it leaked to the press in 1986 and ignited enormous controversy. The document blamed the Yugoslav communists, especially Tito and Kardelj, for cutting Serbia into different administrative pieces to appease the other nationalities. The communists had also ransacked Serbia culturally and economically. The result was that Serbs were being trampled on everywhere and were even in mortal danger in places like Kosovo and Krajina (Croatia).[2]

The Memorandum infuriated and frightened non-Serbs. They saw in it a dangerous proclivity among Serbs to accept conspiracy theories and revive historical agendas. But its "straight talk" fell on increasingly receptive ears among the ever more alienated Serbian population. As a yardstick of the kinds of accumulated grievances that Tito's society had been incapable of airing or relieving, and as a reminder that the second

Yugoslavia was indeed predicated upon avoiding Serbian hegemony, the Memorandum is a historically accurate document. It also entered history as a provocation, on account of the storm of controversy its elite authors released. In these same years, some Serb historians were using their increased freedom from censorship to publish wild and unfounded accusations about the Croats, such as that they were by nature a set of genocidal schemers bent on destroying Serbia.

Other incidents from the 1980s attest to the rising disillusionment and passion among Serbs. There were numerous petitions, exposes, and protest marches by Serbs from Kosovo and by Orthodox church leaders. Many of their charges—for instance of rape campaigns against Serbian women, massive emigration of Serbs, and massive illegal immigration from Albania—were unsubstantiated but were lent credence by uncritical acceptance in the media and most intellectual circles. The most bizarre incident involved a Serbian farmer from Kosovo, Djordje Martinović, who turned up in a hospital emergency room in May 1985 with severe injuries to his anus. He claimed that Albanians had tortured him with a bottle; government officials and local Albanians said the wound was self-inflicted. Mentioning this sad incident would be gratuitous if it were not for the symbolic importance it came to have among the Serbian media and intellectuals, who adopted it as a metaphor for the martyrdom of their people. To many people it had echoes of the medieval Ottoman practice of impalement (which also figured in some of the work of the great writer Ivo Andrić).[3] An unfortunate link to the situation of Serbs in other parts of the country was provided by an irresponsible academic who said that the bottle incident was Martinović's personal Jasenovac, a reference to the atrocities committed against Serbs at the most notorious Croatian concentration camp during World War II. Various investigative bodies came to different conclusions about how Martinović sustained his injury, and there were many lurid speeches and fiery exchanges in the press. But, in the end, most Serbs took two things out of the incident: a very concrete image of the kind of threats they felt from Albanians (and others) and a strong suspicion that the police, party, and medical authorities in Kosovo were working against Serbia and Yugoslavia.

One should not forget the progressively more dismal and frightening economic picture in all of Yugoslavia by the mid-1980s. Real wages were falling by almost 10 percent per year. Decades of borrowing from other countries and international institutions had kept Yugoslavia's consumption of consumer goods high, but debts were mounting ($20 billion by 1983). Inflation soared from an already high 200 percent in the mid-1980s to 2000 percent by 1990. Unemployment and underemployment (offi-cially as high as 18 percent)—despite being statistically masked and also offset somewhat by the exporting of a million "guest workers" to West-ern Europe—were in double digits and created a largely silent legitimacy crisis for a socialist country. Strikes were frequent. There were some huge corruption scandals involving banks and industries, most notably the Agrokomerc affair in Bosnia. Economic problems such as these tend to make people insecure and impatient, delegitimating the existing political system and paving the way for politicians to be able to manipulate the country with ever more radical ideas.

Eventually Serbia placed an economic boycott on Slovenia to punish it for its talk of secession. Major economic reforms were held up at the federal level by the constitutional requirement for unanimity among the eight political units. And perhaps most confounding to the hopes of those who still hoped to bolster the sagging economy, Milošević ar-ranged for the "transfer" of about $1 billion from the Yugoslav National Bank to the government of Serbia on December 28, 1990. This money grab not only sank the ailing economy but also bolstered the growing movement for secession in the northern republics.

In the meantime, the news had not been all bad for Yugoslavs: the 1984 Olympics in Sarajevo had gone very well, and in 1987 a reform-minded federal premier, Ante Marković, began to implement just the kind of economic reforms that were necessary to allow Yugoslavia to come to terms with its stagnant economy and its massive foreign debt; later, he would form a federalist political party to counter the growth of political nationalism. But the trickle of good news proved to be too little, too late.

THE RISE OF SLOBODAN MILOŠEVIĆ

It was under these conditions that a mid-level Serbian official named Slobodan Milošević was rising to prominence in Serbia. Born in Požar-evac of Montenegrin parents, Milošević earned a law degree in 1964 and was married to a professor of sociology, Mirjana Marković. They were both party stalwarts. Milošević's career progressed rapidly, buoyed by powerful friends, and he held leadership positions in several companies. In 1984, his chief patron, Ivan Stambolić, promoted him to the important job of Belgrade party chief. In 1986, when Stambolić advanced into the position of president of Serbia, he saw to it that Milošević moved into his old position as Serbian party chief. Milošević had already begun plac-ing his loyal followers into important positions in the media, government, and party, and in late 1987 he sidelined Stambolić and moderate Serbian officials. Milošević was now the boss of Serbia.

Tension over Kosovo was ratcheted up on April 27, 1986, when Milošević, then the head of the League of Communists of Serbia, made a controversial speech on the medieval battleground near Priština. His ostensible goal was to smooth over relations in the province, but he encouraged the angry local Serbs with the now notorious phrase "nobody will ever dare to beat you again," aimed at both the local Albanians and the government security forces trying to contain demonstrations. This was his public "shot across the bow" at the existing Titoist structure. From this point on, Milošević seems to have been ever more attracted to the idea of using nationalism to secure his own power.

Milošević organized huge rallies (called "meetings") to foment nationalist support for himself; he took over the media in Serbia and, in late 1988 and early 1989, engineered the fall of the governments of Vojvodina, Kosovo, and Montenegro and declared martial law in Kosovo. Milošević touted his "anti-bureaucratic revolution" against the administrative caste that had divided and crippled Serbia. Given the fact that there were in essence eight positions or "votes" in the post-Tito federal power arrangements, Serbia—that is, Milošević—now controlled four, enough to block changes he did not want or to prevent federal opposition to changes he did want.

On June 28, 1989, the 600th anniversary of the Battle of Kosovo was celebrated by a half million Serbs. Prince Lazar's body was interred near the battlefield. Milošević, newly installed as president, presided over the ceremonies in a paroxysm of nationalism. He then moved quickly to remove the fifteen-year-old legal guarantees of Kosovo's and Vojvodina's internal autonomy. He also arrested leading Albanian politicians, such as Azem Vllasi, on charges of treason and counterrevolution. There were bloody riots in Kosovo and great alarm in the rest of Yugoslavia; the Serbian government imposed and maintained martial law on the province, and its poverty and general misery would mount enormously over the next eleven years. Although humanitarian concern for Kosovars was great, especially in Slovenia and Croatia, non-Serb politicians might have thought that they were appeasing Milošević by letting him take control over Kosovo. By 1989, both Serbia and Slovenia unilaterally passed laws in violation of the federal constitution; Slovenia began passing laws that asserted its right to secede, while its leaders spoke of turning Yugoslavia into a confederation of sovereign states with voluntary, functional connections between them. Whether or not they saw a loose confederation as a real solution or as a stepping-stone to full independence remains a debated point. Serbia, at any rate, made known its plans to turn the clock back to a tighter, not looser federal structure—something that might have made sense if real reform was the goal. But any talk of "centralization" from Serbia alarmed Slovenes and Croats, who remembered the assimilation pressures from Royal Yugoslavia and who were convinced that their own economic rationalization would be intolerably slowed by casting their lot in with the Serbs.

Milošević did not suddenly become a full-blown nationalist and turn his back on communism overnight. Instead he performed an amazing, if malevolent, balancing act. He appealed at once to the Titoist legacy *and* to the new, anti-Titoist nationalism beginning to emerge among Serbs in Kosovo and the Serbian Academy of Science and Arts. He cleverly sat on the fence and worked both crowds; at other times, he switched from one tactic to the other. To the large numbers of Serbs who held military or state jobs, or who were pensioners, Milošević played himself off as the upholder of Yugoslavia; he would preserve the status quo and they would preserve their positions, pensions, and pride. To the others, he promised to correct the injustices of the Titoist system and see that Serbs got their fair share of the pie—that is, that Serbia would dominate Yugoslav politics or else gather all of its co-nationals into a state to call its own. His power base became increasingly rural, rooted in agricultural areas which the alternative media of Belgrade did not reach and where the privation caused by sanctions and hyperinflation had the fewest effects. Of course, the SPS had supporters elsewhere, but many of them tended to be older or less educated, and they often shared a distrust of cosmopolitan, urban Serbian (and Yugoslav) culture. Meanwhile, many young and better educated people, the ones most likely to become dissidents, fled the country.

In the crucial early years of his control of Serbia, Milošević profited greatly from the SPS's alliance with two other parties whose programs and size reflected the general tendencies within the society. The Yugoslav United Left (YUL) was a small, crypto-communist holdover party run by his wife, Mirjana Marković, while the Serbian Radical Party (SRS) emerged from a revived Chetnik movement in 1990, led by Vojislav Šešelj. With the SPS he shared an antipathy toward reform forces, student dissidents, new-style Titoists, national minorities, and secessionist-minded Croats. By 1992 Šešelj had become a paramilitary leader, a member of the Serbian parliament, and an essential ally of Milošević. Acting as the personal link between such diverse political groupings enabled Milošević to gain support from contradictory quarters.

In summary, one should bear in mind that Milošević's chief objective was for Yugoslavia to stay together. He wanted to restructure the country on his own terms. This would have massively augmented his own power and, depending on your point of view, returned the Serbs to a privileged position within Yugoslavia or fulfilled the long-standing demands of the predominant understanding of the Serbian historical agenda. When secessions became inevitable, Milošević was determined to wrest Serbian regions from Bosnia and Croatia and reattach them to Yugoslavia. The appeal of both of these strategies was that of keeping all Serbs within the borders of one country, where they would be the dominant, if not the only, population group. Before Milošević began using the army or militias to do his bidding, he manipulated the media to set the public agenda and rally support. Memories of World War II were still fairly fresh, and the legacy of the Serbs' struggle against the Turks was enshrined in folklore. These types of awareness did not make conflicts inevitable, however. The violence was spurred by the leaders who stood to gain from it. History does not automatically generate conflicts; human beings do, and as Milošević discovered, they break out over specific issues. This personal and national Serbian drama played itself out against a backdrop of other peoples seeking their own self-determination, a horribly sick economy, an ideological vacuum left by the erosion of communist legitimacy in the rest of Eastern Europe, and a society fragmented in everything from its political structure to its professional organizations.

SERBIA'S PROBLEMS IN YUGOSLAVIA

Few people in the West are familiar with the Serbs' complaints about the former Yugoslavia. It has become common currency among journalists and diplomats simply that the Serbs succeeded in dominating the first (royal) Yugoslavia and constantly tried and almost managed to dominate the second (Titoist) Yugoslavia. From the point of view of the country's smaller national groups, these conclusions are not entirely unjustified, given the Serb population's size and influence. But the Serbian experience in Yugoslavia cannot be understood without giving an ear to the long list of mistakes and injustices that they feel were perpetrated upon the Serbian people and its patrimony. This is not to imply, however, that in the search for historical truth everything simply depends on point of view; many, though not all, issues have two sides, but they are not always equally relevant or valid. Coming to a scholarly consensus on controversial issues can be a long and painful process, but it is worthwhile. For people from outside a certain culture, it can also sometimes be frustrating to discuss in an unemotional way issues that are painful or precious to other people; sometimes the historian hears the exasperated cry, "But you would agree with us if you *really* understood the situation." As discussed earlier, in the section on Serbian epic poetry, certain interpretations of history gain significance simply because they are believed, and acted upon, by large numbers of people. They need not be fully true to begin leaving their own footprints in history. Two troubling characteristics of many of these perennial complaints are that they assume the existence of global and local anti-Serbian conspiracies and that they are "reductionistic," boiling down complex historical phenomena to monocausal explanations. Thus, they can contribute to Serbs' victim complex, to the belief that people are "programmed" to be and act a certain way, or to the denial that Serbs as a group, like all nations, must make important choices and bear ethical responsibility for them.

One of the biggest complaints Serbs have voiced since 1918 is that Yugoslavia has been sabotaged by the Croats, who are said to have obstructed its Parliament in the 1920s and who did in fact assassinate King Aleksandar in 1934 and massacre vast numbers of Serbs and others during World War II. Many believe that any dominance Serbs might have had within Yugoslavia can be justified by the fact that Serbia lost about one-fourth of its population in the three wars from 1912 to 1918 that made Yugoslavia possible and Serbs gave up their relatively advanced constitution when their government threw in its lot with the other peoples in the new Yugoslavia. They also believe that Tito was foolish to lead Yugoslavia into a close relationship with countries in the developing world (the so-called "Third World") through the Nonaligned Movement and thus siphoned important resources out of Serbia and hampered integration with the rest of Europe.

Another nexus of complaints revolves around the LCY's denigration of Serbian national pride forbidding free cultural expression and accusing the Serbs constantly of being domineering, intolerant, and chauvinistic. The discrimination against the Serbian Orthodox Church and the Marxist and pan-Yugoslav reinterpretation of famous Serbian literary works are part of this "cultural denaturalization" of the Serbian people. What is more, the communists sought to efface important parts of the historical record, such as the progressive aspects of the Serbian multiparty system before World War I. The Ustaše crimes during World War II were downplayed, while Mihailović's collaboration with the Germans was exaggerated.

Another anticommunist argument is that the LCY abdicated its responsibility for ensuring fair play among the republics and tried to compensate for its weakness by a policy of "divide and rule." The linchpin of this policy was summed up in the phrase "Weak Serbia, Strong Yugoslavia." Serbs were dispersed, without special rights, over several republics, while Bosnian, Albanian, and Macedonian nationalism was fostered. Even worse, Serbs sometimes feel their very existence as a nation is threatened by their low birth rate and by the high birth rate and political ambitions of some of their neighbors. The people who officially identified themselves as "Yugoslav" through the 1980s are seen as former Serbs who were pressured by the communist government to cut their ties to their mother culture so that they could now be assimilated by other groups.

Few people today believe that the South Slavic peoples are really just one big nation, as was commonly held 100 years ago. But as they build separate countries today, the Balkan peoples are faced with overlapping historical claims to large swaths of territory. It is also not uncommon to hear both Serbs and Croats claim that the Bosnian Muslims were originally "their" people and that they do not have the right to independence. The fact that migrations throughout history have taken the Serbs so far north and west of their most prominent medieval homelands (which have, in turn, become repopulated with other national groups) has set the stage for a colossal cross-hatching of conflicting territorial claims based on ethnic, historic, and strategic rights. Serbian nationalist leaders say they are justified in using force to win their claims, since Serbia has been a bulwark protecting Europe from Muslim and then communist invaders for centuries. They also tend to use self-serving, distorted logic to argue their claims for certain irredenta, or unredeemed lands. Serbs in the Krajina argue that Zagreb has no right to rule their territory (which has long been a traditional part of Croatia) because Serbs are in the majority there; in Kosovo, Serbs reject that same argument coming from Albanians. There, they assert that Serbia's historic rights are more important. Complicating this welter of conflicting claims is the fact that the international community always strongly discourages the alteration of existing legal boundaries, especially when countries or empires break up. Serbs also question the validity of a country's splitting up right at a time when the rest of Europe is coming together in the form of the European Union (EU) (formerly the European Community or the Common Market).

SECESSION

In 1989, revolutions toppled communist governments throughout central and eastern Europe. The revolutionary spirit spread to Yugoslavia and helped lead, unfortunately, to devastating civil wars, the most tragic of which has been the conflict in Bosnia-Hercegovina. But of course the country was well along on its own path toward disintegration when the East European "domino effect" made itself felt. In early 1990, the Slovene and Croatian communists "seceded" from the federal party. In April 1990 Slovenia held free elections. The Croats followed suit. The Communists were swept from power and replaced by parties determined to pursue national self-determination. Although many plans were floated in the 1980s about ways to reform or loosen the Yugoslav federation, by 1990 Slovenes and Croats no longer felt that the Serbs were a reliable partner. If the Serbs under Milošević were not going to "play by the rules," then it was going to be impossible to resist the urge for greater self-rule. Rounding out what can only be called a year of ultimate significance, the Slovenes held a referendum on independence on December 23. A resounding 88 percent of the voters expressed a wish for independence, so in the new year the Slovene government modified its constitution to give Slovene law precedence over federal (Yugoslav) law. The Croats got their own referendum and amendments in 1991, and on June 25, both republics declared their complete independence.

The Yugoslav National Army (often called the JNA, after its Serbo-Croatian name, the *Jugoslavenska Narodna Armija*), dominated by Serbs, responded aggressively to halt the disintegration of the country. Slovenes deserted rapidly from the JNA, and Slovene police and territorial defense units (a kind of national guard formed by Tito after the Soviet invasion of Czechoslovakia in 1968) seized control of the border crossings into Italy and Austria, in a bid for international recognition and for a source of hard currency. The JNA, acting on its own initiative, rushed military units to the borders also and fighting broke out. The Slovenes were counting on help from Croatia, which was not forthcoming, but they had also been able to purchase some weapons on the black market. Just as importantly, they had set up all kinds of media connections to announce their independence to the outside world and focus attention on the fighting, to embarrass the JNA. The Slovenes only had about 15,000 men in their old Territorial Defense Force, while the JNA at this time consisted of 200,000 soldiers in all branches and had great superiority in armaments. In the two weeks of fighting along the borders, at military bases, and near Ljubljana, about fifty people were killed and close to 300 injured. Under a peace brokered by diplomats from the European Community, the JNA pulled out of Slovenia, but this was not a setback for the main Serbian goal of keeping all Serbs in one state, since almost no Serbs lived there.

One of the most hotly debated issues about the breakup of Yugoslavia is the role played by international recognition of the breakaway republics. Some people argue that for Western European countries, led by Germany, to promise and then grant recognition to Croatia, Slovenia, and Bosnia emboldened those republics to act rashly and provoke fighting with the JNA. Others think that the new countries deserved recognition, that delaying it would have only encouraged the Serb forces to commit further atrocities, and that recognition may have even come too late as it was. Pushed by the government in Bonn, the European Community recognized Slovenia and Croatia on January 15, 1992. The United States recognized them, plus Bosnia, on April 6, 1992.

It is worth noting that Germany's motives were not exactly based on idealism or principle. The Germans withheld recognition from Macedonia, because its NATO ally Greece was quarreling furiously with the government in Skopje. The German government was also evidently blindsided by the lingering bitterness of many people in the Balkans over the atrocities of the Nazi regime there in the 1940s. This bitterness was not lost on many German citizens, however, who were concerned that their government was too eager to show its strength abroad. Newly reunified Germany under Chancellor Helmut Kohl was also eager to play an expanded role in world politics. Many Germans thought it was time to end their country's refusal to send troops abroad, a policy limitation that of course had made good sense while Europe was dealing with the legacy of the Holocaust. Germany felt at the top of its game economically and politically, and it was eager to assert its leadership within the EC.

Serb charges that Germany was out to create a "Fourth Reich," however, are ridiculous. Foreign Minister Hans-Dietrich Genscher had other motives, too, but they were hardly sinister. He was responding to a desire to increase economic investment in Slovenia and Croatia, to pressure from Catholic voters in southern Germany, and to the well-founded belief that Serb forces were behind most of the destruction and were likely to keep on killing if the international diplomatic vacuum around the country were not broken. There were additional reasons for the German haste: the number of refugees heading into their country was enormous, and Germans, with their long history of ties to Eastern Europe, had a good understanding of the dangers of continued unrest there.[4]

THE WAR IN CROATIA

The Croatian path to independence was to take a much more tortuous route. The republic's nationalist president, Franjo Tudjman of the Croatian Democratic Union (HDZ in Croatian), had been in power since April

1990. Unrest in the Serb-populated areas of Croatia had already begun by the late summer of that year. Fearing a revival of the kind of Croatian nationalism that had run amok in Croatia in the 1940s, Serbs formed paramilitary defense groups; they received arms (and eventually tactical support) from the JNA, and they were joined by bands of irregular troops from Serbia proper. They also had their own political party. The spring of 1991 was a frightening, bloody time in Croatia, as confrontations between Serb and Croat forces took place at Pakrac and Borovo Selo in Eastern Slavonia, in the Plitvice Lakes National Park, and in the rugged area around Knin. The Serb population in Croatia, which had migrated into the region for the most part several hundred years before during the Turkish wars, numbered nearly 600,000, or more than 12 percent of the population of 4.7 million. This was a sizable minority, and in many places a concentrated one, capable of stiff resistance to the central government.

Croatia did not lurch into full-blown war when Slovenia did, but by September, tension and bloodshed were mounting as JNA barracks throughout the country were surrounded. Tudjman commanded, at times loosely, a kind of territorial guard like that of the Slovenes but early on there were also neo-fascist Croatian militias that operated outside of his direct control. Some of these, such as Dobroslav Paraga's HOS (Croatian Defense Forces), the fierce but thuggish military wing of the Croatian Party of Rights grew to be an embarrassment or threat to Tudjman, and he eventually shut them down. Still, by the end of the year, rebel Serbs in Croatia had taken over one-third of that republic. Brutal ethnic cleansing of Croats took place in the Krajina and Slovenia. This process involved robbery, murder, rape, and expulsion. Over the next three years, the capital city of Zagreb was occasionally hit by Serbian rocket and artillery fire, and it was flooded with refugees.

The two most famous Serb-Croat confrontations occurred in the autumn of 1991. The multiethnic Slavonian city of Vukovar was besieged by Serb forces, shelled extensively, and then captured in brutal street-to-street fighting. During the eighty-seven days of the assault, a Croatian reporter named Siniša Glavašević broadcast poignant reports to the outside world. He was killed as the city fell on November 19. In all, hundreds of Croats died during the seige or were executed afterwards, in a pattern that would soon be repeated with chilling frequency in Bosnia. The other prominent confrontation was over the Dalmatian city of Dubrovnik, which was besieged by JNA and Montenegrin troops. The airport and much of the countryside were plundered and the city center, an exquisitely preserved medieval walled town, was bombarded for weeks from the high mountains just inland. The world was horrified to watch the "jewel of the Adriatic," as Dubrovnik has been called, being shelled. But a ground assault on Dubrovnik never took place, and the Croatian politician Stipe Mesić, who was then still technically the president of Yugoslavia, organized a flotilla of private boats that succeeded in breaking the navy's blockade of the city. By May 1992, a truce was signed for that area. The battles of Vukovar and Dubrovnik gave the lie to Milošević's claim that Serbs were just fighting to defend themselves.

The European Community and the United Nations eventually sent diplomats to Croatia to negotiate a cease-fire. Milošević agreed to work with these men, including Lord Peter Carrington and Lord David Owen of Great Britain and Cyrus Vance of the United States (representing the United Nations) once Serbian forces were in control of Serbian irredenta—that is, the lands that Serbs claimed. The peacekeepers would simply copperfasten Serbian control by legitimizing it and putting foreign troops between the increasingly well-armed and motivated Croats and the increasingly disorganized and exhausted Serbs. Non-Serbs were pushed out of those regions, and the message from Belgrade was clear: if Croatia wanted to leave Yugoslavia, it could do so only by giving up large chunks of its historical territory that Serbia now claimed. By January 1992, over 10,000 international peacekeepers were moving into Croatia and the countries of the European Community—but not the United States—gave diplomatic recognition to Slovenia and Croatia. Yugoslavia still existed, but it was now just a federation of four republics instead of six. Even that was not to last long.

For the next several years, the situation in Croatia was at an impasse. The Croatian government under President Franjo Tudjman, a former historian, struggled to win international support. This was a difficult task that was made much harder by Tudjman's authoritarian style of rule and his involvement in unseemly historical revision of the Holocaust. Still, the Croatian armed forces grew considerably. It soon had 105,000 soldiers and 150,000 reservists. Gradually, due mostly to events in Bosnia and Serbia itself, the world lost sympathy with the rebellious Serbs of Krajina and Slavonia, despite Croatian atrocities such as the 1991 massacre of over 100 Serb civilians in Gospić.

The year 1993 was also terrible for Serbs on the home front, because the economy collapsed totally because of the loss of markets and resources in the secessionist republics; the government also printed outrageous sums of money to finance its war effort and to keep local factories afloat. In fact, inflation reached the mind-boggling level of 313,000,000 percent per month, a rate unequaled in human history.

One of the only Yugoslav politicians to condemn the war in Bosnia, the federal prime minister, Milan Panić, lost his race against Milošević for the Serbian presidency and was then forced out of office in late 1992. Panić was not a professional politician, but a wealthy businessman who had American citizenship; he was brought in as window-dressing for the regime but had too many independent ideas for Milošević, who also orchestrated the fall of federal President Ćosić in June 1993. The JNA had been renamed "Vojska Jugoslavije" (the Army of Yugoslavia) and, of course, it now consisted of just Serbs, along with Hungarian and other draftees from the Vojvodina. It still had 135,000 soldiers and much of the equipment it had possessed in 1991, but it was frighteningly expensive to maintain. Meanwhile, Croatia had become the focal point of U.S. policy in the region by 1994; it would be rewarded for its cooperation on Bosnian issues by U.S. military training and diplomatic support.

In May 1995, the push of the revived Croatian military to recapture Serb-held areas began in earnest. Milošević, who had by this point cut the Bosnian and Croatian Serbs adrift in order to show enough cooperation with the United Nations to get the crippling sanctions lifted off of Yugoslavia, allowed chaos to hinder the defense of the Krajina para-state. But the Serbs there had also grown arrogant and spiteful, even toward Belgrade. "Operation Flash," as it was called, quickly overran western Slavonia (the eastern portions of that occupied area would be returned under United Nation-sponsored peacekeeping agreements later). In impotent but deadly retaliation, Serb forces fired rockets into the capital city of Zagreb, shocking Croats and outsiders. But acts of revenge were not the domain of Serbs alone. Thousands of Serbs were driven from their homes, and unknown numbers were killed. Terror tactics of plunder and expropriation were now turned against Serbs, of whom some were recent arrivals and others longtime residents of Slavonia. In late July, the Croatian army intervened in Bosnia and, in cooperation with the rejuvenated Bosnian Muslim army, decisively defeated the Serbs there. That set the stage for the most dramatic, and final, events of the Croatian war.

On August 4, 1995, the Croats began "Operation Storm." They quickly overran Knin, the capital of the Republika Srpska Krajina, which had been one of the focal points of the early conflict in 1990 and 1991. NATO provided air support, putting muscle behind promises to support Tudjman's plans to break Serb resistance provided he cooperated in Bosnia. The Bosnian Serb forces and government collapsed under what many have called a Croatian juggernaut. Nearly 500,000 of Croatia's 600,000 Serbs were soon on the road as refugees, heading east into Bosnia and eventually Serbia itself. This was the single largest forced expulsion of people in Europe since World War II, although the cumulative damage in Bosnia was much greater. While Croats were understandably eager to restore their rule—which the West hoped would be a just one—to the territories that were, after all, inside their historic and internationally recognized legal boundaries, their forces committed many unjustifiable atrocities against Serb civilians. Illegal seizures of Serbian houses, apartments, and other property, as well as killings and beatings, are still being investigated. In 2000 a new government came to power in Croatia in elections held after the death of Tudjman. This center-left coalition under President Stipe Mesić and Prime Minister Ivica Rač an courageously began the process of uncovering what went on during the 1995 operations and discussing what to do about it. Meanwhile, many of Croatia's Serbs lived in bitter exile and wondered how fair it was that the world was so concerned about Serbian treatment of the Albanians of Kosovo while it tolerated the Croats' abusiveness.

THE WAR IN BOSNIA

Political Democracy and the Movement for Secession

Bosnia-Hercegovina's secession in April 1992 brought the most complicated problems in the process of dissolution. Both Croatia and Serbia had ruled Bosnia in medieval times, and there had also been an independent Bosnian state then. So historical claims were overlapping. The long centuries of rule by the Ottoman Empire had left a distinctive culture in Bosnia; there were many Slavic Muslims there, but also a regional identity, manifested in common religious and linguistic practices, food and drink, literature, and customs. Long regarded officially as Serbs (but coveted by Croatian nationalists), the Bosnian Muslims had even been "upgraded" from the status of a religious group to a constituent "nation" in 1961. Serbs considered this a huge provocation in the tradition of the unofficial Titoist policy of "weak Serbia, strong Yugoslavia."

By 1990, as the republic's largest ethnic group, Bosnian Muslims, occupied the leading positions in the new country's government and economy. At this time, the population of Bosnia was about 44 percent Muslim, 31 percent Serb, and 17 percent Croat. The capital, Sarajevo, was famous for being a cosmopolitan, tolerant, ethnically mixed city, although this metaphor of successful coexistence and cultural reciprocity probably applied only to the traditional downtown area of the city, since the suburbs were home mostly to informally segregated recent arrivals. Still, Bosnia had the highest percentage of mixed marriages and of people identifying themselves as Yugoslavs in the whole country, proof that the republic was not just a cultural battleground, as conventional wisdom would have it.

The republic held its first free elections on November 9, 1990, exactly one year after the fall of the Berlin Wall. Political pluralism showed that the Bosnian population was drifting quickly into the same kind of ethnic nationalism as the rest of the country. Six months before the election, the Party of Democratic Action (SDA) was founded by Bosnian Muslims. Selected as its leader was the longtime dissident and now nationalist, Alija Izetbegović, who, contrary to Serbian propaganda, was not an Islamic fundamentalist and did not advocate an intolerant Muslim theocracy in Bosnia.

In the early summer of 1990, Serbs in Bosnia founded the Serbian Democratic Party (SDS), which was affiliated with the Croatian Serbian party of the same name. Its leader was Radovan Karadžić, whose face would become a familiar feature on news broadcasts in the West but who proved to be the bane of Western negotiatiors. He had important connections to Milošević and the ultranationalist Radical Party leader Vojislav Šešelj. The most prominent Bosnian Serb military leader, General Ratko Mladić, had been heavily involved in the organizing in Croatia's Krajina. The small city of Pale, just east of Sarajevo, became the capital of the breakaway Serbian "parastate" of *Republika Srpska* (RS, or the Serbian Republic). Most Croats backed the local branch of the strongly nationalistic HDZ. There were also two other reformist communist parties in the first free Bosnian elections. The SDA came in first with eighty-seven seats, the SDS second with seventy-one, and the HDZ trailed with forty-four. The three parties worked out a tenuous coalition government, with Izetbegović as president.

Many Bosnians were not eager to secede, if only because they feared such a move would spark discord among the republic's ethnic groups. But after Croatia and Slovenia left the federation, the SDA decided to move toward independence rather than remain in a reduced Yugoslavia which Serbia was now able to dominate fully. Izetbegović also did not trust the Serbs to remain loyal or peaceful. After sounding out the prospects for international recognition, Bosnia sought to meet the requirements of the European Community's Badinter Commission, set up to pass judgment on the readiness of the Yugoslav republics for full independence. The EC wanted to see the results of a referendum on secession before supporting it. Meanwhile, the political scene in Bosnia had already fragmented along national lines, as we have seen, and Serbs and Croats were angry that Izetbegović planned to rule in Bosnia on the principle of majority rule, without giving their communities as a whole veto rights over government actions. This does not mean that the SDA would have treated its minorities poorly, especially since most Bosnians were proud of their traditions of coexistence and Izetbegović—who of course badly needed any and all Western assistance—promised to hold Bosnia to international human rights standards. The idea of "one person, one vote" does not sound threatening to North Americans. But many Serbs and Croats, in Bosnia and in their "home countries," believed that Bosnia as a whole was historically theirs, and they saw little reason to accept minority status there, even in a democratic Bosnia and even though minorities in rump Yugoslavia as a whole could expect this same treatment.

Ominously, the SDS prepared for the republic's eventual secession by building up a far-flung paramilitary force and holding a referendum to get a mandate to "counter-secede" when the time came. The JNA also set up units just of Bosnian Serb soldiers, equipped them, and prepared to leave them behind when the federal army pulled out. Throughout the entire conflict, even when political relations between the Bosnian Serbs and Serbia proper were strained, the Bosnian Serb army was paid and equipped by the federal government. Such facts give the lie to the common view that this was a "civil war."

On February 28 and March 1, 1992, the Bosnian government sponsored the required republic-wide referendum on secession. Serbs boycotted the vote, so that the turnout was only 63 percent. But of those who voted, 99 percent favored secession. The die was cast. Between the referendum and the declaration of independence, paramilitary groups such as the "Tigers" of Arkan from Serbia began to terrorize parts of Bosnia; meanwhile, the European Community looked for ways to neutralize the threatened rebellion of Karadžić and the SDS. On April 6, Bosnia declared itself independent and was granted immediate diplomatic recognition by the West European countries and the United States. In many ways, though, the war that would eventually cripple the country had already started.

THE COURSE OF THE WAR: "ETHNIC CLEANSING" AND THE SIEGE OF SARAJEVO

The war in Bosnia broke out in the spring of 1992 because most Serbs and Croats of Bosnia vowed that they would not live under a government dominated by Muslims. This was the case even though the Bosnian leaders promised to respect democratic norms and guarantee full civil rights to all of Bosnia's inhabitants. First the Serbs rebelled, with support from the adjacent republic of Serbia (the main part of what was called "rump Yugoslavia") and the *Republika Srpska Krajina* in Croatia. A horrific war began, which lasted until late 1995. Bosnian Croats soon entered the war, aided enormously by the government of independent Croatia next door. At first the Bosnian Croats fought both Serbs and Muslims to seize territory for occupation only by Croats. It soon became apparent that Tudjman and Milošević had made arrangements to split Bosnia between them. Izetbegović rejected partition, a stance in accordance with international law, a conception of Bosnia as a historical territory, and a belief that the new government would be a democratic one, nonetheless earned the Sarajevo government bad press, in which it was cast as provocative and unreasonable.

There were few pitched battles in the Bosnian War. In 1991, the heavily armed Bosnian Serb forces easily crushed their opponents. The Bosnian Serb army had about 80,000 men by the summer of 1992. They soon found themselves in control of 70 percent of the Bosnian territory. One of their most fearsome weapons was the militias, or paramilitaries, who also played an infamous role in the Croatian War. The "Tigers" of Željko Ražnjatović (aka Arkan) and the Šešelj's Chetniks were joined by groups known as the White Eagles, the Knights, the Serbian Guard, the Yellow Wasps, and various kinds of "Ninjas." These groups contained thousands of men and thrived on plunder, rapine, and murder, and their activities, though sometimes tactically beyond the control of political leaders, were endorsed by Milošević and Karadžić. Studies of their motives and backgrounds show that "patriotism" (defending their homes) or even nationalism, was far from being their chief concern. Some men were forced to serve in these militias. But most joined willingly: to supplement their income through the pay and plunder; in search of fame, excitement, or political connections; from peer pressure; or in order to satisfy their own sadism.[5]

The Bosnian defense forces consisted of militias such as the Patriotic League, the Dragons of Bosnia, and the "Green Berets," as well as a rudimentary army built, as was the case in Slovenia and Croatia, on the foundations of the old republican Territorial Defense Force. Its commander was Sefer Halilović, who could do little against the huge force at Mladić's command, especially since an international arms embargo was in effect for all of ex-Yugoslavia. It was also unable to protect the vast number of villages and cities where Bosnian Muslims lived. These civilians, it turned out, were the main targets of the Serb forces. While international attention zeroed in on Sarajevo, the once grand Turkish and

Olympic city, "ethnic cleansing" in the provinces was becoming "the defining characteristic of the war"; tens of thousands of refugees were soon flocking out of Serb-occupied zones because "their expulsion was the whole point of the war."[6] There exist many scholarly and journalistic studies of this policy of ethnic cleansing, so it need only be summarized here.

Victims were selected on the basis of their nationality. In some parts of Bosnia there are ethnic "enclaves," while in other places national groups lived together but tended to live in separate villages or at least parts of a town. When an area was to be "cleansed," military or paramilitary units sealed it off and then often shot it up first, to frighten the inhabitants. Sometimes community leaders were shot right away, as were any men who appeared to be members of an opposing military unit, whether they were armed or not. Often large groups of people were executed for no reason. Houses were robbed and then torched, women and girls were raped, and then the civilians were sorted into columns and marched out of town. Some went to camps of various types, while others were pushed across the front lines or into Croatia, until it closed its borders.

In bigger towns and cities, such as Foča, Prijedor, Banja Luka, and Bijeljina, the Karadžić government set up a bureaucratic apparatus to force Muslims and Croats to leave. They were segregated and subjected to sporadic violence until they were willing to sign over all of their property—cars, houses, furniture, bank accounts—to Serbian warlords and board a bus out of town. In Sarajevo itself, Serbian artillerymen dumped 500,000 shells onto the city between 1992 and 1995. They were joined by snipers who picked off people on streets and in windows. An international airlift was eventually begun by July 1992, but medicine, fuel, electricity, and water were in critically short supply. Some Sarajevans managed to flee the city, but most remained. The veteran journalist and reformer Kemal Kurspahić, editor of the city's main newspaper *Oslobodjenje* (*Liberation*), and his courageous staff put out a paper every day of the siege, to keep Sarajevans connected to the outside world and to demonstrate their determination to outlast the gunners on the mountains. The Serb forces seemed to enjoy torturing the residents of the city, but they did not attempt to storm it outright; they seem to have had in mind ultimately partitioning it.

The camps in the summer of 1992 were numerous and varied. There were transit camps such as Trnopolje and Manjača and detention camps such as Omarska, Keraterm, and Ripač. All were usually called "concentration camps" by Western reporters, who got access to them and publicized the plight of the internees. The first big story of this type was reported on July 19 by *Newsday*'s Roy Gutman, who later published a book of his articles.[7] The conditions in these camps were appalling, and the world was reminded of Hitler's atrocities during the Third Reich. These were not "extermination camps" on the order of Auschwitz, but places where bestial tortures and beatings were administered and where Muslims were humiliated, robbed, raped, starved, and often executed. Eventually, there were some Croat camps for Muslims, too; Muslim ethnic cleansing aimed at the other two groups was of a lesser magnitude, though it was still bloody and reprehensible and only served as fodder for the arguments of people who claimed that all sides were equally "guilty" in the war. There are three possible reasons why the embattled Bosnian Muslim forces did not carry out much ethnic cleansing: they were too weak, they did not consider non-Muslim civilian populations a threat, or they were restrained in the hope of attracting Western support.

In 1992, the UN Security Council set up a war crimes tribunal in the Hague to investigate the atrocities in Bosnia. Its brief was to prosecute people suspected of crimes against humanity and genocide. It issued lists of indictments, which eventually totalled over 100, although there were also secret or sealed indictments. Karadžić and Mladić remain on the list (and on the loose) at the time of this writing; Milošević, by contrast, was not put on the list until his campaign against Kosovo kicked into high gear in 1999. In addition to Serbs, there were quite a few Croats on the list and some Bosnian Muslims. Eventually, the United Nations for the first time defined rape as a war crime in response to the thousands of rapes reported, mostly by Bosnian Muslim women.

International response to the fighting in Bosnia in the rest of 1992 was to try to isolate Serbia by issuing sanctions and by kicking it out of the United Nations. In September, a new United Nations Protection Force (UNPROFOR) peacekeeping force for Bosnia was formed, and a "no-fly zone" was defended over the country by NATO planes.

By 1993, in many parts of Bosnia, forced expulsions had pushed large numbers of Muslims together into pockets. The United Nations helped bus people into these areas (or out of the country altogether, when possible), creating the ethical dilemma of whether it was saving lives or simply helping Serbs empty Bosnia of "unwanted" people. These refugee areas were usually around a city or large town in a valley. Naturally enough these cities usually sat astride a road, but that made them strategic targets for Serbs. When Serb forces surrounded the refugee areas and began shelling them, civilian casualties were high and the fear of massacres grew. The Bosnian government was too weak to send help to the remote, embattled pockets. In April 1993, Mladić's forces very nearly overran the town of Srebrenica. (They would do so, with disastrous results, in July of 1995.) After much bloodshed, it was saved when the United Nations designated it a "safe area." Later in the year, the United Nations would apply this designation to other Bosnian cities: Žepa, Goraž de, Tuzla, Bihać, and Sarajevo itself. But it too lacked the means to defend them. No outside force could persuade the Serbs even to let aid convoys carrying food and medicine reach the stranded refugees; humanitarian workers were regularly harassed and threatened and evacuations were often delayed or even fired upon. In one of the most shameful tactics of the entire war, Karadžić and Mladić repeatedly used the civilians in the safe areas as hostages and bargaining chips, threatening to destroy them outright anytime too much international pressure was placed on them.

The new U.S. president, Bill Clinton, responding to public pressure, gradually began to fulfill one of his campaign promises by taking a greater interest in Bosnia than his predecessor. He avoided committing U.S. troops as peacekeepers, but he proposed a policy of "lift and strike," or lifting the arms embargo on the Bosnians and using NATO air strikes to force Serbian cooperation. Meanwhile, the Bosnian government experienced the absolute low point in its fortunes in the war. Its control of the country was limited to an archipelago of mostly disconnected regions around a few key cities. It now came under full-scale attack from Croats; another para-state was set up, this time for the Croats. It was called "Herceg-Bosna" and had its capital at Mostar in the southern part of the country. One of the most memorable events of the Croat-Muslim conflict came on November 9, when Croat gunners succeeded in destroying a splendid old Ottoman bridge across the Neretva River. The bridge had stood for well over 400 years, and, like the bridges in the works of the great novelist Ivo Andrić, it had been a symbol of connectedness between people of different cultures and religions. The Bosnian Croat military was called the HVO (Croatian Defense Council). It had about 50,000 soldiers, but it was significantly reinforced by elements of Tudjman's regular armed forces. The Croat leaders had started setting up their state in 1992 and had originally fought the Serbs some, too. But large-scale attacks by Croats on Muslims did not start until April 1993, when dozens of Muslim civilians were massacred in Ahmići, not far from Sarajevo.

But 1993 was also the year that the Bosnian Muslims began to fight back in earnest. Paramilitaries (led by gangsters such as Caco and Čelo) that had both defended Sarajevo and terrorized its inhabitants were brought under government control. The Bosnian Army soon had 200,000 men and now outnumbered Mladić's Serb forces. But the Bosnian Serbs still had material advantages and the predatory paramilitaries. Some of the Bosnian units consisted mostly of men who had seen their home cities and villages destroyed by Serb forces; these brigades were known for their determination and their explicitly Islamic brand of Bosnian nationalism. Eventually *mujahideen,* or Islamic guerrilla fighters, sneaked into Bosnia from the Middle East and elsewhere and attached themselves to various military units. Izetbegović had little choice but to accept both such volunteers and financial assistance from other Muslim countries. The UN was not willing to protect Bosnia's civilians, but it was maintaining the arms embargo that prevented the Sarajevo government from purchasing weapons legally.

In Serbia, Milošević moved to shore up his own power. There were riots in Belgrade, sparked by dissatisfaction over the war and the economic misery caused by the international embargo. Milošević began to downplay nationalism and play up his own leftist legacy. A rift opened between him and the Radical Party leader Šešelj. An even bigger confrontation took place with the Bosnian Serbs over the Vance-Owen Peace Plan, which would have "cantonized" the country, reorganizing it into ten large districts and ending dreams of a separate Serbian statelet. The Bosnian Serbs rejected the plan, which Milošević supported. His lack of devotion to the ideals of greater Serbia was also shown in his willingness to turn his back on the Croatian Serbs. He was interested in using them as a bargaining chip with Tudjman.

1994: THE TURNING POINT

In the three-and-a-half-year history of the Bosnian war, there was no single more momentous month than February 1994. The situation on the ground had reached something of a standstill. The United States, Russia, and West European countries differed over how to solve the crisis, and Milošević was confident that he could bluff and bluster his way through any confrontation. But power was about to shift on the Bosnian scene.

On February 5, a mortar shell landed on a marketplace in downtown Sarajevo. Sixty-nine people were killed, the news and accompanying photographs were broadcast immediately around the world, and the uproar in countries like the United States was enormous. This incident tipped the scales of world opinion in favor of decisive action against the Serbs, who by this point had besieged Sarajevo for nearly two years. The world assumed that the shell had come from Serbian guns, something that Karadžić denied. There were theories among Serbs that the Bosnian government might have shot at its own people (as the Canadian UNPROFOR general Lewis MacKenzie accused it of doing in May 1992, when twenty-two people were killed outside a bakery) and then blamed the Serbs in order to attract international sympathy. Military analysts now say that it is impossible to tell who fired that specific shell. Be that as it may, it—and the next big civilian slaughter of 1995—became a symbol of the cold-blooded siege that took 10,000 lives in the city. It also acted as a catalyst for outside action.

Over the objections of Lord Peter Owen, the European Community negotiator who dreaded alienating the Russians, and Lt. General Michael Rose, who headed the United Nations peacekeepers, NATO issued an ultimatum to the Bosnian Serbs, without UN approval: within ten days, the artillery around the city must be pulled back or put under UN control. All kinds of frantic negotiations took place next, as UNPROFOR tried to get Karadžić and Mladić to comply. Had Russian president Boris Yeltsin not stepped in, NATO would likely have had to bomb. But Russian troops entered Bosnia for the first time and joined the other UNPROFOR soldiers around Sarajevo, and the Serbs removed or stopped firing their heavy weapons. There was no clear winner in this diplomatic confrontation, because the city of Sarajevo was still blockaded, with the Serbs controlling the high ground around it. But the Russians had not foiled NATO plans, and the Western alliance was now playing a more direct role. And, finally, but not permanently, the civilians of the mangled city were relieved of daily attacks.

The other big news of February 1994 was the rapprochement between Bosnia's Muslims and Croats. The UN Security Council finally issued an ultimatum to the Tudjman government to pull its forces out of Bosnia or else face strict sanctions like those placed on Serbia. U.S. officials also worked quietly but with great skill to change Zagreb's policies. On March 2, 1994, in Washington, D.C., the Muslim-Croat Federation came into existence. It never developed into the full-fledged organization that was intended, but it did stop all fighting between the two groups.

Later in 1994 another international controversy erupted over Serbian efforts to overrun the UN safe area in Goražde. As Serb forces bombarded and then closed in on the town, UNPROFOR's commander, General Michael Rose, reluctantly requested a limited number of NATO air strikes. Only a few Serbian vehicles were destroyed by American planes, but this was the very first time that NATO forces had ever fired a shot in the forty-five-year history of the alliance. More strikes were threatened, especially by the United States. A miserable and much smaller "safe area" at Goražde eventually survived the Serbian assault, due mostly to the arrival of Ukrainian and British peacekeepers.

In retaliation, Mladić's forces took 150 UN peacekeepers hostage on Mount Igman near Sarajevo. These kinds of retaliations might have paralyzed NATO into refraining from further strikes, but the Serbs overplayed their hand. On April 19, they snatched away a big battery of heavy artillery from UN peacekeepers in the Sarajevo district of Lukavica. Meanwhile, Karadžić snubbed both Milošević and Russian diplomats, all of whom were urging him to stop the assault on Goražde.

After this showdown, relations between Belgrade and the Bosnian Serb government in Pale chilled considerably. The state-run media in Serbia had already begun painting the SDA leadership as egomaniacs and as bandits who were dragging Serbia into needless confrontation with the West. Milošević suddenly invoked the need for peace, and he tried to stir Serbian national pride by asking the rhetorical question, "Why should this one far-off group of insurgents be allowed to dictate policy to all of Yugoslavia, a nation of 10 million?" This image of Karadžić and Mladić is nothing short of dumbfounding, since Milošević's government had supported and praised them enormously as defenders of the Serbian nation in the early 1990s. The shift was occasioned by simple pragmatism. Milošević wanted no rivals, especially powerful ones, and he also wanted to end the UN sanctions against rump Yugoslavia, because they were making life so miserable there that he feared public discontent might weaken his hold on power. There is also evidence that Milošević was bothered by Karadžic's closeness to the Serbian Orthodox Church establishment and his desire to bring back the Serbian monarchy. The media campaign was followed up by a much more powerful tactic in August: a blockade by Serbia of the RS. Much was made in the international press of how Milošević was now cooperating with the West against the "renegade" Bosnian Serbs, and he even allowed international observers to monitor traffic along the Drina River between the two countries. Even though the military of the RS continued to get assistance from Serbia, the blockade did add to the political isolation of Karadžić.

Meanwhile, a new international grouping had developed in response to the conflict. Called simply the "Contact Group," it represented the United States, Russia, France, Germany, and Great Britain, and it set in motion the final wave of peacemaking that would eventually result in the Dayton Accords of 1995. The proposals put forward by the Contact Group abandoned the "cantonization" of the Vance-Owen plan and also the outright partitions of the intervening plans. The goals, beyond stopping the fighting, were to preserve both the international boundaries of

Bosnia-Hercegovina and the fragile but promising Muslim-Croat Federation within it. The plans called for the Muslims and Croats to have joint administration over 51 percent of the country. Karadžić vehemently rejected this idea, which even had Russian support, because it meant Serbs would have to give up important chunks of recently conquered territory. The Muslim government also spurned the plan at first, saying it legitimized Serbian rule over large areas they had overrun and brutally "cleansed." Ultimately, Izetbegović accepted the plan, because he was dependent upon Western support and he doubted that the Serb assembly in Pale would approve it. He was right, and the international isolation of Bosnian Serbs deepened.

MILOŠEVIĆ MAKES PEACE

The impasse in Bosnia shattered in July 1995. Bosnian Serb forces attacked yet another UN "safe area," this time at Srebrenica. If the "safe areas" were "sitting ducks" for Serbian gunners, then the Serbian forces themselves were easy targets for international media attention focused on the plight of the overwhelmingly Muslim refugees. The United Nations was also concerned for the safety of its military and civilian personnel inside the "safe areas" whenever Serbs attacked.

Srebrenica contained about 40,000 refugees from Eastern Bosnia. Muslim military units were also there. When the Serbs began their attack on July 6, they did so under the guise of eliminating this military threat and of rooting out the city's criminal elements. There were fewer than 400 Dutch peacekeepers in the city; they succeeded in protecting about 25,000 civilians, but another 15,000 fled into the woods to avoid the Serbs. A round of NATO airstrikes—the second in the alliance's history—arrived too late to stop the Serbs, and the town fell on July 12. In the following days, something like 7,000 Bosnian Muslims were hunted down and killed in and around the city by Serb forces. This catastrophe galvanized opinion in the West for a military blow at the Serb forces.

The massive rout of the Croatian Serb forces in August was accompanied by successful Croat and Bosnian offensives against the Serbs. Mladić's forces overran another UN "safe area" in Žepa and then, on August 28, another mortar attack on the Sarajevo marketplace—this one killing 37 people and demonstrated to have been fired by Serbs—outraged world opinion. This time, NATO and the United Nations were ready to lower the boom on Karadžić. A large air assault (Operation Deliberate Force) was unleashed on August 31. One of the cease-fire conditions put forward by the United States was the unambiguous withdrawal of all Serbian artillery from around Sarajevo, to make sure once and for all that the siege was broken. The Serbs complied after two weeks. A guiding basic principle for a peace was also accepted by all sides: the country was not going to be partitioned but the Muslim-Croat federation would rule only 51 percent of it, with the RS ruling 49 percent.

On November 1, representatives of the warring parties and members of the Contact Group assembled at Wright-Patterson Airforce Base in Dayton, Ohio, to create a peace treaty. Karadžić, having been indicted for war crimes, could not attend, but other Bosnian Serb officials were there, as was Milošević himself. Tudjman, Izetbegović, U.S. Secretary of State Warren Christopher, and special envoy Richard Holbrooke were the other chief negotiators. What emerged was not only a cessation of the fighting, but plans for how the new country of Bosnia-Hercegovina was to be structured. Agreement over maps—who got what contested region—was the hardest part of the negotiations. It was agreed that the fate of the city of Brčko, a vital transportation link between large swaths of Serbian territory in the west and east, would be decided later under international arbitration. Mostar would be shared by Bosnians and Croats. NATO would have the leading role in an Implementation Force (IFOR) of 60,000, which would also include troops from Russia, Romania, Poland, Pakistan, Malaysia, Morocco, Bulgaria, Greece, Egypt, Finland, the Czech Republic, Austria, and the Baltic states.

More complicated than the peace would be the setting up of a new government. Free and fair elections had to be held under strict international observation and in a bewildering variety of jurisdictions. There was a government for each of the two entities plus a federal structure, in which the high positions were shared or rotated by all three ethnic groups. It was hoped that international aid and pressure, along with the sobering exhaustion of the long war, would overcome memories of the disastrous results of the post-Tito rotation system and of the prewar Bosnian power-sharing arrangements in 1992. Even if the economy could be repaired, it would be fragmented and in need of privatization—three tasks that still loom ahead for Bosnia.

Even trickier were the issues of the prosecution of war criminals and the resettlement of refugees. By 1997, the Hague Tribunal had indicted seventy-five people, of whom sixty-five were still at large.[8] By February 2001, the number of arrests and indictments had increased considerably, but Karadžić, Mladić, and many other politicians and soldiers on the Hague's list of indictments were still on the loose. The Bosnian Serb politician Biljana Plavšić gave herself up. There were also some spectacular captures, especially by British forces, and the new government in

Croatia moved quickly in 2000 against a number of indictees on its territory. But it was widely speculated that IFOR did not go all out to capture Karadžić and Mladić for fear of angering Bosnian Serbs, who might then sabotage the Dayton arrangements. It remains to be seen whether Bosnia is a viable country. It would be a grand symbol of hope for all of Europe if it did survive. If nonnationalist parties do not take root and the flow of international aid does not continue, however, partition or outright absorption by one of its neighbors will most likely be the fate of this young, awkward state. Many refugees remained fearful of returning to areas dominated by other national groups, and the local governments were often uncooperative in such matters. At the end of 2000, more than 500,000 people had still not been resettled.

CONCLUSION: THE EFFECTS OF THE WAR

The most important effect of the war was on individual human beings. Between 150,000 and 200,000 people were killed in the Bosnian war, most of them civilians. By late 2000, more than 20,000 people were still unaccounted for, 85 percent of whom were Muslims. Refugees and displaced persons numbered about 2 million, close to half of the population of the country; so many rapes, especially of Muslim women, were reported that prosecutions for rape and sexual slavery are now being carried out by the Hague War Crimes Tribunal.

Historians will long argue over whether Bosnia's quest for independence was unnecessarily provocative, whether European recognition of the secessionist states made things worse, and whether Serb and Croat fears over living in independent Bosnia were justified. But there is no doubt that Serb forces started the killing and prolonged it for years. There is also no doubt that all sides ended up perpetrating shocking acts of violence, but this does not translate into an "equality of blame," a thesis that became one of the mantras of noninterventionists in the West. Finally, there is also no doubt that the Muslims, because of huge campaigns of rape and "ethnic cleansing" aimed at them, have suffered the most, as a group, in quantitative terms. They are the real "losers" of this war against civilians, in terms of human casualties and the damage done to their mosques, libraries, and educational institutions.

The distinctive regional culture of Bosnia was also a casualty of the war. After the fighting broke out, many people of all three nationalities understandably fled the country in terror and disgust, never to return. The ones who stayed have identities now in which Serb, Croat, or Bosniak (a new term being used to signify Bosnian Muslims as a national group) are the prime elements, and not the historical term "Bosnian." All the civilians of Bosnia have lost a great deal in the fighting, but the Bosnian Muslims lost the most, since Serbs and Croats can at least look across the borders of the country to Belgrade or Zagreb for support. Sarajevo is still the capital of Bosnia, but it is hard to say just what Bosnia is. Is it still multiethnic and will it ever effectively rule the internationally recognized boundaries of 1992? Or is it really just a much reduced but mostly Bosniak state in the center of the country? How will the Bosniaks balance their dual attachment to Europe and to the Muslim world in culture and politics?

The war also left the world with chilling reminders of the potential cruelty and duplicity of politicians. Milošević helped start the war and then helped stop it when it served his interests. But Karadžić brazenly "blamed the victims" and then blamed everyone who tried to help them for escalating the conflict. Looking straight into television cameras and speaking good English, he time and time again stated, with outrageous deceitfulness, that he only wanted peace and democracy. Because the world was ignorant of Bosnian affairs and ready to believe that all parties there were equally at fault, it believed the seemingly rational and urbane Karadžić for months.

The war in Bosnia was a huge challenge to stability in Europe. Since it created so many refugees, the generosity of governments from the United Kingdom to Sweden to Hungary was put to the test. And since the United States was so slow to respond to the conflict, negotiations to end the war were a severe trial for the European Community (now the European Union). The breakup of Czechoslovakia and even of the Soviet Union had not caused as much turmoil as the dissolution of Yugoslavia, and Europeans found it hard to come up with a effective and mutually acceptable policy toward it.

The United States ended up playing a huge and constructive role in the Bosnian crisis. Fears of "another Vietnam" proved utterly unfounded. It was U.S. muscle and negotiating skill that finally stopped the fighting. From July 1992 to January 1996, furthermore, the U.S. Air Force flew 4,200 loads of supplies into Sarajevo in Operation Provide Promise; it also evacuated hundreds of wounded people. President Clinton also initiated night-time airdrops over rural Bosnia. By August 1994, the United States had parachuted into Muslim areas more than 2,200 loads of food and medicine over eighteen months. Other countries mounted smaller airlifts, too. U.S. ground forces initially comprised one-third of IFOR, and by 2001, there were still over 4,000 U.S. personnel in Bosnia, and, though there were some deaths due to accidents and land mines, not one American life had been lost in combat.

The war put the seal of finality on Yugoslavia's dissolution. By the end of 1992, only two of the country's former six republics were still part of the country. "Rump Yugoslavia," as the Serbian-Montenegrin federation was sometimes called, has also been referred to as "Serbonegro" or "the third Yugoslavia." The post-Dayton country of Bosnia is an unsure and artificial entity at present. On good days it has two constituent parts and on bad days, when Croats and Bosniaks are arguing, there are three. Just how long Western aid to Bosnia will last remains to be seen. Eventual admission to the European Union will require not just peace among the national groups and a rebuilt economy but also proof that the Tito-era political and economic systems have been effectively reformed. Those tasks will be too much for the weak central government as it is currently constituted. The rise of nonethnic political parties, such as the Social Democrats of Zlatko Lagumdžija (a former SDA official), is an optimistic sign, however, as is the positive attitude of the new governments in Zagreb and Belgrade, which is slowly bearing fruit among their co-nationals in Bosnia. IFOR has been transformed into SFOR, the Stabilization Force, and has 20,000 soldiers.

Despite concern that the Dayton Accords have rewarded Serbs territorially for some of their aggression in Bosnia, and regardless of the fact that Slobodan Milošević long retained his control over Serbia's politics and economy, the decade of conflict has had a profoundly demoralizing effect on most Serbs. Indeed, as this text has tried to point out, Serbs have lost a great deal, too; their suffering, reflected in myriad personal and family tragedies and massive economic misery, has been tremendous. The wars have benefited some extreme nationalists, war profiteers, and the ruling elites, but many people's lives are in chaos now because of decisions for aggression made above their heads. Most Serbs today do not feel like historical or geopolitical "winners," a label given to Serbia by some international pundits, at least before the 1999 war over Kosovo.

NOTES

1. See Dennison Rusinow, "The Avoidable Catastrophe," pp. 13–37, in Sabrina Petra Ramet and Ljubiša S. Adamovich, eds., *Beyond Yugoslavia: Politics, Economics, and Culture in a Shattered Community* (Boulder, CO: Westview Press, 1995), p. 14; and Mark Thompson, *Forging War: The Me-*

dia in Serbia, Croatia, and Bosnia-Hercegovina, rev. ed (Luton: University of Luton Press, 1999).

2. See Gale Stokes, ed., *From Stalinism to Pluralism*, 2d ed. (London: Oxford University Press, 1996).

3. Tim Judah, *Kosovo: War and Revenge* (New Haven, CT: Yale University Press, 2000), p. 47.

4. See Misha Glenny, *The Fall of Yugoslavia: The Third Balkan War*, 3d ed. (New York: Penguin, 1996), pp. 188–192.

5. Marie-Janine Calic, *Krieg und Frieden in Bosnien-Hercegovina*, rev. ed. (Frankfurt: Suhrkamp, 1995), pp. 143–147.

6. Laura Silber and Allan Little, *Yugoslavia: Death of a Nation*, rev. and updated ed. (New York: Penguin, 1997), p. 244.

7. See Roy Gutman, *Witness to Genocide* (New York: Macmillan, 1993).

8. John B. Allcock et al., *Conflict in the Former Yugoslavia: An Encyclopedia* (Denver: ABC-CLIO, 1998), p. 325.

11

Successor State or International Pariah?

The question of how Milošević retained power in Serbia is a complex one. The journalistic shorthand is that Milošević is a radical nationalist and most Serbs are too, so they obeyed him. Another explanation is that he was a fascist who ruled through terror. While Milošević did rise to power in the late 1980s by highlighting Serbian nationalist issues, he quickly revealed himself to be more of an opportunist, concerned with his own power, than an ideologue. Recent Serbian governments did not meet definitions of fascism. Despite their authoritarianism, scapegoating, militarism, and constant foregrounding of nationalist issues, the SPS did not shut down all alternative voices and centers of power and its platform was not anticommunist or antimodern.

Milošević probably allowed some of the trappings of democracy to continue to exist because Serbs would not (for cultural and historical reasons) tolerate a full-blown dictatorship, because he did not have the power to shut down the opposition completely, because he wanted Serbs to be able to vent some of their frustrations, or because he calculated that he won propaganda points in the West for operating behind democratic window dressing. Thus, some independent media continued to function in Serbia, though with government-imposed limitations that prevented them from reaching all parts of Serbia. There were also some independent activists' organizations and human rights groups such as the Anti-War Center and the Women's Center. There are also, of course, many opposition parties, some of whom received support from the West, in hopes of destabilizing the Milošević government and building on Serbia's more democratic traditions and its significant economic potential. During his rule, demonstrations, especially but not only by students, and elections were held. But there was often significant and sometimes brutal government interference with these elements of democracy.

A major problem the opposition faced was division within its own ranks. The decades of one-party rule in Yugoslavia left Serbia with few civic organizations that could mobilize and unite concerned citizens. Also, many of the opposition leaders, in Serbia as in other East European countries, were intellectuals and dissidents. These people are usually highly intelligent, of course, and morally courageous, but the very qualities that made them good intellectuals or dissidents—pronounced individualism or commitment to a narrow set of principles—often hindered their ability to form durable alliances or to connect with rank-and-file voters.

Opposition groups in Serbia also represented a broad spectrum of views. Some groups are highly nationalistic and blame Milošević for caving in to the West. Other groups are nationalist but willing to be more pragmatic in cooperating with the United Nations, NATO, and the countries of the European Union, so that Serbia can be rebuilt. Others focus on creating a full-fledged democracy within Serbia's existing borders (almost always still including Kosovo). These many differences, along with personal rivalries, long prevented any one opposition candidate from galvanizing anti-Milošević feeling, although at times men such as Milan Panić and Dobrica Ćosić seemed likely to mount a serious challenge to Milošević.

Another way to account for Milošević's hold on power is to blame the West's isolation of Serbia. The government has been able to deflect much of the population's economic misery onto the actions of foreign powers. Many of Serbia's economic problems have actually been caused by the breakup of Yugoslavia and by the massive price tag of the wars of succession, but international sanctions have also created great hardship.

Proponents of sanctions claim that the Serb government brought them on themselves by their aggressive actions and that it was important not to let Belgrade act with impunity. To many Serbs, however, the sanctions against their country were outrageous, because they punished people for the blunders of a political elite over which they had no influence. Some Serbs also resented what they call the West's double standard in applying sanctions: if all the parties in the hostilities shared the guilt for the outbreak of war (or the atrocities committed within it), then why were Serbs singled out for sanctions?

A final tactic Milošević used to keep power was control of the economy. Privatization began in Serbia in 1991, around the time it was starting to take place in other East European countries. But Milošević stopped the process, thus halting the growth of a reform-minded middle class and turning the economy into a kind of feeding trough for his party and its allies. Many workers and retirees depended on the government for their income, and so they remained generally reluctant to support the opposition. Special "police" forces from the Ministry of the Interior were kept well paid and well supplied and functioned as a sort of loyal palace guard. Opposition mayors would find their city's gas or electricity reduced, while independent editors might not be able to secure enough paper for their print runs.

THE LATE 1990s

By 1996 Milošević's unusual dictatorship had grown brittle. The government's attempt to steal the elections of November 17 provided the spark for great unrest and resistance, but there was also economic dissatisfaction. Most sanctions had been lifted after Milošević cooperated in the Dayton process, but there had been little structural change. Serbs knew that their neighbors in Eastern Europe had already begun their reforms; prosperity was starting to arrive elsewhere but Serbs' expectations were going unmet.

In the local elections, Milošević and his allies faced an opposition alliance formed earlier that year called *Zajedno* ("Together"). It consisted of three parties: Drašković's Serbian Renewal Movement, Djindjić's Democratic Party, and the most progressive and liberal of all the parties, the Civic Alliance of Serbia, which was led by Vesna Pešić. Zajedno won control over many Serbian municipalities, including the biggest cities of Belgrade, Novi Sad, Niš, and Kragujevac. But Milošević moved to have the results declared void, and the Zajedno celebration rallies turned quickly into protest marches. The student demonstrators egged government buildings, mocked the regime's leading figures, and kept up its demonstrations—some of them with 100,000 people—for eight weeks. Milošević responded by canceling a session of the Serbian parliament, arresting and beating protest leaders, sponsoring counter-rallies, and shutting down opposition media. Ironically, many people in the West were led to believe that the demonstrators were "nationalists" who were angry at Milošević's "selling out" of the Bosnian Serbs, while within Serbia the government-controlled media depicted the students as antinationalists and foreign lackeys. The students received support from the Montenegrin Parliament; the leader of the Serbian Orthodox Church, Patriarch Pavle; teachers and professors; and citizens of Belgrade.

As electrifying as the sometimes joyful, sometimes frightening protests and plaza "sit-ins" were, many Serbs were not interested in supporting the students. They were keeping their heads down, working hard to make ends meet, or waiting for better economic times. Still, the demonstrations continued, until Milošević ordered his government to accept the election results. International support for the students and Zajedno seems to have helped Milošević make up his mind. On February 15, 1997, after eighty-eight days, the students stopped their daily marches, although sporadic demonstrations continued for another month until the rector of the University of Belgrade was forced to resign. But almost immediately, the opposition began to lose its hard-won momentum.

Later in 1997, Milošević's term as president of Serbia ran out. He became, instead, president of Yugoslavia in elections held that September. He took his power apparatus with him into the new position. This kind of transferable, informal control through party, police, and military connections is a pattern seen in other authoritarian states and has been labeled "sultanism." It was the power of the man that mattered, not the authority of the office or constitution. The September elections highlighted the divisions between the anti-Milošević forces. Some of the opposition groups boycotted this election—rendered unfair in advance by a reapportionment of seats to reduce the representation of opposition strongholds and after the fact by "phantom voting"—and by Albanians in Kosovo, who were boycotting everything because of their total loss of faith in the system after almost a decade of martial law in their province. The SPO, of course, ran, as did Hungarian and Sandžak minority parties. The SPS won its lowest number of votes ever, but it was still able to rule in coalition with Šešelj's Radicals. The opposition's divisions meant that it could not win at the polls; it was also unable to have the elections annulled because of low voter turnout.

KOSOVO IN THE LATE 1990s

The beginning of the end for the Milošević regime came when events in Kosovo began spinning out of his control. Tensions in the province had remained high since the imposition of martial law in 1989. The 1.7 million Albanian Kosovars were denied education, health care, and access to jobs in an effort to make them politically pliable. They boycotted Serbian elections, refused to pay taxes to the Serbs, and set up an underground "parallel" government of their own, in hopes of gaining international support. The most prominent politician was Ibrahim Rugova, head of the Democratic League of Kosovo (DLK). Rugova favored negotiations and nonviolent resistance against the Serbs. But there were more militant voices among the Albanians, and as the political frustration and economic misery of the region rose, so did the volume of their demands. By the mid-1990s, even Rugova was in favor of eventual secession and not just a return to the autonomy prescribed in the 1974 constitution; this course, if conscientiously followed, would eventually have brought him into even sharper conflict with Milošević. Of more immediate significance in heating up the situation were the facts that Albanians working abroad were now returning with guns and money as volunteer fighters, while the Serbian radicals were unstinting in their anti-Albanian threats.

By 1995 the Serbian population (200,000) had been augmented by the arrival of some refugees from Croatia and Bosnia. The Kosovar Serbs, well aware of the role they had played in the SPS's rise to power, continued to support Milošević, for instance by providing pro-government demonstrators at distant rallies. But after the Dayton Accords, these Serbs began to wonder if Belgrade might not jettison their cause the way it had turned its back on Serbian nationalists in Croatia and Bosnia; meanwhile, the Albanians were emboldened by hopes that the Dayton implementation process might be broadened to include their province. Eventually, they also hoped that Montenegro's drive for increased autonomy would make it easier for Kosovo to exit the federation. Many Albanians were growing increasingly restive under the leadership of Rugova, whom the international community had not supported despite all his hard work and nonviolent views.

The crisis that was to result three years later in NATO air strikes began on April 21, 1996. An Albanian student was shot and killed in a dispute with a Serb in Priština, and soon after thousands of Albanians held a demonstration to demand that his killer be punished. Much more ominous was a wave of bloody reprisals against Serb civilians and policemen, which resulted in at least six deaths. A new underground organization, the Kosova Liberation Army (KLA or UCK), founded in 1993, claimed responsibility for the killings. The KLA had taken years to coalesce from a welter of smaller groups separated by clan identity and ideology; getting weapons and military training was also very difficult. But money, guns, and volunteers stirred up by Albanian-language newspapers in Switzerland, Germany, and the United States, were flowing back to Kosovo from emigres abroad. Furthermore, there was an important connection with Albania proper: training could be carried out there, with small groups of fighters moving back and forth across the mountainous border, and when widespread rioting in Albania put thousands of weapons into circulation on the black market, the KLA was able to obtain many of them. KLA leaders such as Hashim Thaçi took advantage of Serbia's political crisis in the winter of 1996–1997, when the Serbian security forces were distracted, to organize and build up their strength.

In mid-1997, Serbs in the province formed the Serbian Resistance Movement. Their goal was to publicize the plight of the Serbs in the province and mobilize assistance against the increasing terrorism. The group was, however, surprisingly moderate in its approach, emphasizing that dialogue and compromise with the Albanians was crucial.[1] Two other important political figures of the late 1990s in Kosovo were Veton Surroi, a respected journalist and editor of Priština's daily paper *Koha Ditore*, and Adem Demaci, a writer-turned-human rights activist who has been called "the Mandela of Kosovo." Demaci, who wrote the novel *Serpents of Blood* (1958) on progressive themes, became active in the political underground in the 1950s. He was first arrested in 1964 and spent most of the next thirty years in jail. His ideas since his release have reflected the concerns of both nationalism and coexistence with the Serbs; he has been a leader in human rights monitoring and an active participant in discussions with the Serbian opposition about changing the structure of the Yugoslav federation. (After the NATO occupation of Kosovo in 1999, Demaci would stick to his unpopular position that the rights of Serbs in the province needed to be respected and that democracy needed to be created there in a multiethnic context; likewise, after the fall of Milošević in 2000, Demaci was to be the first Kosovar leader to visit Belgrade and initiate a dialogue with the new government.)

The Milošević government tried to control the situation by deflecting international concern over the mounting violence. It argued vociferously that, while it was a reliable partner in the implentation of the Dayton Accords, it would not submit its domestic problems to international meddling. Serb-controlled courts sentenced large numbers of suspected UCK operatives. Belgrade also sponsored the activities of pro-government organizations.

In November 1997, open fighting broke out between the Kosovo Liberation Movement and Serbian police in the isolated Drenica Valley. The Kosovar Albanian forces—national freedom fighters to some and brazen terrorists and thugs to others—now maintained a public profile and ef-

fectively wrested control of the Drenica region from the Serbian government. They were bolstered by large displays of public support, especially
at funerals of Albanians killed by Serbian security forces. The reluctance
of Western governments to support the Albanians merged with accusations from Serbs that the UCK were wild drug traffickers and Islamic
extremists to give Milošević a free hand to seek a military solution to
the crisis. The border with crime-ridden Albania proper was admittedly
porous. It is also unsurprising that the overwhelmingly Muslim Kosovars would also eventually accept volunteers (*mujahideen*), weapons, or
money from other Muslim countries; like the Bosnians, when the Kosovars found their plight ignored by the West, they availed themselves of
whatever help they could find. But this does not translate into being
"anti-European" agents of revolutionary theocracy. Incendiary accusations such as these merely masked the need for negotiation and
accommodation by both sides in Kosovo. Like other revolutionary movements throughout history, and especially in the twentieth century, the
UCK did not shy from murdering civilians—including Albanians whom
it viewed as traitors. It claimed, rightfully or not, that Serbian oppression
was so great that only violence could bring an answer.

In late February 1998, Milošević, gambling on Western inaction,
moved against the UCK. Dozens of Albanians and Serbs were killed in
the Drenica region. When Serbian forces finally caught up with one local
UCK leader, Adem Jashari, a huge shoot-out took place and fifty-eight
Albanians, including twenty-eight women and children, were killed at
their family compound in Donji Prekaz. Jashari had cultivated the colorful but fearsome persona and dress of a traditional *kaçak* (rebel) leader;
his violent death meant that "the KLA had gained a martyr."[2]

The crisis in the province helped solidify the new government in Belgrade into a coalition of the SPS, YUL, and Šešelj's ultranationalist radicals. Milošević cracked down on opposition media who were reporting
on the bloodshed and arranged a strange referendum to justify his tactics. On April 23, 1998, Serbs voted on whether or not they wanted "the
participation of foreign representatives" in the Kosovo crisis. This loaded
question netted the desire result (95 percent in support of the government position), giving Milošević a "mandate" to continue what was escalating into a miniature domestic war.

By the fall of 1998, NATO was once again threatening to bomb Serbia
as punishment for aggression, this time against a population group fully
within its own borders. Something like 300,000 Albanians had been
turned into refugees in their own province, fending for themselves in
squalid camps and in the mountains, in the fear that winter would bring

mass death by exposure, disease, and starvation. In October, Milošević made an agreement with NATO to pull some troops out and allow human rights monitors in, but he only slowed the Serbian offensive long enough to short-circuit the threat of air strikes. NATO negotiated with the UCK as well to try to get that group to lay down its arms. The UCK rejected the deal outright because it did not stipulate independence for Kosovo; the insurgency spread and deaths mounted. On January 15, 1999, Serbian army and paramilitary units killed forty-five people, at least some of them civilians, in the village of Račak. This gruesome incident, which drew the attention of the European monitors in Kosovo, was widely publicized and had a galvanizing effect on public opinion in the West. Like the marketplace bombing in Sarajevo in 1995, this mass killing made intervention on human rights grounds a public relations necessity for NATO governments.

The crisis peaked in February and March 1999, when Serbia refused to sign the "Rambouillet agreement," named after the French town near Paris where it was drawn up. A group of Western diplomats had invited representatives of the Serbian government and the UCK to France to hammer out an arrangement to stop the fighting for the short and the long term. It called for a great deal of autonomy for Kosovo and for the insertion of about 28,000 NATO-led troops into the province, but Serbian sovereignty was not to be abrogated—at least not immediately. The ultimate fate of Kosovo was to be decided in three years by a plebiscite on independence. The Albanians, impatient for complete victory and very mistrustful of Milošević, were barely persuaded to sign the Rambouillet agreement; the Serbs steadfastly refused to. Ignoring an eleventh-hour warning from U.S. representative Richard Holbrooke, who had distinguished himself in the Bosnia negotiations, Milošević prepared to stare down NATO over what had become for him a nonnegotiable issue. He had "bent" on other issues of international importance before, but Kosovo's weighty history and his insecurity on the increasingly tumultuous Yugoslav political scene combined to make him dig in his heels.

Once the bombings of Serbia started on March 24, ordinary Serbs also became increasingly defiant of NATO and supportive of their government. Their anger at the damage being done to their homeland was fueled by the belief that the West was selectively enforcing human rights standards, ignoring both the viciousness of UCK attacks and the massive expulsions of the Croatian Serbs in 1995.

In seventy-eight days, NATO forces dropped 23,000 bombs and missiles on Serbia, killing as many as 3,000 civilians and soldiers and causing enormous damage to buildings, roads, bridges, power plants, refineries, factories, communications centers, and other targets. (No Americans were killed by Serbian forces.) At first only military targets were hit, but Milošević dug in and tried to weather the "surgical" strikes by waiting for internal tensions among the NATO allies to pull the plug on "Operation Allied Force." Soon the bombing was greatly expanded to include a variety of targets throughout Yugoslavia; the goal was no longer just to disable the Serbian military in Kosovo, but to bruise the whole society's morale and standard of living enough to make Milošević make peace or find himself deposed. The many civilian targets hit caused uproar among Serbs and some people in the NATO countries—for instance, it was hard to see why bridges spanning the Danube in far-off Novi Sad were important to anyone's war effort, and hundreds of civilians died in damage that seemed anything but "collateral" to people on the ground. NATO mistakes included bombing a passenger train, a refugee convoy, and the Chinese Embassy in Belgrade. Serbs closed ranks, patriotically condemned the attacks, and pledged to fight to the end to defend their country. This attitude lasted for most of the campaign, although Milošević must have detected a major erosion of loyalty as well as a drastic diminution of economic potential (which he needed to fuel his patronage network) by the end; this accounted for his sudden willingness to accept NATO's terms.

In the year before the bombing started, Serbian forces had killed about 2,000 Kosovo Albanians. As we have seen, a wide-scale push to crush the increasingly assertive KLA ("Operation Horseshoe" in Serbian military parlance) was well under way. But after the NATO intervention began, the Serbs' ethnic cleansing magnified almost beyond comprehension. As many as 1.3 million Albanians were driven from their homes and approximatedly 800,000 were forced out of the country altogether.[3] Most went to Albania or Macedonia, while some went to Montenegro or even Serbia proper. Thousands were flown out of the Balkans altogether in a humanitarian airlift. The plight of these civilians, hungry and wet, leaving behind burning homes and bodies of murdered loved ones, slogging on foot through mountain passes or piling off trains in muddy no-man's-lands between border crossings, was broadcast around the world and bolstered public support for the NATO action, even though critics now claim that it was the bombing campaign that pushed Milošević into committing atrocities on a colossal scale. Some estimates are that 10,000 Albanians died during the escalated phase of Serbian attacks. So far, well over 2,000 bodies have been found. After a consensus on the number of casualties has been reached, historians will have to discuss whether the timing of the air campaign was a blunder. But the fate of Kosovo's Albanians was not likely to have been enviable, whatever NATO did, and today, most of them are back in their homes.

By the second week of May, Milošević had expressed his willingness to negotiate, and American, Russian, and European diplomats were holding talks with each other to create a united approach. In May NATO began hammering out plans for a ground invasion and the KLA resumed large-scale fighting with its force of 15,000 to 20,000 men. On May 27, Milošević and four other top Yugoslav leaders were indicted by the International Tribunal in the Hague for crimes against humanity in Kosovo. Some speculated that this move would steel his resolve to keep fighting, but others have argued that it may have pushed Milošević to make peace while he was still in control and could still protect himself with the trappings of office. Many Serbs found it hypocritical that the West would label Milošević a criminal while NATO's leaders sent bombs into civilian neighborhoods near targeted barracks, communications centers, airports and bridges.

By this point, the president of Finland, Martti Ahtisaari, and Russian Foreign Minister Viktor Chernomyrdin were meeting with Milošević in Belgrade, and the Serbian government approved NATO's peace terms on June 3. The bombings continued for another week as military leaders worked out and signed the concrete details of the cease-fire, in the form of the "Kumanovo Military-Technical Agreement." On June 10, the bombing stopped and the United Nations passed resolution 1244, which authorized the entry of 50,000 NATO-led troops (called the Kosovo Force or "KFOR"). By the end of the summer, most refugees had returned home.

After the war, the Serbian economy was totally devastated. Tens of thousands more Serbs lost their jobs, so that a total of about half of the work force was unemployed; the transportation and communications networks were wrecked. The U.S. Department of Defense claimed that it had destroyed 100 percent of Yugoslavia's petroleum refining capacity and 100 percent of the rail connections to Kosovo and Montenegro, as well as more than half of both the rail and road bridges across the Danube and the military industry and infrastructure.[4] Actual losses of Serbian tanks, trucks, and antiaircraft units seem to have been greatly overestimated by NATO officials during the war, but in all Belgrade probably lost 10 percent or more of its military hardware. Environmental damage around factories and in the Danube River is also extensive. The price tag for rebuilding Kosovo has been put at about $1 billion and for the rest of Serbia at about $100 billion.

The stated justification of Western leaders for the attacks on Kosovo and Serbia proper were twofold. On the one hand, they said that intervention was necessary to stop the slaughter and expropriation of Albanian civilians. They also stated that they acted in the interests of regional stability and NATO's credibility. But there remain many unanswered questions. Was there perhaps also the objective of removing an emboldened Milošević before he was able to wreck the peace in Bosnia or move against the Vojvodina, Montenegro, or even Macedonia? Could the refugee crisis have destabilized the Balkans enough to have brought NATO members Greece and Turkey into the conflict on different sides? Are "humanitarian interventions" becoming camouflage for national self-interest? Is the term "radical nationalist"—so often used to describe the leaders of "rogue states" such as Yugoslavia, Libya, and Iraq—being mutated into an all-purpose epithet to arouse indignation at their "unwillingness to submit to the will of the powerful" West?[5]

The war was relatively popular among the public in the United States, France, Britain, Germany, and Italy, and the Serbian maltreatment of the Albanians was well documented—as was earlier Serbian aggression in Bosnia. The earliest critical voices in the United States simply claimed that America had no vital interests in the area and thus should not risk casualties there. Such neo-isolationist views did not win out; in general the 1990s saw a diminution of the "Vietnam syndrome," which made Americans justifiably wary of getting bogged down in foreign conflicts but also made the country reluctant to use its enormous military muscle to accomplish straightforward humanitarian tasks. It should be noted that U.S. involvement in Bosnia and Kosovo has not resulted in a single American combat fatality, though there have been some deaths and injuries caused by accidents and mines.

With the arrival of nearly 50,000 foreign troops in the province—including contingents from most NATO countries, Russia, and also 6,000 from the United States—Serbia lost de facto control of Kosovo. According to United Nations Resolution 1244, no decisions are to be made on the future legal status of Kosovo until three years after democratic rule there and in Serbia. KFOR has not been able to prevent 300 or so revenge murders by Albanians against Serbs and Gypsies (who are said to have collaborated with the Serbian forces). There has been vandalism to Serbian churches and there is great fear of more once NATO leaves. About half the province's 200,000 Serbs have fled to Serbia. Bloody riots have shaken many towns, especially Mitrovica. A low "buzz" of beatings, arrests, weapons confiscations, denunciations, shootings, and bomb throwings—involving Albanians and Serbs—constantly dominates the news coming out of Kosovo. About 80 percent of the KLA was disbanded and the rest converted into the Kosovo Protection Corps, under Commander Agim Ceku. But NATO collected or confiscated mostly small arms and grenades, meaning that there is still a lot of military hardware in Albanian hands. This spells trouble for the Serbs in the long run. The Albanian spelling of the name of the province, "Kosova," is now gaining popularity among Western media and governments. Soon, the world can expect to witness an obstreperous debate in Yugoslavia and in the United Nations about what exactly "self-determination" means in Kosovo: will the "historic" rights of Serbs take precedence, even though only 2 percent of the total Serbian people lived in Kosovo before the war? Or will the "ethnic" rights of Albanians be given the green light, since their population of 1.7 million represented 90 percent of the province's prewar total? What would it mean for poor, landlocked Kosovo to be independent, since it is almost as populous as the even poorer country of Albania next door?

The goal of the international community now is to allow democracy to develop under conditions of autonomy in Kosovo. All sorts of aid from foreign governments and NGOs (non-governmental organizations) have arrived. Still, Kosovo's history of underdevelopment and over-population makes economic prospects dim, even apart from the confusion over its future legal status. Serbs are uniformly adamant in their determination to retain at least titular control over Kosovo, while the Albanians there just as vehemently refuse to consider ever living under Serbian rule again. For the international community, the easiest solution is obviously for the new democratic government in Serbia to agree to give the Kosovars broad autonomy, and for the Albanians, in turn, to forego independence or enosis with troubled Albania. The recent electoral victories of Koštunica (Yugoslavia), Djindjić (Serbia), and Rugova (Kosovo), along with the cooperation in Kosovo of the usually moderate or pragmatic Serbian National Council (headed for its first year by Momcilo Trajkovi and Bishop Artemije), bode well for a dialogue. But no one is yet promising to compromise. It could be a long haul for the peacekeepers in Kosovo, and the effort could falter if the new U.S. President George W. Bush should attempt to "europeanize" the issue and pull out American troops.

OPPOSITION TO WESTERN INVOLVEMENT IN THE BALKANS

From scholars such as Noam Chomsky of the United States to writers such as Peter Handke of Austria, many people in Western Europe and

North America opposed NATO's intervention in Kosovo and, to a lesser extent, President Clinton's efforts to create a settlement in Bosnia. There were many reasons for this opposition, most of them, frankly, having nothing to do with pro-Serbian feelings. Many outsiders believed, erroneously, that the history of the Balkans and the motives of its peoples are too complex to understand. Another set of myths used to support noninvolvement claims that all Balkan peoples are equally guilty for the war, that they are all similarly murderous and unreliable, that the Bosnian nightmare was a civil war and thus off-limits to the international community, and that the (supposedly) "ancient ethnic hatreds" in the region would make choosing sides or reaching a peaceful settlement impossible.

Many pacifist voices have also been raised, reminding the world of an important moral and ethical issue: Can humans really use war to make peace? Can violence effectively stop violence, or does it perpetuate itself against our best intentions? NATO's right to attack a sovereign state, Serbia, because of its behavior to its own province of Kosovo has been often, and justifiably, called into question since the bombing campaign of 1999.

Germany's participation in the recent actions in the Balkans has upset some Europeans—not least among them Germans. They fear a reawakening of aggressiveness and militarism in the prosperous and newly reunified Germany, which since 1990 is once again the largest country in Europe west of Russia. Some critics—Michael Ignatieff and Zbigniew Brzezinski among them—have even focused on the nature of military technology. The sophisticated electronic hardware used by NATO forces—which let the destruction shower down on Serbia from ships safely offshore and from planes flying at 15,000 feet—shows that it is possible for the rich countries of the world to destroy more people and infrastrucure than ever before. The fact that countries can be so massively assaulted with ever fewer NATO lives being put at risk adds another concern: that such force is more likely to be used than in the past. Finally, some observers in the West, such as the Austrian novelist Peter Handke, have rebelled against the "feeding frenzy" of the Western news media that they claim have presented the Serbs in an unfair light.

It is important to remember, however, that the violence in Kosovo and Bosnia had long been of great interest to international human rights groups. The overwhelming verdict coming from these private-sector watchdog groups is that the majority of atrocities were committed by Serbian forces. Groups from Amnesty International to Doctors without Borders agree on this. The Croats, Bosnians, and Kosovars have also committed atrocities, and grave abuses have been inflicted upon Serbian populations and their property. War crimes are never justified. But does the fact that all groups have committed some of them truly render unnecessary a frank analysis of who escalated the conflict to the level of violence, who prolonged it, and who profited from it the most, until international intervention altered the equation?

The wars have divided world popular opinion. Pleas for understanding, sympathy, and even apologia for the Serbian side were especially abundant in the early 1990s. Having fought against the Germans—and thus on the side of the British, French, and Americans—in both World Wars, Serbs had a positive reputation and a reservoir of goodwill in most parts of the world. Famous travel writers such as Rebecca West also helped shape a very favorable image of Serbs; her monumental classic *Black Lamb, Grey Falcon* (1940) written as the Nazi danger loomed ever larger over Europe, praised Serbs as resolute defenders of freedom and virile opponents of tyranny.

NOTES

1. Robert Thomas, *The Politics of Serbia in the 1990s* (New York: Columbia University Press, 1999), p. 401.

2. Tim Judah, *Kosovo: War and Revenge* (New Haven, CT: Yale University Press, 2000), p. 140.

3. Ivo H. Daalder and Michael E. O'Hanlon, *Winning Ugly: NATO's War to Save Kosovo* (Washington, D.C.: Brookings Institution Press, 2000), p. 200.

4. Ibid., p. 3.

5. Noam Chomsky, *Rogue States: The Rule of Force in World Affairs* (Cambridge, MA: South End Press, 2000), p. 19.

12

After Milošević: A New Beginning

THE FEDERAL ELECTIONS OF SEPTEMBER 2000

In late July of 2000, Milošević called a federal election for September 24. He was eager to propel himself into the new category of president provided for by his constitutional amendments. Elections would also be held for the federal parliament seated in Belgrade. In early August the various parties began announcing their candidates. Milošević, of course, was the candidate for the Socialist Party of Serbia. The little-known mayor of Belgrade, Vojislav Mihajlović, was nominated by Drašković's Serbian Renewal Movement; this was considered a weak choice for that party. Despite the fact that he is the grandson of the famous Draža Mihajlović of World War II, he is little known himself aside from rumors of corruption. The most important electoral news, even before his eventual victory, was the nomination of constitutional lawyer Vojislav Koštunica to run for the coalition known as the Democratic Opposition of Serbia (DOS). That this grouping of fifteen—eventually eighteen—parties could finally settle on just one candidate meant that the opposition might finally be able to marshal enough votes to turn out Milošević. Infighting among the small opposition parties in previous elections has been frequently cited as one of the reasons for the failure to send Milošević packing; the opposition, and its foreign backers such as the United States, were buoyed by the Koštunica nomination, even though he was known as a strong nationalist himself. There were also more problems that DOS might face in the future, such as the lack of political experience of many of its members and the uncertainty of its appeal outside large metropolitan centers such as Belgrade and Novi Sad. The opposition summed up its plans for change in a program entitled "Contract with Serbia," which focused on instituting the rule of law and democracy. It is important to stress that much of the Serbian opposition was "nationalistic" and also that Serbs could not be expected to be anything but nationalistic. Most Serbs see their country as being in a life-or-death crisis, and the citizens of any country in such a position would act in "nationalistic" ways. Whatever the demographics of Kosovo, any student of diplomatic history can tell you that countries never voluntarily give up land. During the campaign, Milošević was characterized not only as a criminal in his behavior toward other Serbs, but also as an unsuccessful nationalist with regard to the recent conflicts in which Serbia has been embroiled.

Milošević evidently believed that he would win the election. But he also took underhanded steps to ensure his victory. Had he known just how soundly he was to be defeated at the polls, however, he might have taken even nastier measures against his opponents or engineered a crisis big enough to warrant calling off the election altogether. In vintage Milošević form, the manipulation of public information and low-grade terror were the hallmarks of the regime's interaction with Serbia's stunted democracy. Opposition activists, especially students, were often harrassed and arrested. Independent-minded journalists were jailed for supposed treason or libel and often labeled the "stooges" of Western powers. As if to prove that Milošević's strong hand was needed against the forces of international conspiracy, Dutch, Canadian, and British citizens were arrested on technicalities and charged with espionage.

The elections were held, as scheduled, on September 24, amid reports of widespread irregularities. By the next day, Koštunica was claiming victory over Milošević by a margin of 55 percent to 34 percent. Meanwhile, Deputy Prime Minister Nikola Sainović stated that Milošević had won by a margin of 45 percent to 40 percent. International commentators noticed that the Federal Election Commission (FEC) had suspended work earlier than expected on election day, perhaps indicating a wish to slow down the tabulation and dissemination of unfavorable results. The dispute over the percentages of the vote was to last another two weeks, but the SRS and SPO were already getting in touch with the seemingly victorious DOS and the ever-unpredictable Drašković said that not joining the opposition coalition had been a mistake. That same day, from his home in London, Crown Prince Aleksandar Karađorđević urged Milošević to accept the people's wishes and step down; his was but the most prominent in a crescendoing chorus of such voices that included Montenegrin President Djukanović and the moderate Bosnian Serb leader Milorad Dodik. One of Milošević's chief associates, Yugoslav Prime Minister Momir Bulatović, resigned because of his boss's poor electoral showing in Montenegro, where only 24 percent of eligible voters even went to the polls.

The day-to-day tide of events rolled on, and tension rose inside Serbia as the world watched developments turning against Milošević. How would the autocrat react? Would he sweep the opposition from the streets, flee to some country where he had his millions stashed, or be swept away in a Ceauşescu-like bloodbath? On September 26, Serbian Archbishop Pavle recognized Koštunica as the winner even as the FEC claimed that Koštunica had indeed led Milošević in the voting by 48 percent to 40 percent, but that since neither candidate passed 50 percent, a run-off election would be necessary on October 8. Political leaders in France, Germany, and the United States were already beginning to talk about lifting sanctions and sending millions of dollars in aid to a newly democratic Serbia. Koštunica wisely rejected, with complete firmness, the possibility of any run-off election. Delaying a final decision in the presidential contest would have simply given Milošević time to harass and divide his opponents, to bolster his own profile through dramatic actions to resolve some self-created crisis or through the distribution of largesse and favors, or to cancel the elections on the grounds of national security.

On the next day, demonstrations began in the streets of Belgrade and other Serbian cities. Tens upon tens of thousands of protestors, once again, called for Milošević to step down. DOS was now citing an electoral victory of 52.5 percent to 35 percent. Koštunica made public statements that were both brave and clever: he refused to make any deals with Milošević, but he also stroked the egos of the Serbian military. He said he did not fear a massacre of demonstrators because these same security forces that had fought so bravely in the recent war over Kosovo would not fire on their own people. Over the next several days, strikes broke out across the country and Russian President Vladimir Putin, who was growing ambivalent in his support of Milošević, offered to send mediators to work with Milošević and Koštunica.

On October 2, a general strike began across Serbia. Police did little to prevent or contain the manifestations of dissent, and photographs of heavily armed riot police chatting casually with demonstrators were seized upon by the Western media as indications that the regime's grip was weakening. Major strikes froze work at refineries and coal mines, most notably at Kolubara, south of Belgrade. By this time, Milošević was rapidly losing control of previously loyal media as well. Two days later, the last gasps of the regime began. In a desperate maneuver, the highest court in Yugoslavia, known as the Constitutional Court, declared that new elections were necessary. The thought that victory might slide down the drain brought hundreds of thousands of Serbs into the streets on October 5. Belgrade was teeming with as many as 500,000 protestors. Tens of thousands of people drove to the capital from other Serbian cities for maximum effect. Equally dramatic were the events at the Kolubara coal mines—the site termed "our Gdańsk" by one local opposition leader (a reference to the Polish shipyards where the Solidarity labor movement was born). Riot police turned up to force the workers back to their jobs. Instead, 25,000 protestors also showed up and forced the police to leave. By the end of the day, protestors had braved walls of tear gas and stormed the federal parliament in Belgrade and the official radio and television studios. These buildings were damaged and some people—on both sides—were beaten. But now-President Koštunica was able to address the crowds from the balcony of Parliament and *Politika*, formerly a solid pro-Milošević daily, referred to him as "President."

That night the streets remained full of jubilant Serbs who basically felt that they were safeguarding their revolution. Praise for the change of power flowed from foreign capitals in unstinted measure. News commentators in America were quick to refer to the events as "Serbia's version of 1989," referring to the final ouster of authoritarian communist governments in other East European countries after the fall of the Berlin Wall and the multiparty elections in Hungary and Poland.

The next day, Friday, October 6, brought a reversal by the Constitutional Court, which now declared the election valid and endorsed Koštunica's victory. Milošević met with Russian Foreign Minister Igor Ivanov, then with Koštunica; despite widespread concern that he still had the plans and means to undermine the election, he conceded his loss. But he did not leave the country, and his party quickly began reshuffling its leaders and preparing for elections. Just how much unseen power—for corruption and obstruction and perhaps terror—the SPS retained and would use to fracture DOS remained to be seen. But the military did not intervene, and perhaps the most important military figure in the country, chief-of-staff Nebojša Pavković, even congratulated Koštunica. Showdowns were sure to occur later, if DOS tried to shake up the military structure and move in officers more compatible with its ideas, but for now the military leadership was at least publicly acquiescing in the arrival of new civilian bosses. In dicey transitions of power like this one, announcements of congratulations from potential foes can be read as endorsements of the new status quo. Thus Koštunica's power can be seen to have been spreading through the rest of the government on this day, since the governor of the National Bank and the president of the Serbian Parliament indicated their acceptance of the election results. Two of the British citizens and one Canadian recently arrested on espionage charges were released, and Russian President Putin finally sent an official message of congratulations.

The most important formal event of Saturday, October 7, involved Parliament, which met—not in its own building because of the riot damage, but rather in the large "Sava" conference center in another part of the city—to inaugurate Koštunica. Milošević's wife, who won a seat in Parliament on the ticket of the United Yugoslav Left, did not attend the ceremony; meanwhile, her son Marko and his family flew to Moscow, where Milošević's brother, Borislav, was ambassador. Milošević himself was only making bland utterances to the effect that he appreciated being relieved of the burden of running the country and that he now hoped to spend more time with his family.

By Monday, October 9, the lifting of oil and air traffic sanctions was under way; Western governments indicated that they would soon be lifting visa restrictions on Yugoslavs (except Milošević's allies accused of war crimes or corruption) and unfreezing assets abroad. Very quickly, procedures were to begin for restoring full diplomatic relations with Belgrade and readmitting Yugoslavia to the Organization for Security and Cooperation in Europe, the European Council, the International Monetary Fund, the World Bank, the World Trade Organization, and to the United Nations, from which it had been excluded in June of 1992. At this point, the anti-Milošević currents reached beyond the federal government and began to affect the Serbian republican government. This was a logical development when one remembers that Belgrade was both the federal and republican capital, and far and away the dominant metropolitan area in the entire country. The Serbian government actually resigned; new elections were called for late December, and negotiations among the various parties began for the construction of some sort of caretaker government.

After the fall of Milošević and the outpouring of international support for Koštunica, the Serbian political scene was dominated by five major sets of concerns: the future of the Yugoslav federation involving Montenegro; the status of Kosovo and neighboring regions; a worsening energy crisis; the future of Slobodan Milošević, especially in regard to his indictment by the Hague Tribunal; and Serbia's republican elections, scheduled for December 23, 2000, which would present an opportunity for DOS to solidify its hold on police, media, and economic power bases.

As Serbia moved into the winter of 2000–2001, its electrical power situation grew increasingly grim. There was, of course, lingering damage from NATO's seventy-eight-day bombing campaign in 1991. But the country was also in a drought that began in early 2000 and affected generating plants, especially hydroelectric ones. Yugoslavia's disastrous balance of trade induced Russian gas companies, which supply most of the country's energy imports, to reduce deliveries by about 25 percent because of unpaid bills. Some observers worried that perhaps company managers loyal to Milošević were handicapping the country's power production in order to embarrass Koštunica. Unemployment was running at abou 40 percent and the country had a huge foreign debt of over $12 billion.

Another issue that was important at this time was the so-called "Balkan Syndrome." This was, purportedly, a medical phenomenon relating to the harmful after-effects of NATO ammunition containing depleted uranium. Tens of thousands of such shells were used against Serbs in Bosnia and in Kosovo; their purpose is not to spread radioactivity, but to enhance the armor-penetrating capability. In late 2000, several Italian soldiers who had served in Bosnia died of leukemia, and there was widespread worry in NATO countries that their deaths were caused by exposure to depleted uranium. Most NATO countries began medical screenings of their personnel and launched investigations of conditions in the Balkans; the United Nations continued its environmental assessment of the war in Serbia and Kosovo. Some NATO countries even tried, unsuccessfully, to put in place a ban on the use of such munitions until investigations were complete. The United States insisted that the weapons could not have serious health effects, but many people—not least of all Serbs, who will of course be exposed to far more of the dust than NATO soldiers in the long run—wondered if a case could be made for banning such weapons under international laws protecting civilians during war. Meanwhile, a bewildering variety of rumors circulated, some labeling the uranium scare a ruse to justify the early departure of American troops and others calling it a Milošević-era ploy to make the NATO bombing raids look even nastier than they were.

WHO IS VOJISLAV KOŠTUNICA?

The man who has emerged as the new president of Yugoslavia is a complex figure with a long history of public involvement. While Zoran Djindjić has been the single most active and prominent figure in the anti-Milošević opposition of the past ten years, Koštunica, a constitutional lawyer, emerged in the summer of 2000 as a kind of "supra-party" compromise candidate on whom the many various groupings within DOS could agree. He coauthored a book on dissent in the early Tito years (released in the United States in 1985 as *Party Pluralism or Monism: Social Movements and the Political System in Yugoslavia, 1944–1949*) and is reputed to be a scandal-free, honest, and relatively moderate politician given both to pragmatism and scrupulous respect for the rule of law. Most of these qualities, of course, set him far apart from most of the political class in the Milošević regime. One often hears it stated in the Western press as well that Koštunica is a "nationalist." This term is only of limited use in describing Koštunica, who reminds Westerners that he is a "nationalist" in the same way an American or German or Spanish or any other politician is a "nationalist": he puts his country's interests first. All this means is that he, like most Serbs, believes that Serbia probably got the short end of the stick in the breakup of Yugoslavia and that it is right and natural for the Serbs—and their government—to be concerned about the welfare of their co-nationals living in Croatia and Bosnia. It also means that he (again, like nearly all Serbs) appreciates the historical and cultural significance of Kosovo to his country's identity and that he resents the suffering the NATO air war brought to his country. As a scholar, Koštunica is doubtless also aware that NATO's intervention in Kosovo can be disputed on the basis of international law and that, more generally, governments never give up territory willingly, so the Serbian desire to retain Kosovo should not be written off by the West as some sort of historical obsession or ethnic fanaticism. While sharing in the basic Serbian consensus on these issues, Koštunica can nonetheless be said to differ from the politicians of the country's other main parties—the SPS, the SPO, and the SRS—in terms of his probity and of what one might call his "procedural moderation," that is, his search for just and appropriate methods to reach his goals. Koštunica seems to stand for a rejection of the maxim that "the end justifies the means." Time will tell if this is so.

Although Koštunica is universally seen as an enormous improvement over Milošević and Serbs seem to appreciate his bold statements and his boundless confidence, his young government faces a number of serious issues and problems. Simply heading up DOS when Milošević tumbled from power will not be enough to earn Koštunica his spot in history. He must deal effectively with a long list of challenges such as gaining international acceptance and assistance for his country and fighting the corruption, cronyism, and violence that has increased enormously in Serbia of late. Before he can begin to reform the Yugoslav economy in the direction of a post-communist transition, he must rebuild it; sadly, Serbia and Montenengro have been rocked by three massive waves of dislocation, starting with the disruptions caused by the breakup of Yugoslavia, continuing through the decade of sanctions, and climaxing in the war over Kosovo. He must hold the DOS coalition together, because Milošević's Socialist Party of Serbia is still the biggest single vote getter in Yugoslavia, and he must find enough politically savvy, loyal administrators to put his ideas into force. And he will have to work assiduously for the return both of Serbian security forces (which would reassert Belgrade's sovereignty over the region) and of Serbian refugees (on humanitarian grounds) to Kosovo.

The United States and its allies are watching eagerly to see whether Koštunica assists the Hague Tribunal in prosecuting indicted war criminals, including Slobodan Milošević and Radovan Karadžić. So far, Koštunica has refused even to recognize the validity of the International Court of Justice. He claims that its motives are unacceptably politicized and that Yugoslavia is not allowed to extradite its citizens. Still, his government has allowed the court to open an office in Belgrade and he grudgingly met with chief prosecutor Carla del Ponte in Belgrade in January 2001. Serbia's neighbors, especially Bosnia and Croatia, are eager to hear Koštunica admit Serbian guilt in starting the wars that raged there from 1991 to 1995. Although he has said he regrets the human rights abuses that occurred in those wars and made his intention clear not to repeat them, Koštunica ascribes to the "equality of blame" thesis, abjuring special Serbian responsibility. He has also raised questions about the "legality" of the 1995 Dayton peace accords. He is also now greatly concerned with preventing the secession of Montenegro. Meanwhile, he will not be able to make progress on any of these issues if he does not have effective control of and cooperation with the Yugoslav and Serbian governments. It is not yet known if he has powerful opponents in the police, army, and economic sectors. It also remains to be seen whether his previous support for Serbian separatists in Bosnia and his current denial of Kosovo's right to secession will undermine his ability to bring peace to the Balkans. He has admitted that Serbia's behavior is now the major factor in equations of war and peace in the region.

Koštunica's attitude toward the United States and Russia is also complex. He makes no secret of his anger at the NATO countries, and there is no reason to think that he sports this anger simply for public consumption. Strong statements about NATO and Kosovo without a doubt increase his popularity with Serbs but also seem to be more than the product of calculation: Koštunica seems viscerally angry over what he might call his country's manhandling by the West. He also shares in a certain kind of traditional Serbian historical and literary Russophilia and has stated that he admires the writing of Alexander Solzhenitsyn, a Nobel Prize-winning Russian author who is known not only for his literary craftmanship and his criticism of the communist dictatorship in the Soviet Union, but also for his censure of the materialism and moral laxness of democratic capitalist countries.

One of the biggest issues that Serbia faces as it moves toward greater integration into Europe has nothing to do with Koštunica: the creation of a political atmosphere in which process is valued as much as result and in which goals other than traditionally conceived nationalism stir public enthusiasm and command the long-term attention of the government. In short, Serbia needs to be concerned about more than just its borders and its outlying population groups. It needs socioeconomic development and friendly relations with its neighbors. In order to get sustained international cooperation and to mature into a full-fledged and stable democracy, Serbs will at some point need to come to terms with the role of the Milošević regime and its supporters in the recent wars. As one leading observer of the Serbian scene has put it, "If anything, most Serbs' problem with Milošević is not that he started wars but rather that he lost them."[1] Corroboration for this view comes from the fact that, even among Serbs who want the leaders of the previous regime put on trial, Milošević and his clique are hardly viewed as war criminals. Rather, they are seen as subverters of Serbian democracy and as failed leaders who exploited their constituencies through corruption, duplicity, terror, and inefficiency. There are exceptions, of course, among civic leaders, the new government officials from DOS, and the public at large. Once again, Zoran Djindjić seems to have said it best when he noted recently that the biggest political wish of most Serbs, to forget the past ten years, cannot and should not come true. The ideal settling of accounts with the Milošević period can only occur once he is off the political scene for good and once Serbs are willing to heal the international, as well as the domestic, scars of his aggression. It will be very interesting to observe how Koštunica balances his strong personality and unabashed patriotism with the many political demands now being placed on him. In the following typical statement, however, one can certainly see a heartening combination of pragmatism and honesty: "This is not Greater Yugoslavia or Greater Serbia. This is Real Serbia, cut to the measure of our interests, values, abilities, ambitions, and wishes."[2]

THE MONTENEGRIN PROBLEM

One of the thorniest issues facing Serbs was the status of Montenegro. In practical terms, the Montenegrin republic was a junior partner to the Serbs in the Federal Republic of Yugoslavia. It made up less than a tenth of the Yugoslav population and its people had traditionally considered themselves cousins (if not closer relatives) of the Serbs. Montenegro is also a poor region. It has a significant Albanian majority and a smaller Slavic Muslim one as well, in the Montenegrin portion of the historical region known as the Sandžak. Long controlled by Milošević ally Momir Bulatović (who was the ill-fated Yugoslav prime minister during the federal elections of 2000), Montenegro plunged into uncharted political territory around 1997 when a reform-minded politician named Milo Djukanović was elected president. Working with the new prime minister, Filip Vujanović, Djukanović began gradually loosening Podgorica's ties to the federal government in Belgrade.

During the war of Kosovo (March–June 1999), NATO planes hit only a few—and exclusively military—targets in Montenegro, because Djukanović had become such an ardent critic of Milošević. Throughout 1999 and 2000, the Montenegrins—always to the accompaniment of protests and threats from Serbs—began distancing themselves from the Milošević-dominated Yugoslavia in other ways. Perhaps the most important steps they took were opening diplomatic offices abroad and rejecting the Yugoslav *dinar* for the German *mark* for their local currency. Even though moves such as these helped to stabilize Montenegro's economy and put them in a position to win even more sympathy and attention abroad, not all Montenegrins favored this higher, autonomous profile. Djukanović and his company of reporters were walking through a political minefield, especially because Western support was unlikely to include military protection should Milošević intervene with security forces or the army. Still, the government in Podgorica enjoyed fairly warm relations with the NATO countries and a tentative, but pathbreaking, relationship with the Albanian government in Tirana.

The government of Milošević set off one minor crisis after another in Montenegro, and there were constant conflicts over who should be running the customs and border control stations and military airports. There were naval provocations on the Adriatic Sea and Lake Scutari. Since Djukanović only has a small police force to protect him, he is trying to limit the presence of the federal armed forces in his republic. He seemed to live in constant fear of a putsch by forces loyal to Milošević. Even holding his country together was a challenge: certain clans in the north of Montenegro, long known for their fiery, independent behavior, have threatened to secede back to Serbia should Djukanović seek independence; meanwhile, efforts in the assembly to strengthen the legal status and raise consciousness about "Montenegrin" citizenship (as opposed to Serbian or Yugoslav) were barely under way. But the government of Montenegro has participated in regional meetings with Slovene, Bosnian, and Croatian leaders; abolished many visa requirements for visiting Westerners; and announced that it will field its own Olympic team by 2004 and its own Balkan League basketball team sooner than that. Montenegro has also moved further than Serbia in privatizing its state-owned and socially-owned property and has a better recent record on human rights and media freedom. The United States and its allies have exempted Montenegro from some of the sanctions placed on the rest of Yugoslavia, and some Serbian businesses have relocated there to take advantage of the business climate. But Milošević actually put in place an economic embargo against Montenegro to punish it for its growing autonomy. Still worse, the violence and bizarreness of Serbian politics frequently spilled over into Montenegro, as when the mercurial Serbian politician Vuk Drašković survived an assassination attempt in his house on the coast in 1999. Two brothers from Belgrade were suspected of the crime, but their motives were unclear. Drašković, originally a writer of historical novels and now the head of the Serbian Renewal Movement has a history of run-ins with Milošević, of surviving assassination attempts, and of incendiary political commentary.

Perhaps the most daring move that President Djukanović made in 2000, however, was his meeting with the Croatian president Stipe Mesić in Cavtat, a suburb of the beautiful Croatian coastal city of Dubrovnik. In the fall of 1991, Dubrovnik's suburbs had been plundered by Montenegrins, and the city itself was badly shelled. In June 2000, however, Djukanović apologized to Croatians for the emotional and physical damage done by Montenegrin soldiers at this time. Later, the president even offered unspecified monetary reparations. The Milošević government was outraged, because it admits to no aggression against Croatia. This was an important confidence-building measure vis-à-vis other European countries, even though many Croats at the time wanted even more, such as an admission that the Croatian secession had been justified and that

a promise that Djukanović would help round up war criminals sought
for trial in the Hague.

After Milošević pushed devastating constitutional amendments
through the Yugoslav parliament in July 2000, laws that would drastically undermine Montenegrin autonomy, Djukanović declared that as far
as he was concerned, Yugoslavia had ceased to exist.[3] He urged Montenegrins to boycott the September elections and incurred the mystified
ire of most Serbian oppositionists, who urged him to support their unified platform known as the DOS. This opposition group—a loose grouping of small parties—won the election, as we have seen, without
Montenegrin help. Milošević has been sidelined, but now relations continue to cool between Belgrade and Podgorica, even though the two governments seem to share a lot of ideological ground.

After the election of Koštunica, which Djukanović greeted lukewarmly,
Montenegro began moving toward a referendum on the question of independence. The Montenegrin president sees the new Yugoslav president as pretending that their relationship can be patched up as usual
and as dead wrong in his assertion that Montenegrin independence is
out of the question; after all, the Montenegrin constitution does allow
for secession from Yugoslavia if it is the will of the people. His government made announcements to the effect that the current arrangements
were only provisional until either a new federal relationship could be
hammered out between full equals or the two states broke apart entirely.
Bolstered by opinion polls that showed nearly half the Montenegrins in
favor of independence (with 40 percent against), Djukanović declared
that the two countries should seek separate seats in the United Nations.
He also committed himself to making some sort of limited, functional
alliance afterwards, though, a move that is strongly favored by most
Montenegrins. The Montenegrin president, along with Prime Minister
Vujanović and the leader of the republican assembly, held numerous
meetings with Koštunica in the months after the federal elections. The
federal president did see fit to address one of the Montenegrins' chief
security concerns: he abolished the 7th Military Police Battalion, a force
of about 1,000 pro-Milošević soldiers first put together in 1999 to pressure Djukanović into submission. The Montenegrins also demanded the
removal of several pro-Milošević generals.

In early 2001, Djukanović even stated that a referendum would definitely be held by June 2001, and if the results were negative, he would
resign. Koštunica, an avowed opponent of Podgorica's secession, continues to attempt to engage the half-rebellious republic in dialogue about
future constitutional arrangements. The existing Yugoslav constitution

also calls for a Montenegrin delegate to the Federal Assembly to be prime minister if the president is Serbian; thus, Koštunica was considering naming a politician from Montenegro's Socialist People's Party (SPP) to that post. This presented further problems for Djukanović, since his "Coalition for a Better Life" did not participate in the September elections and has no delegates in the federal assembly; the SPP is Djukanović's main competition inside Montenegro. A final consideration for Djukanović in the postelection period is whether his republic's stint as "the darling of the West" is now over, since Serbia itself is now well on the way toward reform; in early 2001 he began to come under NATO pressure to cooperate more fully with Koštunica. Rumors began circulating that Djukanović was tied to smuggling or even war crimes. Evidently, NATO support for Montenegrin independence can be read as a barometer of the alliance's confidence in Koštunica's cooperation. At this point, it would seem that the chances are tilted rather against a Montenegrin exit from Yugoslavia. Meanwhile, the Montenegrin experiment is producing echoes elsewhere in the region. In the Vojvodina, north of Belgrade, where the "Montenegrin model" has recently been touted as a template for its own possible autonomization or secession, radical reformers have a much steeper row to hoe. Despite the presence of a large and well-organized Hungarian minority, the Vojvodina has long belonged to Serbia proper (and not just to the federal entity of Yugoslavia). Kosovo—or the southern part of it—is the most likely region to depart from Yugoslav and Serbia in the near future.

KOŠTUNICA IN ACTION

Anyone expecting a quick and far-reaching "revolution" in Yugoslavia after Milošević's fall met with quick disappointment. It is debatable, even, whether or not the events of the autumn of 2000 can be called "Serbia's 1989," in reference to the raft of changes that swept almost all of Eastern Europe's communist parties from power more than a decade ago: Serbia had already changed enormously since the days of the communist monopoly on power, and Yugoslavia (in its meaningful and original forms) had long since disappeared.

Against the backdrop of continued unrest in Kosovo, the spillover of hostilities into the Preševo region, and the uncertain status of Milošević, his associates, and their fortunes presumed to be abroad, Koštunica took many concrete—if small and sometimes controversial—steps aimed at stabilizing Serbia. He released imprisoned journalists and some Albanian activists, such as the poet and doctor Flora Brovina. His general amnesty for deserters and draft evaders was also a positive step toward erasing some of the scars of the 1990s, but it also created problems for Koštunica: he came under fire in the West for not pardoning the approximately 700 Albanians still being held on political charges, and there were riots in the three largest Serbian prisons, evidently by common criminals who felt the amnesty should apply to them as well. He met many foreign leaders and envoys, including the U.S. ambassador to the United Nations, Richard Holbrooke, who had played such a pivotal role in U.S. Balkan policy under President Clinton. He negotiated constantly, though usually unfruitfully, with the Montenegrin leadership. Although Koštunica agreed to meet with Albanian leaders from Kosovo, he avoided meeting U.S. Secretary of State Madeleine Albright in Vienna.

The victory of DOS at the federal level in September represented, in effect, a vote of no-confidence in the Milošević-dominated republican government in Serbia. This was an important ripple effect because Serbia dominated the federation, and politics in the two entities were not really separable. Representatives of the major parties agreed to hold new Serbian elections on December 23, 2000. But it was also decided to scrap the existing Serbian government—or at least much of it—in favor of a compromise "caretaker" administration. Here DOS agreed to work with the discredited parties of Milošević and Vuk Drašković. Milan Milutinović, the president of Serbia, refused to step down and was not pressured to do so by Koštunica, even though he had been indicted as a war criminal; evidently Milutinović was cooperating with DOS despite his associations with the previous regime. But the prime minister was replaced on October 24, 2000, and the ministerial portfolios were apportioned among the SPS (12), DOS (6), and SPO (6). The new prime minister remained an SPS member, while there were deputy prime ministers from the other two parties and joint administration of the ministries controlling the police, judicial system, and finances. Many outside observers felt that this system allowed Milošević and his associates to retain far too much power and possibly to earn renewed legitimacy in the public's eye.

In contrast to the provisional Serbian government, the elected DOS federal government acted strongly on its mandate. By early November, the important positions of foreign minister, interior minister, and justice minister had gone to loyal DOS leaders Goran Svilanović (Civic Alliance of Serbia), Zoran Živković (the mayor of Niš), and Momčilo Grubac, respectively. The new governor of the National Bank is Mladjan Dinkić, a prominent member of the Serbian economic think tank called G-17. Numerous portfolios went to Montenegrins, such as the prime ministership (required by law if the president is a Serb) and the ministries of defense and finance. In general, these men are not the most reform-minded, since they are members of the Montenegrin branch of the SPS; Djukanović's party boycotted the elections and was not eligible for appointments. Koštunica did not carry out a general housecleaning of the police or military, a policy epitomized by his leaving in place the security chief Rade Marković and the army's chief of staff Nebojša Pavković. Koštunica may have been trying to win such powerful men over to his side, whereas sacking them might have provoked rebellion, but he irritated many of his supporters by letting so many Milošević allies keep their jobs. In January 2001, he eventually ousted several prominent members of the military's "old guard" such as former Defense Minister Dragoljub Ojdanić; DOS also promised to cut the heavily armed Serbian police forces, which had functioned as Milošević's well-supplied praetorian guard, by two thirds. His government initiated criminal investigations of the former heads of the information ministry, the customs agency, and the electoral commission.

Meanwhile, Milošević did not exactly disappear from the political scene in humiliation, as one might expect. Several prominent figures from the SPS retired or founded new parties, and the SPS itself broke its long-standing alliance with the YUL. But, despite rumors that he would step down, Milošević was reelected party leader in late November and made a speech roundly condemning his long list of foes from the Hague to the former oppositionists (now the leaders of the federal government). He appeared on television and met twice with Koštunica. It remains to be seen if Milošević still commands a powerful following. The prospects for Mira Marković's YUL look even worse. After some delay she showed up in the Federal Assembly to take her seat as a delegate, but from her party headquarters have come other politicians' more vituperative speeches and news of defections.

The heavily monitored republican elections in Serbia on December 23 resulted, not surprisingly, in a clear victory for the DOS slate. They won 65 percent of the vote and 176 of the 250 seats in the assembly. It would be easier to hail this result as a splendid victory for democracy and stability if DOS were not an eighteen-party coalition, but the biggest single party remained the SPS with 14 percent, or thirty-seven seats. The Serbian Radicals, led by Vojislav Šešelj, who was recently removed from his professorship at Belgrade University and harrassed in public by demonstrators but is still a member of Parliament, brought in 8.6 percent, or twenty-three seats. Finishing astonishingly high was the dark-horse Party of Serbian Unity (SSJ), founded by the now-dead paramilitary leader Arkan and headed by Borislav Pelević; the SSJ finished with 5.3 percent, or fourteen seats. The overall picture left by these election results is a sobering one: parties steeped in the aggression and corruption of the recent past won 28 percent of the popular vote. The installation of the new government was delayed by the necessity for a revote in nineteen precincts.

On January 22, the new Parliament was seated. Zoran Djindjić, the longtime dissident who had been Koštunica's campaign manager in the federal elections, took office as prime minister and immediately begin sparring with his former boss; while not budging on the issue of Kosovo, Djindjić did take a more cooperative stance with the Hague Tribunal about possible extraditions, as did the new justice minister, Vladan Batić. Interior Minister Dušan Mihajlović said that he was placing Milošević under round-the-clock surveillance and that he would have no problem arresting him; he also said that he wants to open the secret police files on Serbian citizens and eliminate the police's political functions. The new speaker of the Serbian Parliament was Dragan Marsičanin. The Djindjić government also had the cooperation of the Hungarian minority in Vojvodina, as Jozsef Kasza became a deputy prime minister.

On January 23, the chief prosecutor for the Hague Tribunal, Carla del Ponte, arrived in Belgrade. Her meeting with Koštunica was as stormy and unproductive as expected. She adamantly refused to allow Milošević to be tried in Yugoslavia and hinted that she might find it easier to arrange his extradition through Serbian Prime Minister Djindjić than through Koštunica. During her stay in Serbia she met with Serbs from Kosovo, families of war victims from 1999, and political leaders such as Djindjić and Dinkić.

SERBIAN CULTURE IN THE NEW MILLENNIUM

The sanctions against Serbia in the 1990s had the unfortunate effect of cutting off Serbian artists, actors, musicians, and writers from much of the international contact they had previously enjoyed. It was hard, for instance, for theater and music festivals in Belgrade—which were a showcase for new Serbian works as well as a forum for contact with foreign artists—to continue to attract participants. Meanwhile, "political kitsch" proliferated[4], as did "turbo-folk," a neo-traditional musical manifestation with nationalist themes supported by Milošević and his allies.[5]

Still, many renowned writers continued their work during the 1990s; these include Momo Kapor, Vida Ognjenović, Svetislav Basara, and David Albahari. New authors appeared on the scene with critically acclaimed novels, such as Radoslav Petković's *Destiny and Commentaries*, and Goran Petrović's *The Siege of the Church of Holy Salvation*, both of which treated historical themes in new and creative ways. Naturally, some works mocked Serbia's leaders, such as Mileta Budanović's short story "The Queen with the Screeching Voice," a play on Mirjana Marković.[6]

The years of sanctions also made it very hard for Western libraries to update their holdings of Yugoslav books and periodicals. By the same token, Serbian presses found it hard to get the materials and financial backing to print translations into or out of the Serbian language. The difficult international political situation of the country polarized its citizens, so that every political statement or implication carried with it a set of associations that put an artist in the government camp or on the side of the opposition; such a pressurized atmosphere is hardly conducive to artistic freedom and subtlety of expression. On the positive side, Serbian artistic institutions survived, even if the cultural scene was stagnant for a decade; there are now many new private presses and the Serbian arts scene, having survived a very difficult period, will probably flourish in the near future. The fate of cultural monuments in Kosovo and Bosnia remains of great concern to most Serbs.

EVENTS IN KOSOVO

The 40,000-strong NATO force in Kosovo, known as KFOR, remained in place after Koštunica's election. The United Nations civilian director temporarily in charge of the province was Bernhard Kouchner, who was replaced in January 2001 by Hans Haekkerup, the former foreign minister of Denmark. There was of course no large-scale fighting in Kosovo, but kidnappings, assassinations, and the vandalizing of cultural monuments continued. There were also reports of continued Serbian emigration from Kosovo and of Albanian immigration into the area from adjoining districts of southern Serbia. In the Serbian elections of December 23, Milošević's party won a plurality. When local elections were held, however, the Serbs boycotted them. The results of the elections were intriguing, because the most radically nationalist Albanian party, the Alliance for the Future of Kosova, headed by Ramush Haradinaj, received only 8 percent of the vote. The more moderate Democratic Party of Kosova of the former military leader Hashim Thaci won 27 percent, but the biggest vote getter was the Democratic Alliance of Kosova, headed by veteran peacemaker Ibrahim Rugova. Such a result might possibly have pleased Serbs, except that all of the Albanian parties are agreed in their unconditional opposition to the reimposition of Serbian control over the region. That is to say, they all want independence. Some United Nations and European Union administrators were urging that Kosovo now have another round of elections, for some sort of provincial assembly, but Haekkerup wisely pulled the plug on this idea until it becomes clear just what the functions of such an assembly would be—that is, until the relationship between Kosovo and the rest of Serbia is clarified. The much-quoted UN Resolution 1244 calls for the province's legal status to be decided once democratic systems are operational in both Serbia and Kosovo.

Two patterns of events in Kosovo greatly concerned Serbs in this period. One was a set of trials, in courts with mostly Albanian judges, of Serbs accused of genocide and other war crimes. The first conviction, for fourteen years in prison, in such a case came in January 2001 and immediately met with protests. Even more disturbing was the spillover of fighting from Kosovo into southeastern Serbia. An Albanian group calling itself the Liberation Army of Preševo, Medvedja, and Bujanovac (three cities in the predominantly Albanian-populated region) began moving troops into the area and attacking Serbian police and government installations in mid-November 2000. The Serbian army could not be used against them, because the attacks took place in the five-kilometer buffer zone around Kosovo created by the Kumanovo Agreement of 1999, which ended the war with NATO. KFOR tried to crack down on Albanian fighters and weapons stores, but the Serbs urgently requested a change in the buffer zone so that they could drive out the Albanian insurgents themselves. There was also speculation that Milošević holdouts had ordered Serbian police to retreat from the buffer zone in order to make the new DOS governments look bad. Understandably, Serbs feared a de facto enlargement of Kosovo, with all of its secessionist wrangles. The fighting in this area south of Niš was on a small scale but elicited a passionate response from Serbian politicians of all stripes. By year's end, twenty-four people had been killed and fourteen kidnapped in 313 armed incidents in the region.

In the spring of 2001, NATO commanders began to let Serb forces gradually reoccupy the buffer zone. They did this as a gesture of good will to Koštunica's government and to help stop the movement of diehard Albanian rebels throughout the region, especially into Macedonia where they began a major uprising in March. The small Macedonian army was hard pressed to contain the rebels around the village of Tanusevci and the city of Tetovo; although a cease-fire held for most of April, by May the rebels were again attacking government forces. Many Serbs and other critics of NATO said that Western support of the Kosovars was leading to the aggression; others said that granting Kosovo independence would choke off the rebellions.

Although polls showed that Serbs still overwhelmingly favored retaining sovereignty over Kosovo, some people within Serbia and abroad began floating the idea of partitioning the province. The northern fifth, with Mitrovica, could be attached to Serbia, and the western fifth, with Peć, to Montenegro. That would leave most of the province, with the cities of Prizren and Priština, in Albanian control. Whether important Serbian churches could actually be moved or reconstructed elsewhere could be discussed, if Serbs continued to feel that Kosovar Albanians would not provide appropriate care of or access to the monuments. Likewise, population movements might occur. As drastic as this action would be, it might hold the best hopes for a peaceful future in the region. The United Nations and NATO are hardly likely to support such an idea right away, however, because of the precedent it would establish for Bosnia, where official policy is still determined to construct a unitary, multiethnic country. And unlike the prosperous small states of Western Europe, such as Monaco and Luxembourg, Kosovo would not be economically viable by itself. Its survival would require a sustained economic lifeline from the West, and the political will for that might fade. Independence would also present Kosovars with the dilemma of deciding whether to carry out enosis with neighboring Albania, a country that is already massively poor and rent by crime and sectional disputes.

In the early morning hours of April 1, 2001, Serbian special police units arrested Slobodan Milošević at his home in Belgrade. President Koštunica continued to deny vehemently that Milošević would ever be sent to the Hague, but other key Yugoslav and Serbian officials gave mixed messages about if, when, or where Milošević would stand trial on war crimes charges. What was apparent, though, was the careful planning that went into the ex-president's arrest. The government leaked hints of the move for several weeks, probably as a trial balloon to gauge public reaction. Key allies of Milošević were also arrested, and the number of charges against him was gradually increased. The timing of the move seems to have been determined largely by Serbia's desire not to miss out on a further $50 million in U.S. economic aid, which President Bush had linked to cooperation with the Tribunal. Even though Serbian Justice Minister Batić agreed not to deliver Milošević to the Hague immediately, two other suspects had recently been turned over, and so the U.S. aid was granted.

Important parliamentary elections in Montenegro cast the future of

Yugoslavia into doubt. On April 22, the "Victory for Montenegro" coalition of President Djukanović won a narrow plurality and was expected to put together a government with the help of another pro-independence party. Djukanović came under intense pressure from Western leaders not to secede from Yugoslavia, this time for fear that it would encourage the Kosovars to do so too; although he was earlier encouraged by the international community to explore secession, he stated after the election that his government would move with prudence and that a referendum might be pushed back from its promised June date.

In April it also came to light that the Yugoslav army was investigating the alleged war crimes of some of its soldiers in Kosovo, a process that Milošević would never have initiated. On April 25, the Yugoslav government finally released the "Djakovica group" of 143 Albanian men arrested in 1999. Koštunica had long acknowledged that the men were innocent but that public opinion and "the rule of law" would not allow their earlier release. Such equivocation alarms human rights advocates in Serbia and abroad and has been labeled "childish" by Croatian President Mesić, who has taken bold steps to come to terms with Croatia's nationalist excesses. President Koštunica's promising Truth and Reconciliation Commission, designed to investigate the excesses of the Milošević regime, got off to a troubled start when several of its prominent potential members backed out; Vojin Dimitrijević, an international law specialist with the Civic Alliance of Serbia, and the historian Latinka Perović stated that its mandate was too weak and its composition not representative. It is possible that Koštunica no longer represents a pragmatic compromise with Serbian nationalists and the military but that he is out of tune with the population's overwhelming desire for reform. Whether he will go down in the history books as an important transitional figure, an obstruction to modernization, or a courageous and progressive leader remains to be seen.

NOTES

1. Patrick Moore, in *RFE/RL Balkan Report* 4: 77; (October 17, 2000), Internet edition.

2. *Free B92 News*, October 26, 2000, Internet edition.

3. *RFE/RL Newsline* 4; 131 (July 11, 2000), Internet edition.

4. Comments by Vida Ognjenović at the Denver meeting of the American Association for the Advancement of Slavic Studies, November 2000.

5. See Eric Gordy, *The Culture of Power in Serbia* (University Park: Pennsylvania State University Press, 1999), Chapter 4.

6. Comments by Aleksandar Jerkov at the Denver meeting of the American Association for the Advancement of Slavic Studies, November 2000.

13

Conclusion

The foregoing chapters suggest two general conclusions as well as several sets of questions about Serbian history. One important fact to remember is the tenacity of the Serbian identity. National identities are not genetically predetermined or divinely bestowed; they are constructs and they change over time. But Serbia's cultural legacy is a long one, and its claims on the hearts and minds of contemporary Serbs should not be dismissed as an impulse that either "globalization" or NATO's military strength will eradicate.

Milovan Djilas characterized what it meant to be Serbian in one of his short stories. In this passage, Serb Partisans are on an expedition into Hungary during World War II. They do not expect to stumble across any Serb families, since they are not inside Serbia. But they do:

> We were uneducated and did not know that there were, that there could be, Serbs in Hungary . . . So when on one occasion, on the outskirts of a village, we came upon a house with our Orthodox icons and a *kandilo* [votive candle] burning before Sveti Nikola, we looked and wondered. Speaking in Magyar, as we always did except among ourselves, in order to hide our tracks more easily, we asked: 'Where did you get those icons?' The householder replied,

also in Hungarian: 'We are Serbs, Orthodox.' 'Serbs? How can there be Serbs in Hungary?' But so it turned out. We began to speak in Serbian, and they spoke good Serbian. Then we asked them about Kosovo, and our Serb rulers and our Serb saints. They knew about them, and they knew all the *slava* [name-day] customs. They were true Serbs, no question of that.[1]

This passage gives a compelling portrayal of the cultural and linguistic borders of "Serbdom." As we have seen throughout this book, the zone of Serbian cultural identity and the borders of an independent Serbian state have seldom matched up since the fourteenth century. The negative side of many Serbs' preoccupation with their history of national suffering is that it has aided in the growth of exclusivist, ethnic nationalism. There were, of course, many other causes of the kind of violence that swept Serbia and its neighbors in the twentieth century. But the biggest challenge facing Serbia today is configuring its own identity; the country still needs to sort out the relationship between ethnicity, historical legacy, democratic culture, and economic modernization.

Another conclusion is that there are conflicting interpretations of Serbian history. Fortunately, Serbian history is not really reducible just to the simple formula of many hard-core nationalists. A traditional but in many ways counter-productive schematization of Serbian history runs thus: the glories of the medieval kingdom were followed by the "long night" of slavery to the Turks and then a meteoric reappearance as a state and development into a regional power from 1804 to 1913; after World War I came "Yugoslavia" in its two forms, which resulted in a partial deculturalization and a thoroughgoing economic exploitation of Serbia by the other Yugoslav peoples.

A more objective conceptualization begins also with the impressive Serbian medieval culture and multiethnic empire. But the chief effect of Ottoman rule was to "flatten" the society, depriving it of its aristocracy and ensuring that most Serbs were peasants. The Ottoman isolation, further, largely prevented the growth of secularism and cities in the Serbian lands, which set the society on a different course of development from West European countries. In the absence of church-state rivalry and intellectual and merchant classes to spur change, most Serbs conceived of the future of their state in terms colored very heavily by historical lessons and legends. When Western currents of thought and economic change crept into the moribund Ottoman Empire, Serbs embarked on a century of "catch-up" nationalism. This nationalism was predominantly "ethnic" rather than "civil," but its manifestations were neither monolithic nor antithetical to Serbia's domestic democracy. The twentieth century, in turn, has seen the Serbs, willingly or not, experiment politically with Yugoslavism and communism, which greatly affected their state-building arrangements. Once again Serbia stands at the threshold of nation-state status, as it did at the time of the Balkan wars nearly a century ago. Along the way the society has become considerably more modern, urban, industrial, and secular, but the tumult accompanying the collapse of communism has not yet allowed observers to verify the degree to which democratic tendencies have expanded in Serbia.

Some of the questions that scholars are considering today include the following: What could have improved the common life of Yugoslavs and made their country more resilient? How long will it be before Balkan peoples can cooperate enough to spur their own economic development and allow closer ties with Western Europe? Is it really true, as many claim, that peoples need to be allowed to be fully "national" before they can be expected to be cosmopolitan and internationalist? Last, and most concrete, is the question of "who killed Yugoslavia?" One can make reasonable cases that events in Slovenia, Kosovo, and Serbia each pushed the country beyond the point of no return. In Slovenia and Kosovo, hints of secession emerged in the 1980s, and Yugoslavia's territorial integrity was indispensible to its existence; in Serbia, the rise of nationalist public opinion and demagogic leaders quickly convinced the other republics that Serbs were no longer playing fair and were not reliable partners. As government archives become available in years to come, the historiography of this period will be considerably enriched.

It is reasonable to hope that future Serbian governments will move away from both expansionism and ethnic nationalism. Indeed there has long been an "unofficial Serbia," the one sometimes called today "suppressed" or "silent" or "the other Serbia." In literary history, political history, and the recent anti-Milošević opposition movements one finds the story of many Serbs who have eschewed formulaic national programs in favor of humanistic worldviews. One could begin with such writers as Dositej Obradović, Danilo Kiš, Ivo Andrić, Jovan Sterija Popović, David Albahari, Dragan Velikić, Bora Ćosić, and Bogdan Bogdanović (a famous architect and former mayor of Belgrade). Important cultural trends included pan-Yugoslav cooperation in the arts from the 1880s through the 1960s as well as the "women's poetry" from medieval times through the nineteenth century, which focused on material hardship, heartache, love, and sex instead of the military themes of male-authored epic poetry.

Progressive Serbian political events include the episodes of cooperation with Croats from 1848 through World War I and the activities of the Serbian Social Democratic party and several key turn-of-the-century journalists such as Dimitrije Tucović. Some of the anti-Tito opposition figures also rejected nationalist extremism, such as Latinka Perović, Miladin Životić, Nebojša Popov, Slobodan Inić, and to some degree Djilas.

Today, with Milošević gone, the demilitarization and democratization of Serbia are being well served by the many politicians who are trying to repair the lies and violence of the last twenty years and more. In the past fifteen years, numerous human rights activists and journalists—such as Nataša Kandić, Miroslav Filipović, and the late Slavko Ćuruvija—have spoken out against autocracy and the war crimes committed by Serbian forces. They are joined in their efforts to built a more modern and rational Serbia by economists such as Dragoslav Avramović and Mladjan Dinkić. Some religious leaders are active in such endeavors too, such as Patriarch Pavle and Archbishop Artemije of Kosovo. The journalists of *Vreme* and *Borba* (before its takeover) distinguished themselves by their vision and courage, as did Veran Matić and his associates at B92, Belgrade's alternative radio station. Today civil society in Serbia is being built by writers, academics, small publishing firms, human rights lawyers, and student activists such as those in "Otpor" (resistance).

The writer Dobrica Ćosić once created a telling fictional portrait of the "other" Serbia. This character, a World War I-era politician named Vukašin Katić, appears in the novel *Into the Battle*. Katić is not obsessed with the boundaries of its medieval empire or with revenge for bloody historical wrongs; instead, he supports all kinds of modern causes within Serbia and rejects the village "world of long beards and low ceilings," symbols of the kind of nationalism and peasant values upon which the country's leaders had based their long reign. Here is Katić expounding his views of history and politics:

> Let me just say this: we were driven out of the southern part of the Balkan peninsula when we were defeated at the Battle of Maritsa. Dušan's empire was the Byzantine Empire. We can't found national goals or political programs on this historical debris. We must not go on moldering with our old illusions . . . We should not forget that in our final migrations we Serbs moved northward and westward. I am convinced that our national path lies in that direction, and that it is there that our national aims will be fulfilled.[2]

These are the ideas embraced by a growing number of Serbs today, the thorny issue of the old cultural heartland of Kosovo notwithstanding.

Serbia, with its rich culture and its nineteenth-century experiences with democratic politics, is poised at a crossroads. The elections of September and December 2000, along with the aid of Western governments and philanthropists, might well mark the beginning of Serbia's rebuilding and transformation.

To reduce the likelihood of future violence, Serbs now must be willing to bring war criminals to justice and, at some point, to admit their own leadership's dominant overall role in initiating and perpetuating the violence of the wars of Yugoslav succession. These actions will help democracy sink deeper roots and will set Serbia's neighbors at ease. Meanwhile, the public now knows that Milošević, who ruled in an idiosyncratic dictatorship for more than a decade, was less than a programmatic nationalist; he was a crass manipulator who played upon Serbs' national insecurities to elicit their loyalty or acquiescence. His true aims were personal and material, as Serbs have now realized. No one expresses this realization better than the Belgrade sociologist—now prime minister—Zoran Djindjić, who often quips that, from 1991 to 1999, Milošević sent Serbs out on tanks four times (as soldiers to Slovenia, Croatia, Bosnia, and Kosovo), and all four times they came home on tractors—as refugees. If Djindjić and Koštunica live up to their promise as representatives of the new Serbia, and if other opponents of "long beards and low ceilings" really carry the field, Serbia will be a vastly different place in ten years.

NOTES

1. Milovan Djilas, "An Eye for an Eye" (pp. 86–107), in *The Stone and the Violets* (New York: Harcourt Brace Jovanovich, 1972), translated by Lovett F. Edwards, p. 100. Translations added by John K. Cox.

2. Dobrica Ćosić, *Into the Battle* (San Diego: Harcourt Brace Jovanovich, 1983), translated by Muriel Heppell, pp. 59–60.

Notable People in the History of Serbia

Andrić, Ivo (1892–1975) was a great Serbian writer who won the Nobel Prize for Literature in 1961. Most of his complex, realistic novels and short stories are set in multiethnic Bosnia in various historical periods. He was a cautious supporter of Yugoslav ideals. His work is still very highly regarded by critics. *The Bridge on the Drina* is his best-known work.

Anžujska, Jelena (r. 1276–1314) ruled during a a time of cultural flowering and religious toleration.

Crnjanski, Miloš (1893–1977) was a highly regarded Serbian modernist writer. He spent more than twenty years in London, but continued to write in Serbian. His poetry and novels had both cosmopolitan and patriotic themes. *Migrations*, the story of family conflict and political disillusionment set against the wanderings of a detachment of Serbian frontier soldiers in the service of the Habsburg Empire in the eighteenth century, is his most famous prose work.

Djilas, Milovan (d. 1995) was a Montenegrin political figure and writer. Djilas was a prominent interwar communist and Partisan who got into trouble in the 1950s and 1960s with the Tito government, which he was attacking for its elitist and pro-Soviet attitudes. Djilas wrote four volumes of memoirs, numerous stories and novels based on historical events, and many volumes of political analysis, most of which were translated into English and other languages. His transformation into a believer in social democracy and political pluralism won him the reputation of Yugoslavia's greatest dissident.

Dušan (d. 1355) deposed his father to become king of Serbia. He rapidly expanded the borders of the kingdom and had himself crowned an emperor with international approval. His political dream was to conquer Byzantium; in that he failed but he did create a large, multiethnic Serbian empire that was the dream of Serbia's nineteenth-century politicians.

Jovanović, Slobodan (1869–1958) was Serbia's greatest historian. The son of the liberal nineteenth-century politican Vladimir Jovanović, he wrote a considerable amount on all periods of Serbian history. He was loyal to the Karađorđjević dynasty and served as a member of the government-in-exile during World War II.

Karađjordje (d. 1817) led the uprising of 1804 that turned into the Serbian war of independence. A fiery and talented military leader, he eventually fled to Austria after Russian aid to the Serbs dried up. He was killed by his rival and the founder of Serbia's other royal dynasty, Miloš Obrenović.

Karađjordjević, Aleksandar (d. 1934) was the son of King Petar Karađjordjević. He actually ran the country from 1914 on, although he was not crowned until 1921. Aleksandar was a sincere believer in integral or unitarist Yugoslavism, which meant that he wanted a strong central government and believed that the Serbs, Croats, and Slovenes were basically one people or culture. He ruled as a dictator after 1929. He was assassinated by Croatian and Macedonian fascists during a visit to France.

Karađjordjević, Petar (1844–1921) was king of Serbia during its "golden age," when parliamentary rule was restored and great territorial expansion took place. His wife was Princess Zorka of Montenegro. After the great suffering of World War I, the king's fortunes rose along with those of Serbia when Yugoslavia was created in 1918.

Karadžić, Vuk (1787–1864), a great Serbian intellectual, reformed the Serbian alphabet and language, published many important collections of folk songs, and defined Serbian nationhood in linguistic terms.

Kiš, Danilo (1935–1989) was one of Serbia's greatest writers. His novels such as *Garden, Ashes* and *A Tomb for Boris Davidovich* placed him in the vanguard of European experimental writing. Not always popular in communist Yugoslavia but much admired abroad, he died as an expatriate in Paris.

Lazar, Prince (d. 1389) was the leader of the increasingly disorganized Serbian state at the time of the Battle of Kosovo against the Turks. The battle, which resulted in a draw but which became known as the disaster that eclipsed Serbia's power, has for centuries been the central event of Serbian history. Avenging the "defeat" at Kosovo became the national mission of the Serbs, and this drive was linked to the reconquest of lost territories and to fitful animosities toward people of Muslim faith. Key elements of the Kosovo legend include the treachery of Vuk Branković, who murdered Lazar to aid the Turks, and the heroism of Miloš Obilić, who slew the Ottoman sultan Murad to even the score. In a religious metaphor, Lazar's sacrifice and betrayal fed the hopes that Serbia would soon be resurrected and reign again.

Maksimović, Desanka (1898–1993) was a very popular and prolific Serbian woman writer. She was known mostly as a poet but also wrote stories and novels. Her work was usually based on historical and patriotic themes. Her most famous work is "I Seek Clemency," a long poem in which she elaborates on and modifies Tsar Dušan's famous law code from the fourteenth century.

Mihailović, Draža (1893–1946) was the leader of the Serbian Chetnik movement during World War II. Loyal to King Petar, Mihailović planned on outlasting the Nazi occupation of Yugoslavia, defeating the communist Partisans under Tito, and then restoring the interwar system of government, in which Serbs dominated the country. Mihailović fell out of favor with the Western allies and lost the support of many Yugoslavs because of his narrow nationalist program and his tactical cooperation with the Germans. His movement was overwhelmed by the Partisans and he was executed.

Milošević, Slobodan (1941–) became the head of the Serbian branch of the League of Communists of Yugoslavia in 1987 on the strength of his appeal to Serbian nationalism. He has since held the offices of president of Serbia and president of Yugoslavia. After unleashing great violence in his pursuit of a greater Serbia and after promoting systematic corruption in the Serbian government for years, he was turned out of office in late 2000 by a coalition of opposition forces and by massive street demonstrations. He was arrested by the Serbian government in the spring of 2001, reportedly to stand trial on corruption charges in Serbia. He was soon thereafter flown to the Hague where he faced many charges (including crimes against humanity and genocide) stemming from the conflicts in Croatia, Bosnia, and Kosovo.

Nemanja, Stefan (r. 1168–1196) was the first important Serbian king. He united several small principalities such as Raska and Zeta. After turning his throne over to his son, he retired to a monastery at Mount Athos in Greece.

Njegoš, Petar Petrović (r. 1813–1851) was the most famous princebishop, or *vladika*, of Montenegro. He tried to modernize the country but is mostly remembered for his sophisticated but passionately nationalistic literary works. *The Mountain Wreath* (1847) depicts a furious fratricidal struggle between Orthodox and Muslim Montenegrins; it is a sort of modern version of the myth of Kosovo that puts Serbs squarely into the position of defenders of Western civilization against infidel invaders. The poem is controversial because it abounds in religious hatred and violence as well as patriotism and courage. In his other works, Njegoš demonstrated that the Serbian language was capable of expressing complex philosophical thoughts.

Pašić, Nikola (1845–1926) is the most famous Serbian politician of all time. He dominated the Radical Party and, indeed, the whole country of Serbia for decades. Pašić steered the country through success in the Balkan wars and disasters in World War I, and then into a highly advantageous scenario for the founding of Yugoslavia in 1918. He was known for his Machiavellian tactics but is loved and respected by many to this day.

Pribićević, Svetozar (1875–1936) was the leading politician among the Serbs in Croatia in the last decades of Habsburg rule. He guided the Independent Party into cooperation with liberal Croatian politicians who also opposed Hungarian domination. Although he later became passionately "Greater Serbian," he was able to convince many Croats that they should join Yugoslavia in 1918. Pribićević later reverted to his original, more tolerant political views.

Ranković, Aleksandar (d. 1983) was a Serbian communist who held extremely high positions in the Yugoslav government until he was forced into retirement in 1966. Ranković had been an important wartime leader and then became head of the secret police, often known by its Serbian acronym UDBA. He kept a firm hand on minorities in Serbia and was a strong proponent of centralism in Yugoslavia. He was opposed by liberal communists, especially from the republics of Slovenia and Croatia; his ouster was prompted by Tito's belief that Ranković was abusing his powers as security chief and that he was blocking needed reforms. His funeral turned into the occasion for a huge outpouring of pent-up Serbian nationalism.

Sava (1169–1236) was one of the sons of Stefan Nemanja. He led the Serbian church to independence.

Tito, Josip Broz (1892–1980), who was half Croatian and half Slovene, became the head of the Yugoslav Communist Party in 1937. He led a fierce resistance movement, called the Partisans, against the Nazis and their allies during World War II, after which he created a new Yugoslavia based on federal and socialist concepts. After his break with Stalin in 1948, Tito and his advisors steered Yugoslavia onto a "third course" between the superpowers. His personal prestige and the strong army he built up allowed him to paper over problems among Yugoslavia's national groups. After his death, the country rapidly fell apart.

Glossary

The Balkans The lands of southeastern Europe occupied for several centuries by the Ottoman Turks. The term has connotations of backwardness and thus is often avoided when used as more than a geographical catch-all. Scholars agree that Albania, Bosnia, Bulgaria, Greece, Macedonia, Romania, and Serbia are Balkan states; some would also include Croatia.

Central Europe Another geographical and historical term with political and cultural overtones. The lands of Central Europe are often considered to be "the lands between," that is, the peoples sandwiched between the German and Russian cultural spheres. These countries, which share a pride in their cosmopolitan cultures, especially with regard to literature, and in their ability to cooperate politically, include Poland, Hungary, the Czech Republic, and Slovenia. Some observers would place Slovakia, Croatia, or (up to 1918) Austria in Central Europe.

Chetniks One of the main armed groups in Yugoslavia during World War II. The name derives from the "ete" (irregular armed bands), which resisted the Turks and aided in the territorial expansion of nineteenth-century Serbia. They supported the former Royal government of King Petar II and are representative of "greater Serbian" national ideas. At first, they fought against the Axis occupiers, but they quickly became more preoccupied with their domestic rivals, the communist-led Partisans of Tito. Today the term is applied to a variety of Serbian paramilitary or radical nationalist groups.

The Croatian Spring A revival of Croatian nationalism in Yugoslavia between 1967 and 1972. Concerns that they were being economically exploited by Serbs and that their language was being unfairly assimilated led Croatian cultural and political figures and students to agitate, with some success, for greater autonomy. The remaining concerns, including a preoccupation with extending Croatian power into Bosnia-Hercegovina, were picked up again in the 1990s by new political parties, especially those of Franjo Tudjman and other right-wing figures.

Eastern Europe A geopolitical term used during the Cold War to refer to the communist states and peoples of Europe, including those that were part of the Soviet Union (Ukrainians, Lithuanians, Estonians, etc.), those that were allied with the Soviet Union (Poland, Hungary, Romania, etc.), and those that were independent but socialist (Yugoslavia and Albania). In the older sense, and now once again, the term basically represents the merger of the sets of Balkan and Central European lands.

Ethnic cleansing A term of recent vintage used as a euphemism for genocide and the forced expulsion of civilian populations. The idea behind it is that different national, linguistic, or religious groups cannot or should not live together in the same country; it is often reinforced by a desire to exact "revenge" for perceived historical grievances from long ago. It is of course condemned by democratic countries and human rights groups, although Serbs rightfully note that crimes against Serbs in the 1990s (by Croats and Kosovo Albanians, mostly) have attracted less attention in the West than crimes committed by Serbs against other groups. The reasons for this judgment include the widely shared belief that Serbian leaders pushed the former Yugoslavia into violence and that Serbian forces were responsible for the largest share of atrocities there.

Federalism A principle of governance especially important in multiethnic states such as the former Yugoslavia. It holds that the powers of the central government—in this case in Belgrade—should be limited by powers retained by local authorities. In the Yugoslav case, the local authorities represented the six South Slavic nations (Serbs, Croats, Slovenes, Bosnians, Macedonians, and Montenegrins) and a number of smaller nationalities. The First Yugoslavia (1918–1941) was not very federalist, and as a result, many non-Serbs felt threatened. One of the signal accomplishments of Tito's socialist Second Yugoslavia (1945–1991) was a federal structure that guaranteed wide-ranging rights to various ethnically and regionally identified groups.

Feudalism A medieval political system based on political hierarchy and the economic system of manorialism (estates worked by serfs). Under feudalism, all land was technically owned by the monarch (usually a king or queen, or, in the Ottoman case, the sultan), but it was used by nobles (lords, aristocrats, or, originally, knights) who owed political and military loyalty to the monarch. Often the nobles became at least as powerful as their monarchs. The rise of cities, the development of agricultural and eventually industrial technology, and the economic changes that took place during the era of European colonial expansion after about 1500 undermined feudalism and manorialism. In Western Europe they eventually gave way to capitalism, but feudal conditions lasted much longer in Eastern Europe.

The Great War A European expression for World War I. Today this war stands in the shadow of World War II (which includes the Holocaust and the use of the atomic bomb and signaled both the permanent emergence of the United States as a superpower and the beginning of the Cold War). But countries like Great Britain and France suffered many more casualties in the First World War than in the Second, and the war had massive effects, such as pioneering technologized mass warfare (with ghastly results), expanding governmental powers in propaganda and economics, weakening European empires in Africa and Asia, and spreading pessimism, irony, and alienation. For Serbia, World War I is usually considered together with the Balkan wars of 1912–1913; it was a bloody but ultimately successful period of national expansion which, with the creation of Yugoslavia in 1918, resulted in the first modern country to contain all Serbs, albeit mixed with other significant populations.

Hajduk A traditional term for a bandit or highwayman, especially one who protected Serbian peasants against the depredations of the Ottoman landowners or officials. Many hajduk heroes, exalted in folk tales and epic poems, have come to be portrayed as kind of proto-nationalist freedom fighters, even though in actuality they often victimized poor Serbs too and were sometimes even vassals (warriors in a service relationship) to Turks. Doubtless, however, the restless energy and fighting prowess of the hajduks did contribute something to Serbian military success in anti-Ottoman wars after 1700.

Irredenta "Unredeemed lands" that nationalists in one country seek to take from another country. These lands are claimed on ethnic (population) or historical grounds. Most European countries now have or have had irredenta. For instance, many Germans today still regard parts of the Czech Republic or Poland as German in a historical sense. Until the early twentieth-century, Kosovo and Bosnia-Hercegovina were the most important irredenta for Serbs.

Janissaries Elite Ottoman infantry. They were at first well-equipped, well-trained, and intensely loyal to the Sultan. By the 1700s, they occupied a privileged position in Ottoman society and spent more time protecting and expanding their wealth than they did fighting the sultan's many enemies. They grew so disruptive and presented such an obstacle to reform that they were physically liquidated by Sultan Mahmud in the 1820s.

Krvna osveta (or "blood feud") The Montenegrin equivalent of the Sicilian "vendetta." It also existed in other places in the Balkans, especially Albania. Although blood feuds were supposed to follow a strict code (supposedly to protect "honor"), they were a major drain on the economic and cultural productivity of societies that nurtured these traditions, since they siphoned off a great deal of manpower into violent pursuits. The traditional blood feud died out in the early twentieth century, although some observers say its legacy of revenge and spite continues to make itself felt in Balkan politics.

Millet The Turkish word for "community of faith." Millets in the Ottoman Empire were religious organizations that carried out many important functions in the country's internal administration, especially in finance and jurisprudence. There were separate millets for Muslims, Jews, and Orthodox Christians (as well as some other Christian groups). The existence of millets shows the Ottoman preference for indirect rule, and they put a buffer between the local population and the central government which helped groups like the Serbs retain their culture.

Military Frontier (in Serbian, "Vojna Krajina"). A belt of territories extending across the Balkans from Croatia to Romania. It was part of the Habsburg Empire for centuries and was administered from Vienna as a kind of buffer zone to protect the interior of the Empire from Turkish attacks. Many Serbs moved into the Military Frontier when they fled their traditional homelands to the south and east; the Habsburg emperors gave them certain privileges (such as the right to retain their Orthodox faith in a predominantly Catholic land) in exchange for military service. Many of the Serbs who lived in Croatia until their expulsion in the mid-1990s were descended from these military settlers.

Nationalism A sense of identity perceived by people who share a common language, territory, culture, tradition, and, sometimes, religion or race. Nationalism is a more modern and a more significant bond between people than patriotism, which is a form of local attachment usually restricted to times of (military) crisis. Scholars of nationalism are split into two groups: "perennialists," who believe that national essences have long existed, and the larger group of "constructivists," who hold that nations are created by economic, political, and intellectual elites in the course of social modernization. Nationalism itself exists in two types: "ethnic," which views the nation as an extended kinship group and stresses the importance of a common high and low culture, and "political," which sees the nation as a political population, united by common economic aspirations and governmental preferences. The rise of nationalism after the late eighteenth century was related to the spread of the idea of popular sovereignty, or rule by the people. This same impulse underlies much of modern democratic thinking, although national states are often not founded on respect for due process and toleration of competing interests as in democracies. When nationalism departs from the realm of individual identity and becomes a political force, it usually aims at "self-determination," or the creation of nation-states in which each nation (or people) is sovereign, autonomous, or dominant within its borders. Despite the emergence of a global economy and powerful multinational corporations in the late twentieth century, nationalism remains one of the most powerful forces in world affairs.

Notables Locally prominent individuals in Ottoman times. They were usually merchants, military officers, or government officials. Notables differ from nobles (i.e., aristocrats or gentry) because they had little inheritable wealth. The Serbian nobility disappeared during the Turkish conquest, and both of the competing royal families that emerged after 1804 were descended from new notables.

Old Church Slavonic A medieval language of Europe that split and developed into the modern Slavic languages such as Serbian, Russian, and Bulgarian. It still plays important ecclesiastical functions.

Opština The equivalents of municipalities or townships in Serbia's governmental structure.

Partisans The military forces led by Josip Broz Tito during World War II. This highly effective fighting force was organized and dominated by the Communist Party, and its goals were both to defeat the German, Italian, Hungarian, and Bulgarian occupation forces and the local collaborators and to carry out a social revolution after the war, establishing a people's republic in Yugoslavia. They ended up fighting the Chetniks a great deal, too. The Partisans appealed to many people who were not communists, however—especially to women, minority groups, young people, and federalists and idealists who felt betrayed by the failure of the Second (Royal) Yugoslavia. By 1945, there were several hundred thousand Partisan fighters, and many more support and organizational personnel. They were weakest in Serbia proper but strongest in Croatia and Bosnia where persecuted Serbs joined the Partisan ranks in large numbers. They received considerable material aid from the United States and Great Britain but had little Soviet assistance in liberating the country, a fact that enabled Tito to pursue an independent type of socialism after the war.

Republics Administrative units in Serbian and Yugoslav history similar to American states or Canadian provinces. In Tito's Yugoslavia (1945–1991), they were based on national criteria, unlike states and provinces. In the third Yugoslavia (1991–present), the country consists of only two republics, Serbia and Montenegro.

Socialism In general terms, the philosophical and political belief that true democracy requires the sharing of economic as well as political power. Sometimes the term is used to describe the economic systems (usually based on centralized planning and the rapid growth of basic industries and infrastructure) of countries ruled in the twentieth century by communist governments. A third use of socialism denotes a "milder" form of communist political thought—that is, one that allows for a peaceful and gradual transition from capitalism to a sociopolitical system that is more fair and rational but, supposedly, equally productive in economic terms. Socialist ideas originated in Europe in the late eighteenth century, but they were greatly deepened and popularized by Karl Marx (1818–1883), a German economist, journalist, historian, and sociologist. The first country in the world to establish a socialist form of government was Russia in 1917; the subsequent development of the Soviet Union under Lenin and Stalin is seen by many observers as having a decisive, and usually negative, influence on socialist ideas and policies in other countries. Since the collapse of communist governments in Europe between 1989 and 1991, socialism has slipped under the horizon of most political and academic discourse, except in China, North Korea, and Cuba.

Successor states New countries that emerge from the breakdown of a larger state. For instance, when the Habsburg Empire was defeated in

World War I, the successor states of Czechoslovakia, Hungary, and Austria were formed wholly on its territory. Yugoslavia in that same period was a successor state of both the Habsburg Empire and the Ottoman Empire, since it came to possess territory that had recently been part of both of those defunct empires. Today, Ukraine, Kazakhstan, and Russia are examples of the fifteen successor states of the former Soviet Union, while Slovenia, Croatia, Bosnia, and Macedonia are successor states of the former Yugoslavia.

Ustaše Croatian fascists during the 1930s and 1940s. As Hitler's allies, they were given control over a large "independent" Croatian state, including Bosnia, after the invasion of Yugoslavia in 1941. Led by Ante Pavelić, the Ustaše were responsible for enormous atrocities against Serbs, Jews, and other groups. They were defeated militarily by Tito's Partisans; most were executed or fled after the war.

Vladika The traditional position of prince-bishop in the Montenegrin lands. Combining ecclesiastical and political functions, the title *vladika* gave way in the late nineteenth-century to the position of king, but until the 1920s the Montenegrin population was too dispersed among its mountains to be subject to any significant degree of centralized administration.

Yugoslavism The belief that the closely related South Slavic peoples would benefit from cooperation in the political or cultural realms. It is one of the many variants of Pan-Slavic thinking in Europe, all of which stress the natural similarities of the Slavic-speaking peoples and the advantages of various types of cooperation among them, especially given the precarious geographical position of Europe's Slavs between several strong empires. Bulgarians were generally not included in Yugoslavism, and Serbs were less enthusiastic about it at first, given their individual success in creating an expansionistic nation-state in the nineteenth century.

Zadruga A name for the traditional family farming unit in much of Serbia, as well as in other parts of the Balkans. A zadruga contained several generations of the extended family and had certain protodemocratic customs of governance, including the dispatch of a male representative to a village council. In contrast to the settled life of zadrugas, many Serbs and, especially, Montenegrins lived in clans in mountain societies based on herding.

Bibliographic Essay

This essay only includes items in English. Many of the authors mentioned have written more than one noteworthy book; readers can locate other books by them via on-line catalogs for large university libraries. References to numerous other related works can be found in the chapters and Notes sections. For more detailed searching, consult the bibliographies such as Murlin Croucher, *Slavic Studies: A Guide to Bibliographies, Encyclopedias, and Handbooks* (Wilmington, DE, 1993); John J. Horton, *Yugoslavia* (Santa Barbara, CA, rev. ed., 1990); and Francine Friedman, *Yugoslavia: A Comprehensive English-language Bibliography* (Wilmington, DE, 1993). An invaluable reference work is Željan E. Šuster, *Historical Dictionary of the Federal Republic of Yugoslavia* (Lanham, MD, 1999). A useful guide to the recent Balkan wars is John B. Allcock et al., eds., *Conflict in the Former Yugoslavia: An Encyclopedia* (Denver, 1998).

The most comprehensive work on Serbia in English is Michael B. Petrovich's magisterial *A History of Modern Serbia, 1804–1918* (New York, 1976). A judicious and highly readable contemporary account by the British journalist Tim Judah is *The Serbs: History, Myth and the Destruction of Yugoslavia* (New Haven, CT, 1997). The classic pro-Serbian travel account is Rebecca West's *Black Lamb and Grey Falcon: A Journey Through Yugosla-*

via (New York, 1940); more recent and equally engaging travel accounts are found in Brian Hall, *The Impossible Country: A Journey Through the Last Days of Yugoslavia* (Boston, 1994) and Peter Morgan's *A Barrel of Stones: In Search of Serbia* (Aberystwyth, Great Britain, 1997). Dusko Doder's *The Yugoslavs* (New York, 1978) provides a general, if dated, overview of life in Tito's Serbia, while Vasa D. Mihailovich, ed., *Landmarks in Serbian Culture and History* (Pittsburgh, 1983) chronicles Serbia's contributions to Western civilization. A large and intriguing volume by Serbian scholars about all aspects of life in Serbia in King Petar's day is Alfred Stead, ed., *Servia by the Servians* (London, 1909). For young readers, JoAnn Milivojevic's *Serbia* (New York, 1999) is a good, colorful place to start.

Serbian history in its Balkan context is presented in Leften S. Stavrianos, *The Balkans Since 1453* (New York, 1953); this indispensable book, just republished in 2000, is the ideal starting point for any serious study of Balkan history. Other first-rate treatments of this sort include Charles and Barbara Jelavich, *The Establishment of the Balkan National States, 1804–1920* (Seattle, WA, 1977); Stevan Pavlowitch, *The Balkans, 1804–1945* (New York, 1999); and Barbara Jelavich, *History of the Balkans* (New York, 2 v., 1983). A general political and diplomatic history of Eastern Europe that places Serbia in a somewhat broader context (and that has stood the test of time) is the elegantly written *The Lands Between: A History of East-Central Europe since the Congress of Vienna* (New York, 1970) by Alan Palmer; for more recent events right up through 2000, the four volumes by J. F. Brown are unsurpassed.

An excellent general history of Yugoslavia and Serbia's role in it is John R. Lampe, *Yugoslavia As History: Twice There Was a Country* (New York, 2d ed., 2000). Older but comprehensive and still insightful is Fred Singleton, *A Short History of the Yugoslav Peoples* (New York, 1985). A richly detailed political analysis of Tito's Yugoslavia is Dennison Rusinow, *The Yugoslav Experiment, 1948–1974* (Berkeley, CA, 1978); other solid, standard accounts, some of which move well beyond the political sphere, are Steven L. Burg, *Conflict and Cohesion in Socialist Yugoslavia: Political Decision Making Since 1966* (Princeton, NJ, 1983); Pedro Ramet, *Nationalism and Federalism in Yugoslavia, 1962–1991* (Bloomington, IN, 2d ed., 1992); Wayne S. Vucinich, *Contemporary Yugoslavia: Twenty Years of Socialist Experiment* (Berkeley, CA, 1969); and Paul Shoup, *Communism and the Yugoslav National Question* (New York, 1968); and Melissa Bokovoy et al., eds. *State-Society Relations in Yugoslavia, 1945–1992* (New York, 1995). For economic analysis see Harold Lydall, *Yugoslavia in Crisis* (Oxford, 1989) and Fred Singleton and Bernard Carter, *The Economy of Yugoslavia* (New York, 1982). Tito's foreign policy is explored in Alvin Z.

Rubinstein, *Yugoslavia and the Nonaligned World* (Princeton, NJ, 1970) and John C. Campbell, *Tito's Separate Road: America and Yugoslavia in World Politics* (New York, 1967).

Analyses of Serbian literature can be found in Celia Hawkesworth, *Voices in the Shadows: Women and Verbal Art in Serbia and Bosnia* (New York, 2000); Thomas Eekman, *Yugoslav Literature, 1945–1975* (Ann Arbor, MI, 1978); Antun Barac, *A History of Yugoslav Literature* (Ann Arbor, MI, 1955); Tatyana Popovic, *Prince Marko: The Hero of South Slav Epics* (Syracuse, NY, 1988); and Wayne S. Vucinich, ed., *Ivo Andric Revisited: The Bridge Still Stands* (University of California Press, 1996). All aspects of Serbian culture are treated in the lavishly illustrated but scholarly *History of Serbian Culture* (Edgware, England, 1995) by Pavle Ivic, et al. Good translations exist in English of novels and short stories by Ivo Andrić, Danilo Kiš, and Miloš Crnjanski (sometimes spelled Tsernianski). Interested readers will also be able find English editions of works by many other Serbian writers, most readily Miodrag Bulatović, Bora Ćosić, Dobrica Ćosić, Borislav Pekić, Slobodan Selenić, Meša Selimović, and Aleksandar Tišma. Superb poetry translations with extensive commentary can be found in Milne Holton and Vasa D. Mihailovich, *Serbian Poetry from the Beginnings to the Present* (New Haven, CT, 1988) and Mihailo Đorđevic, *Anthology of Serbian Poetry* (Belgrade, 1988); for contemporary poets, see Charles Simic, ed., *The Horse Has Six Legs: An Anthology of Serbian Poetry* (St. Paul, MN, 1992). Excellent individual editions of the work of Ivan Lalić and Vasko Popa also exist. Two new first-rate literary collections are *The Prince of Fire: An Anthology of Contemporary Serbian Short Stories*, edited by Radmila Gorup and Nadežda Obradović (Pittsburgh, 1998) and *Songs of the Serbian People: From the Collections of Vuk Karadžić*, edited by Milne Holton and Vasa D. Mihailovich (Pittsburgh, 1997). The four collections edited by Branko Mikasinovich are also noteworthy. Three superb North American writers with Serbian roots are the poet Charles Simic and the novelists Nadja Tesich and Negovan Rajic. Svetlana Rakic, *Serbian Icons from Bosnia-Herzegovina: Sixteenth to Eighteenth Century* (New York, 2000) is an important new study of a cultural patrimony endangered by the recent wars. A well-illustrated examination of the Serbian cultural heartland is Gojko Subotić, *Art of Kosovo: The Sacred Land* (New York, 1998).

Medieval Serbian history is treated in John V. A. Fine, *The Early and Late Medieval Balkans* (Ann Arbor, MI, 2 v., 1994). The Battle of Kosovo and the construction of the myths about it receive competent treatment in Thomas Emmert, *Serbian Golgotha: Kosovo 1389* (Boulder, CO, 1990). The best work on the Serbian Revolution is Wayne S. Vucinich, *The First*

Serbian Uprising, 1804–1813 (Boulder, CO, 1982); another wonderfully detailed and erudite study of that period is *The Life and Times of Vuk Stefanovic Karadžić, 1787–1864: Literacy, Literature and National Independence in Serbia* (Oxford, 1970) by Duncan Wilson. Nineteenth-century politics in Serbia are treated in detail and with great analytical skill in several books by Alex N. Dragnich and Gale Stokes. Essays by world-class scholars on World War I and the creation of Yugoslavia are found in Dimitrije Djordjević, ed., *The Creation of Yugoslavia, 1914–1918* (Santa Barbara, CA, 1980), while the conflicting expectations and rocky political scene of Royal Yugoslavia are masterfully depicted in Ivo Banac, *The National Question in Yugoslavia: Origins, History, Politics* (Ithaca, NY, 1984). Peter Radan and Aleksandar Pavković, eds, *The Serbs and Their Leaders in the 20th Century* (Brookfield, VT, 1997) contains a variety of detailed contributions by top scholars, including important information on that most competent and effective of all Serbian monarchs, Petar Karađjorđjević I.

The first political biography of Slobodan Milošević in English was by Dusko Doder and Louise Branson, *Milošević: Portrait of a Tyrant* (New York, 1999). More analytical is Lenard J. Cohen, *Serpent in the Bosom: The Rise and Fall of Slobodan Milošević* (Boulder, CO, 2001) Three other excellent recent works, all demonstrating some degree of sympathy with the anti-Milošević opposition are Robert Thomas, *The Politics of Serbia in the 1990s* (New York, 1999); Mladen Lazić, ed., *Protest in Belgrade: Winter of Discontent* (New York, 1999); and Eric D. Gordy, *The Culture of Power in Serbia: Nationalism and the Destruction of Alternatives* (University Park, PA, 1999).

Readers looking for autobiographies will be impressed by the scope and sense of immediacy in the four volumes of Milovan Djilas's occasionally turgid autobiography, *Land Without Justice* (New York, 1958); *Wartime* (New York, 1977); *Memoir of a Revolutionary* (New York, 1973); and *Rise and Fall* (San Diego, CA, 1983). The American publisher William Jovanovich reflects on Serbs and Montenegrins in the old country and in the new world in *Serbdom* (Tucson, AZ, 1998). The fascinating memoirs of a Serbian scholar who experienced World War II and then emigrated to the United States are found in Dimitrije Djordjević, *Scars and Memory: Four Lives in One Lifetime* (Boulder, CO, 1997).

Three first-rate studies of the breakup of Yugoslavia from within are Nebojša Popov, ed., *The Road to War in Serbia: Trauma and Catharsis* (New York, 2000); Branka Magaš, *The Destruction of Yugoslavia* (New York, 1993); and Jasminka Udovički and James Ridgeway, eds., *Burn This House: The Making and Unmaking of Yugoslavia* (Durham, NC, rev. ed., 2000). A powerful, fact-filled presentation of the Serbian side of these issues is found in Dušanka Hadži-Jovančić, ed., *The Serbian Question in the Balkans* (Belgrade, 1995). The most impartial and readable analyses from outside Yugoslavia remain Lenard J. Cohen, *Broken Bonds: Yugoslavia's Disintegration and Balkan Politics in Transition* (Boulder, CO, 2d ed., 1995); Laura Silber and Allan Little, *Yugoslavia: Death of a Nation* (New York, rev. ed., 1997); and Christopher Bennett, *Yugoslavia's Bloody Collapse* (New York, 1995). Misha Glenny offers a gritty, up-close view of the 1990s in *The Fall of Yugoslavia: The Third Balkan War* (New York, 3d ed., 1996); Mark Thompson, *A Paper House: The Ending of Yugoslavia* (New York, 1992), is engaging and erudite. Roy Gutman's pathbreaking *A Witness to Genocide* (New York, 1993) is one of many journalistic and scholarly treatments of ethnic cleansing. Vesna Nikolić-Ristanović, *Women, Violence and War: Wartime Victimization of Refugees in the Balkans* (New York, 2000) is one of several important works on rape and other war crimes directed at women. An important set of memoirs by a non-Serb about the war in Bosnia is Kemal Kurspahić, *As Long as Sarajevo Exists* (Stony Creek, CT, 1997). A view of life during the 1999 NATO air campaign is found in Jasmina Tesanović, *The Diary of a Political Idiot: Normal Life in Belgrade* (2000). Diplomats' memoirs about the wars in the 1990s include William Zimmerman, *Origins of a Catastrophe* (New York, 1996) and the indefatigable Richard Holbrooke, *To End a War* (New York, 1998).

An informal and lucid account of life in Kosovo before the recent war is Mary Motes, *Kosova/Kosovo: Prelude to War, 1966–1999* (Homestead, FL, 1999). A scholarly overview of Kosovo's history is Miranda Vickers, *Between Serb and Albanian: A History of Kosovo* (New York, 1998). The roots of the recent conflict are compellingly traced in Julie A. Mertus, *Kosovo: How Myths and Truths Started a War* (Berkeley, CA, 1999) and Tim Judah, *Kosovo: War and Revenge* (New Haven, CT, 2000). This latter book also takes the reader into Serbia during the air campaign. A Western perspective on the military and diplomatic aspects of the 1999 war can be found in Ivo H. Daalder and Michael E. O'Hanlon, *Winning Ugly: NATO's War to Save Kosovo* (Washington, DC, 2000).

Index

About the Author

JOHN K. COX is Associate Professor of History at Wheeling Jesuit University. His main research interest is the twentieth-century intellectual history of the South Slavic lands; his teaching interests include World War I and the Holocaust. A former Rotary scholar in Hungary, and a Fulbright fellow in Austria and Slovenia, he knows Serbo-Croatian, Slovene, German, and several other languages of the region. He is the author of several chapters and essays on nationalism, Yugoslav communism, and Balkan fascism, as well as numerous book reviews about the breakup of Yugoslavia.

**Other Titles in the
Greenwood Histories of the Modern Nations**
Frank W. Thackeray and John E. Findling, Series Editors